This book investigates ways 'the Other' can be both a cause of and an answer to religious and cultural fears. The multi-layered question of cultural and religious diversity has received some attention recently both in academic and policy circles. The authors of this work address this issue by focusing on fears and phobias, and the ways they are historically and sociologically produced and reproduced in a Global Era. The volume presents examples of fears related to different cultures and religions from a multidisciplinary perspective. Some of these have been provoked or sublimated by religious fundamentalisms, and a double ignorance, that is, ignorance of and about fundamentalisms, which have helped feed these collective concerns. Through a sample of stereotypes, mystifications and simplifications, the authors look at Islam as a focal lens for showing the current power of globalized collective fears. The collection also explores possible cultural antidotes to these phobias, such as the need for awareness and familiarity with diversities, based on an education accepting of interculturality and plural citizenship. The book will be essential reading for academics, researchers and policy-makers working in the areas of Intercultural Pedagogy, History, Anthropology and Sociology of Religions, Law and Religion, Contemporary Islam, Migration Studies, Interreligious Dialogue, and Ethnography.

**Gennaro Gervasio** is Associate Professor of History of the Muslim Countries at the Department of Humanities, Roma Tre University, Italy. Prior to that, he has worked in Egypt, Australia and in the United Kingdom. He is Research Fellow at the Forum Transregionale Studien in Berlin, and from 2019 to 2021 he was the co-coordinator for Roma Tre University of PriMED international project (Prevention and Interaction in the Trans-Mediterranean Space). His research focuses on: secularism and Marxism in the Arab world, the history and politics of Islam in Europe, and civic activism and social and protest movements in the Arab World (especially Egypt and Iraq).

**Maria Chiara Giorda** is Full Professor of History of Religions at the Department of Humanities, Roma Tre University, Italy. She is the coordinator of the international project "SHARP Lab", and a member of the École Française d'Athènes Project, "Interactions, juxtapositions, imbrications religieuses dans les Balkans (XX-XXIe siècles)" and of the Permanent Seminar on "Religious Diversity in Italian Urban History" (RDIUH), promoted by New York University and Roma Tre. Her research focuses on the following themes: history of religions, geography of religions, religion and urban spaces, shared religious places, history of monasticism.

**Paola Perucchini** is Full Professor of Developmental and Educational Psychology, and Head of Department at the Department of Education, Roma Tre University, Italy. She has been Vice-Director of the same Department and member of the Executive Committee of the Italian Psychology Association, Developmental and Educational Section (2012-2019). From 2019 to 2021 she was the co-coordinator for Roma Tre University of PriMED international project (Prevention and Interaction in the Trans-Mediterranean Space). Her research interests include, among others, communicative infant development; children's social adjustment; children's ethnic prejudice and educational programmes against discrimination.

# Diversity, Fear and Religions:
# Cultural Accommodation in a Globalized World

## Routledge-Giappichelli Studies in Religion, Law and Economics in the Mediterranean Space

*Book Series Direction*

The Director of the Book Series is appointed by the Scientific Council of the Research Center REDESM of the University of Insubria (redesm.org).
The Editorial Board is composed of academics belonging to different scientific and disciplinary sectors of the macro-area involved by the Book Series approved by the Scientific Council of the Research Center REDESM.

*Editorial Board*



The Mediterranean was the cradle of many religious and political models, which transformed themselves into universal paradigms. Much has been written about this geopolitical space and its peoples, within the context of their religious and political institutions and their commercial and cultural exchanges. However it seems that this unitary vision, predominant in the past, has recently been replaced by a fragmented and partial approach; that one focuses on the individual regional actors only, neglecting the overall picture and the connections between the different parts.

This *Book Series* aims to promote an interdisciplinary analysis of the connection between the religious, social, economic, and legal aspects of the Mediterranean world. It emphasizes the role of religious beliefs and institutions as a "discursive heritage", pragmatically used in the construction of political and economic systems. Religious phenomenology will be analysed from a diachronic and dynamic perspective to highlight the interdependence between the diversified cultural forms of the Mediterranean area. The core idea is that contemporary globalization, by re-proposing old questions in new scenarios, deepens and reveals forms of osmosis between different social systems. Globalization, and the pluralism it entails, challenges the post Second World War constitutional and democratic model, which was based on the universality of human rights, with the difficulty of realizing its promises; such a challenge reactivates tensions between contemporary universalistic claims and modern nationalistic reactions. Religion, economy, state politics, international and religious rights, and soft rules are all part of this transformation, which combines in a new way modern and contemporary paradigms.
To achieve these objectives, this *Book Series* is committed to publish works produced in languages different than the English one. Exchanging methods and knowledge in one of the most important languages of globalization, along with a comparative study of the relationships between the two shores of the Mediterranean, shall constitute a further step towards the overcoming of unilateral interpretations and culturally rooted stereotypes. Moreover, the *Series* will be linked to a web platform, created to stimulate a dialogue between researchers, but also to gather and share documents.

The Book Series "Studies in Religion, Law and Economics in the Mediterranean Space" is an integrated academic project, organized by the *Research Centre for Religion, Law and Economy in the Mediterranean Area* of the Insubria University, together with other Italian and foreign academic and research institutions (among others, three Universities of Milan, the Universities of Rome III, Padua, Turin, the Oriental Piedmont and, abroad, the Universities of Carthage, Tunis and Saint-Joseph, Beirut); furthermore, it is also an educational project, aimed at stimulating a cultural exchange between students, teachers, and researchers, on the one hand, and religious, social, economic and institutional actors, on the other hand.

# Diversity, Fear and Religions: Cultural Accommodation in a Globalized World

Edited by

Gennaro Gervasio, Maria Chiara Giorda
and Paola Perucchini

Routledge
Taylor & Francis Group
LONDON AND NEW YORK

G. Giappichelli Editore

First published 2026
by Routledge
4 Park Square, Milton Park, Abingdon, Oxon OX14 4RN

and by Routledge
605 Third Avenue, New York, NY 10158

*Routledge is an imprint of the Taylor & Francis Group, an informa business*

and by G. Giappichelli Editore
Via Po 21, Torino – Italia



*British Library Cataloguing-in-Publication Data*
A catalogue record for this book is available from the British Library

*Library of Congress Cataloging-in-Publication Data*
A catalogue record for this book has been requested

ISBN: 978-1-032-91317-9 (hbk-Routledge)
ISBN: 978-1-003-56256-6 (ebk-Routledge)
ISBN: 978-1-032-91319-3 (pbk-Routledge)
ISBN: 979-12-211-0893-4 (hbk-Giappichelli)

DOI: 10.4324/9781003562566

Typeset in Simoncini Garamond
by G. Giappichelli Editore, Turin, Italy

*The manuscript has been subjected to a peer review process prior to publication.*

*This book is published with the financial support received through the PriMED Program launched by the Ministry of Education, University and Scientific Research (MIUR) through a MIUR call (Directorial Decree n. 3089 of 11/16/2018 – ID 82382) and coordinated by the University of Eastern Piedmont.*

# CONTENTS

# LIST OF FIGURES

*page*

## Figures

### Chapter 5



### Chapter 7



### Chapter 8

# CONTRIBUTORS

**Carmen Becker**, holds a PhD in the Study of Religion. She works at the Institute for the Study of Religion of Leibniz University Hannover where she leads the junior research group "The Reproduction of Religion in Secular Societies" (RelSec) funded by the Deutsche Forschungsgemeinschaft (DFG).

**Marco Catarci**, is Full Professor of Intercultural Education at the Department of Education, Roma Tre University. He holds a PhD in Education and is member of the PhD School in Educational Research and Theory. He has taken part in many national and European research projects in the field of education. His major research interests include intercultural education, cultural mediation and inclusion of refugees and is the author of books, articles and research reports on these topics.

**Iain Chambers**, lives in Naples, where he researches the Mediterranean. He has taught Cultural, Postcolonial and Mediterranean Studies at the University of Naples, L'Orientale. Among his recent publications are *Postcolonial Interruptions, Unauthorized Modernities* (2017), *Mediterraneo blues* (2020) and, with Marta Cariello, *The Mediterranean Question* (2025). In 2022, he was a member of the collective «Jimmie Durham & A Stick in the Forest by the Side of the Road» invited to participate in documenta fifteen. He writes regularly for the Italian daily *il Manifesto.*

**Isabella De Paolis**, is currently a PhD candidate in "History and Cultures of Europe" at the Faculty of Humanities of Sapienza, University of Rome. Her research project investigates young Muslims attending Italian universities. She is a subject expert in History of religions at the Department of Humanities of Roma Tre University and a member of the editorial staff of *EREnews*, European Religious Education newsletter.

**Massimiliano Fiorucci**, is rector of Roma Tre University since 22 June 2022, Full Professor of General, Social and Intercultural Pedagogy. His research interests focus mainly on social and intercultural pedagogy with particular attention to the topic of inclusion of students with a migratory background, social inequalities and dispersion. He is the author of over 300 publications.

**Sara Gabrielli**, PhD, is Post-Doc student at Department of Education, Roma Tre University. Her research concerns prejudice development and reduction in primary school children; teaching Italian as a second language; migrants' inclusion in Italy; resilience development. She has authored different papers, chapters and books, her latest publication is: *Politiche e percorsi per l'inclusione* (2024).

**Gennaro Gervasio**, is Associate Professor of History of the Muslim Countries at the Department of Humanities, Roma Tre University. Prior to that, he has worked in Egypt, Australia and in the United Kingdom. He is Research Fellow at the Forum Transregionale Studien in Berlin, and from 2019 to 2021 he was the co-coordinator for Roma Tre University of PriMED international project (Prevention and Interaction in the Trans-Mediterranean Space). His research focuses on: secularism and Marxism in the Arab world, the history and politics of Islam in Europe, and civic activism and social and protest movements in the Arab World (especially Egypt and Iraq).

**Maria Chiara Giorda**, is Full Professor of History of Religions at the Department of Humanities, Roma Tre University. She is the coordinator of the international project "SHARP Lab", and a member of the École Française d'Athènes Project, "Interactions, juxtapositions, imbrications religieuses dans les Balkans (XX-XXI$^{e}$ siècles)" and of the Permanent Seminar on "Religious Diversity in Italian Urban History" (RDIUH), promoted by New York University and Roma Tre. Her research focuses on the following themes: history of religions, geography of religions, religion and urban spaces, shared religious places, history of monasticism.

**Alberta Giorgi**, is Associate Professor of Sociology of Cultural and Communication Processes at the University of Bergamo. Chair of the research network Political Sociology (European Sociological Association), co-editor-in-chief of the *Journal of Religion in Europe*. Her work explores boundaries and classifications, particularly at the intersection of politics, gender, religion, and science. She has recently co-edited with H. Eslen-Ziya *Populism and Science in Europe* (2022), and with J. Garraio and T. Toldy *Religion, Populism, Gender in the Mediterranean* (2023)

**Massimo Giuseppetti**, is Associate Professor of Greek at Roma Tre University. His main area of research is Greek Language and Literature, with particular attention to Greek poetry of the late archaic and Hellenistic periods. His publications include a monograph on Callimachus' *Hymn to Delos* and an annotated translation of Bacchylides' poem and fragments. He is currently working on the intersection between religion and literature in ancient Greece and on cognitive approaches to literature.

**Manlio Graziano**, is a Geopolitical Analyst who teaches at the Paris Institute of International Affairs, Sciences Po, and the Sorbonne, while also collaborating with various Italian, French, and American universities. He regularly contributes to *Corriere della Sera*, *Appunti*, and the *International Affairs Forum*. He has authored a dozen books, notably published by Columbia University Press, Stanford University Press, and Palgrave Macmillan. His latest book is *Disordine mondiale: Perché viviamo in un'epoca di crescente caos* (2024).

**Bryan McCormack**, is an Irish contemporary artist and activist. Over the past twenty years, he has exhibited his work in more than 30 group and solo exhibitions. In 2017 he founded the Yesterday-Today-Tomorrow (YTT) association. The inception of YTT followed Mc Cormack's impactful exhibition at the $57^{th}$ International Venice Biennale, which showcased the artistic creations of thousands of refugee children. YTT focuses on creating and implementing inclusive educational programs, vocational training, gender-equality education, gender-based violence prevention, and mental healthcare support. These initiatives aim to provide invaluable assistance to individuals in need, regardless of age, gender, or ethnicity.

**Manfredi Merluzzi**, DL and MA (Sapienza University of Rome), PhD (University of Genoa), is Professor of Early Modern History at University of Roma Tre, where is Director of the Advanced program in Historical Communication: multimedia and digital languages. He is member and leader of several international research group. His main research interests are: history and representations of power between Europe and America in the Spanish Monarchy; the role of Religion in the process of construction of viceregal colonial societies. Within his publications are: *Gobernando los Andes. Francisco de Toledo virrey del Perú 1569-1581* (2014); *Para la Quietud del Reino. Negociación y gobierno en el Perú (1533-1581)* (2019); *Conoscenza, governo e narrazione del potere nelle Monarchie Iberiche (secoli XVI-XVIII),* with Sabatini and Tudini (2020); *La Vergine contesa: Roma, l'Immacolata Concezione e l'universalismo della Monarchia Cattolica* (2022), with G. Sabatini and F. Tudini.

**Paola Perucchini**, is Full Professor of Developmental and Educational Psychology at the Department of Education, Roma Tre University and Head of the Department. She has been Vice-Director of the same Department and member of the Executive Committee of the Italian Psychology Association, Developmental and Educational Section (2012-2019). From 2019 to 2021 she was the co-coordinator for Roma Tre University of PriMED international project (Prevention and Interaction in the Trans-Mediterranean Space). Her research interests include, among others, communicative infant development; children's social adjustment; children's ethnic prejudice and educational programmes against discrimination.

**Gabriele Proglio**, is Associate Professor of Modern History at the University of Gastronomic Sciences, Pollenzo (Italy). His work focuses on the history of food, migrations, and mobilities across the Mediterranean in Modern and Contemporary eras, as well as memory studies, also the tools of oral history.

# INTRODUCTION


## Gennaro Gervasio, Maria Chiara Giorda and Paola Perucchini



ABSTRACT: *This opening chapter illustrates the aim of the book by outlining the subject. It approaches the concept of contemporary phobias, trauma and cultural memory, defines the research question and explains the methodology of the study. Furthermore, it provides an overview of the book's structure and briefly introduces the other chapters.*


While we were coordinating the PriMED project (www.primed_miur.it) on social integration and interreligious dialogue, which for Roma Tre University was coordinated by the Humanities Department and the Educational Science Department, we organized numerous educational and outreach activities related to otherness, diversity, and countering racism, xenophobia, and Islamophobia.

Together with those fears, in that period, a new collective fear, unprecedented for almost any living generation in the contemporary world, was able to paralyze millions of people and nail them to a feeling of terrorized panic that lasted for months.

The fear generated by the Covid-19 pandemic was the latest so far in a series of collective phobias that have swept across the world in recent decades and were driven by the feeling that the future held something different (and worse) not only from what we had envisioned and projected as a common expectation, but from what we had grown accustomed to experiencing (see Graziano's contribution in this volume).

The idea of a different and worse life began to feed the collective imaginaries following the eruption of traumas to which, after years of moderate pacification, democratic transition, economic development and social welfare in the so-called Western world, no one was accustomed anymore.

And it is with an awareness of the risk of using the categories of "us" and "them" as the best anthropologists from the past century to the present have taught us, that we want to point out how that "us" consisting of the inhabitants of a certain area of the Earth has ended up becoming a world-wide "us".

Fear has become the predominant feeling not only for a certain part of humanity, irresponsibly relying on the good life to which they are accustomed, but of all the inhabitants of the earth.

It is about splits, tears, disruptions from what is considered the norm and normal.

We know how event-trauma, or rather what is considered trauma, marks history and memory, and conversely, memory is capable of nurturing or dampening the power of trauma.

This happens on both a personal and a collective level and plays out on the double track of remembering and forgetting. One selects what one must and wants to remember but also what one must and wants to forget. As Assmann taught us in his studies on Cultural Memory, it often depends on whether violence was suffered or perpetrated, but not only that. As Alexander (2012, 14-15) writes:

> *"Traumatic status is attributed to real or imagined phenomena, not because of their actual harmfulness or their objective abruptness, but because these phenomena are believed to have abruptly, and harmfully, affected collective identity. (...) Trauma is not the result of a group experiencing pain. It is the result of this acute discomfort entering into the core of the collectivity's sense of its own identity. Collective actors "decide" to represent social pain as a fundamental threat to their sense of who they are, where they came from, and where they want to go".*

The history of trauma is the result of a shared convention and classification that nurtures a collective memory. In this sense there is no history of trauma, but a narrative (or multiple narratives) of a possible history of trauma.

And as he writes later (Alexander 2012, 26):

> *"Experiencing trauma can be understood as a sociological process that defines a painful injury to the collectivity, establishes the victim, attributes responsibility, and distributes the ideal and material consequences. Insofar as traumas are so experienced, and thus imagined and represented, the collective identity will shift. This reconstruction means that there will be a searching re-remembering of the collective past, for memory is not only social and fluid but also deeply connected to the contemporary sense of the self. Identities are continuously constructed and secured not only by facing the present and future but also by reconstructing the collectivity's earlier life".*

What is at stake is the construction of a cultural memory through cultural formations communication and the incorporation of it into an official and public memory. The official history of modern fears will also be constructed and narrated on the basis of personal, cultural and public memory.

One traces, trivial to remember, the detonation of collective contemporary fear to September 11, 2001, when for the first time in decades, in an overt, visible and visualized way, random death invaded the urban space of one of the seemingly safest, most vital, most dynamic, most vibrant cities. Most vibrant and least religious. Yet, it was religion and a certain reading of religion that corroborated the history and memory of that event. September 11, whatever the historically established facts may have been, the day of the deaths of hundreds of innocent victims, marked the beginning of a "terrified collective feeling", not only and not so much by the random and unjustified death made possible even in the safest place in the world, but, to put it briefly, by Islam. That day in 2001 ushered in the spread of a sense of belonging to a cultural (and religious) us that also reached the extreme as dangerous synthesis of us and them, the West and Islam. Even those who wanted to interpret the geopolitics reinforced, if not triggered, by 9/11 in such dichotomous terms did not emphasize that everyone shared the same sentiment: on the one hand fear of Islam, on the other hand fear of the spread of a visceral and unmediated sentiment that would technically be called Islamophobia.

Fear was replacing other feelings, such as hope, trust, serenity. Fear accompanied by aversion, anger, hatred. Fear of the other than oneself was expressed in reference to the culturally and, notably, religiously different. A new era began, in which of the double bond of religion with fear, it was the latter that was consolidated and entrenched. From one side, every culture and religion was born and has been fed by the fear of the loss or impossibility of controlling life, death, illness, pain, the end. From the other side, collective imaginaries feed clichés, stereotypes, in particular toward minorities, diversities and other cultures. Within this frame, religions can be both an answer to, or a cause of fears. Since 2001, religion has been scarier than offering comfort to fear.

Since that time, other collective fears would invade the world, fuelling a feeling of alarm and insecurity resting on diverse and not only cultural factors, intertwining, multiplying, nurturing and allowing stratifications of different fears and for different causes to settle. Diversity induces fear, where difference may be a language, a culture, a religion, but also a social, economic, physical condition compared to what is considered normal, compared to what we are familiar with, compared to what has been normalized, compared to what is taken for granted.

As Zerubavel (2018) taught us among all that we take for granted, customs, cultural facts, language habits, we are not used to reflect on how much our ways of saying, doing and being are always social facts, socially connoted.

Different crises, for different factors, have followed one another since 2001: the economic crisis, the environmental crisis, the pandemic crisis, the crisis related to ongoing wars. None has been overcome, but they have been juxtaposed and have increased the range of collective fears, sometimes narcotized by ephemeral antidotes that have no power over the disruptive force of the various forms of terror that cyclically reappear and re-propose. In the year in which we write this introduction, Islamophobia still exists, as does fear of poverty, terror over war, distrust of the means of environmental protection (Gervasio, Giorda and De Paolis; Giorgi in this book).

Focusing on the many fears that involve people around the world, history, sociology, pedagogy, psychology and anthropology can help to recognize the irrational aspects of such fears and to reflect on the us-them dichotomy by overcoming opposition and prejudice and by considering diversity a factor of empowering our identities as individuals and as social groups (see Catarci and Fiorucci; Perucchini, Gabrielli and McCormack).

The field of research on emotions is in its historical developments and has become increasingly multidisciplinary behind the driving force of the so-called *Emotional Turn* (Stearns 1985; Hitzer 2011): traversed by the humanities, social sciences, psychological and cognitive studies, between universalism and socio-constructivism, with different positions leaving the field open to different perspectives and hypotheses.

Within it, the feeling of fear represents one of the subfields that has attracted the scientific attention of many scholars, especially historians, for several decades (Gironda and Tolomelli 2015). We can consider a pioneer Georges Lefebvre observing the first phase of revolutionary politics in 1932, focusing on the French Revolution, followed by *La peur en Occident, XIV^e-XVIII^e siècles*, in 1978, and *Une cité assiégée* by Jean Delumeau (see Merluzzi in this volume).

If fear is, as Gioronda and Tolomelli remind us citing Bourke, "*a powerful driving force in the history of humanity*" (Bourke 2005, XII), it can be studied not only from different disciplinary perspectives, but by considering different spatialities of vantage points, in a historical frame: individual and collective fear, private and public fear, social, cultural, political and religious fear, fear from below, of citizens and fear from above, of institutions. These are physical and symbolic spatialities that this miscellaneous volume ambitiously sought to occupy and investigate.

In particular, within such an ocean of fears, this volume focuses on some examples of cultural fears related to different cultures and religions in a diachronically perspective (Merluzzi; Chambers; Proglio), starting from Ancient Greek models (Giuseppetti) and from a multidisciplinary perspective, which includes Religious Studies (De Paolis, Gervasio and Giorda; Giorgi; Becker), political science (Graziano), psycho-educational (Peruchini, Gabrielli and McCormack) and pedagogical (Catarci and Fiorucci).

Some of these forms of fear were provoked or sublimated by religious fundamentalisms and a double ignorance (ignorance *of* and *about* fundamentalisms) and have been contributing to feeding these collective worries and despair.

Through a multiple sample of stereotypes, mystifications and simplifications, the authors look at the power of nowadays globalized collective fears. Massimo Giuseppetti explains how in the broader context of the multiple religious experiences in place in the Ancient Greek world, the fear of the gods was a crucial factor in the conceptualization of proper ethical behaviour. Fear of divine powers was a social standing but also was used to implement very different political agendas.

In his chapter, Manfredi Merluzzi stresses how, from modern times, fear has been used as an important factor in constructing social and cultural consensus and social unity, to endorse policies, to strengthen power systems. Continuous perception of external and internal threats have been generating a widespread feeling of fear as a widespread social sentiment.

In his contribution Iain Chambers suggests to link present-day fears over migration to deeper histories in the forging of Europe through elements usually considered extraneous and foreign: Islam, Arab culture and the Ottoman Empire.

In the same path, the chapter of Gabriele Proglio analyzes from a historical perspective some mobilities of food and people in the Mediterranean to dismantle a white-European imaginary in the area and stressing how many different interruptions have marked its history so far.

Manlio Graziano focuses on the dynamic of a increasing collective fear in the last decenies: a great international disorder triggered by the collapse of the Yalta order, was further exacerbated by the crises of 2008 and 2020, generating a state of uncertainty, confusion and apprehension

Alberta Giorgi explains how the Muslim Question essentializes Islam as a homogeneous actor through the 'othering' processes which combine gender, religious, and ethnic dimensions in complex identity assemblages of 'us' and 'them'. Exploring one Italian iteration of the narrative of replacement she focuses on how it is articulated by the First report on Islamization of Europe, published in 2019 by a think tank connected to the current leading party in the Italian government.

Marco Catarci and Massimiliano Fiorucci in their chapter focus on the use of intercultural approaches to education to promote dialogue and cultural exchange amongst natives and foreigners, tackling various forms of diversity (cultural, gender, social class, etc.) and different intercultural approaches: political, critical and transformative.

Carmen Becker theorizes the figure of the refugee in order to provide the conceptual framework for a case study based on some refugees' histories. Mixing the coded, analyzed, and theorized data from her ethnographic participant observation with the help of maxqda, a software for qualitative data analysis, she aims to connect the micro level of daily interaction and practices to the meso and macro levels of discourses, structures and institutions.

Paola Perucchini, Sara Gabrielli and Bryan McCormack reflect on the fear created by migration flows both in 'us' and 'others'. They present the Yesterday-Today-Tomorrow's (YTT's) learning program to promote human rights, which has been used with displaced populations in refugee's camps and with primary school children to reduce prejudice toward migrants.

Isabella de Paolis, Gennaro Gervasio and Maria Chiara Giorda shed light on the self-representations and the fears emerging from within the Muslim communities in Italy today. Thanks to a privileged corpus of primary sources made of interviews realized within the activities of PriMED project.

The chapters of this volume explore the possibilities of some cultural antidotes to phobias, such as new awareness and knowledge related to diversities, based on an open education to interculturality and plural citizenship, that can be "another" way to tackle the fear.

## References

Alexander, J.C. (2012). *Trauma: A Social Theory*. Polity Press. Kindle edition.

Bourke, J. (2006). *Fear: a cultural history*. Shoemaker Hoard, Publishers Group West, Emeryville, CA.

Gironda, V. and Tolomelli, M. (2015) *History and Emotions: On Social Constructions and the Politics of Fear*, in V. Gironada and M. Tolomelli (eds.). *Representations of Fear in History: Empirical / Practical evidence and Methodological Issues. Storicamente*, available at https://storicamente.org/dossier-doss_paura/gironda_tolomelli_history_fear.

Hitzer, B. (2011). "Emotionsgeschichte – ein Anfang mit Folgen". *H-Soz-Kult*, available at http://www.hsozkult.de/literaturereview/id/forschungsberichte-1221.

Lefebvre, G. (1970). *La grande peur de 1789*. Armand Colin, Paris.
Pamlper, J. (2015). *History of Emotions*. Oxford University Press, Oxford.
Rosenwein, B.H., (2016). *Generazione di sentimenti. Una storia delle emozioni, 600-700*. Viella, Roma.
Stearns, P.N. and Stearns, C.Z. (1985). "Emotionology: Clarifying the History of Emotions and Emotional Standards". *The American Historical Review*, 90(4), 813-836.
Zerubavel, E. (2018). *Taken For Granted – The Remarkable Power Of The Unremarkable*. Princeton University Press, Princeton.

Chapter 1

# FEAR IN WESTERN SOCIETIES? AN HISTORICAL APPROACH TO OCCIDENTAL CONSTRUCTION OF "FEAR"

**Manfredi Merluzzi**

ABSTRACT: *This opening chapter illustrates the aim of the book by outlining its subject. It approaches solidarity from a legal perspective, defines the research question and explains the methodology of the study. Furthermore, it provides an overview of the book's structure and briefly introduces the other chapters.*

SUMMARY: 1. An increasing sense of fear. – 2. Provincializing Europe increases Western fears? – 3. History and the politics of Fear. – 4. A step backward in the past: Plague and other pandemics. – 5. What about wars, slavery, religious and political persecutions? – 6. The new information eve. – 7. Fear it's not only in the West. – 8. Age of crisis and melancholy: war, pestilence, climatic change, revolutions, economic decline, international relationship in 17$^{th}$ century. – 9. A recent fear: climatic change. – 10. The fear of losing the superabundance. – 11. More than fifty years of concerns. – References.

## 1. An increasing sense of fear

There is no doubt that, at the moment we are writing this book, what we usually consider "Western societies" are experiencing a growing sense of fear. Terrorism, economic crises, pandemics, wars, and their most dramatic potential consequence: nuclear disaster, are adding threats to the more recent "global fears" related to climate change and its impact on human societies, and migration (as a result of famine, wars – again – and political persecution). Many scholars agree that the continuous perception of external and internal threats is generating a widespread feeling of fear (Todorov 2009) that eventually prevails over other widespread social sentiments, to the detriment of constructive and shared political actions (Antonelli 2019; Monod 2006; Borgna 1997; 1995).

This sentiment of fear acts like a fire consuming a portion of international and media attention, affecting economics, finance, influencing public opinion, election results, and everyday life in Western (and not only Western) societies. And fire is difficult to manage; it can expand very quickly and run out of control.

Moreover, the Hamas terrorist attack on October 7, 2023, has brought the dramatic situation in the Middle East back into people's minds. It seems to have set the international Middle East situation back several years, demonstrating the fragility of the diplomatic efforts to achieve the so-called "Abraham Accords" as a strategic solution to the Israeli-Palestinian issue. The events, occurring on the 50$^{th}$ anniversary of the Yom Kippur War, had a symbolic aspect and have been described as the 9/11 of Israel. During a one-day visit to Tel Aviv, US President Joe Biden appealed to Israel not to be "consumed" by rage in its response to the attack by Hamas, while pledging steadfast support for Israel's self-defense. Israeli Prime Minister Benjamin Netanyahu promised to allow aid into Gaza via Egypt. In his speech, Biden compared Israel's predicament after the massacre of more than 1,300 of its citizens to the US's crisis 22 years ago after the 9/11 attacks. His country had "sought and got justice", but also "made mistakes", he said. The suggestion of the US President is relevant, and the consent us to point out at least three topics related to our contribution.

1) Biden compared the attack of 7/10/23 to the atrocity of 9/11/01, as a shocking event that influenced the international politics of the US nourishing a "rage response" to the fear of having been attacked and to the quest for justice as this atrocity caused in the public opinion;
2) he affirmed that 10/7 could have an impact on Israeli society 15 times greater than 9/11 for the US;
3) the quest for reparatory justice after 9/11 led the US to commit mistakes relevant to the situation in Israel. Nevertheless, he asked the Israeli Prime Minister and Government not to ignore these mistakes.

President Biden was directly connecting to one of the most relevant and shocking events of the last 20 years, the impact of terrorism following 9/11/2021, and the role this played in the international economy, politics, and world order.

'It is clear that the threat of terrorism has fed the construction of an enemy based on radicalized Islam and has been one of the most pressing aspects of internal and international politics in Western society (Monod 2006). This closely connects with the notion of 'otherness' along with the changing composition of Western societies' (Furedi 2019; Catarci *et al.* 2022).

4) On October 20th, 2023, the UN Secretary António Guterres wrote on Twitter/X from the Rafah Crossing:

*"It's impossible to be at the Rafah crossing & not feel heartbroken.*
*Behind these walls there are 2 million people in Gaza with no water, food, medicine, fuel.*
*On this side, these trucks have what they need.*
*We need to make them move – as soon as possible, as many as necessary".*

This is a significant metaphor for the crisis of Western globalized societies: not a lack of resources, but an overabundance of them, coupled with an unequal capability to use them adequately and to redistribute them properly. The strong liberal and capitalistic idea that increasing resources would address all the needs of human societies, and that the redistribution of this wealth could weaken tensions within different human groups and eventually make them dormant, has proven to be untrue (Ostili 2023).

## 2. Provincializing Europe increases Western fears?

Recently, in *Civilization: Is the West History?* Niall Ferguson (2018) argues that, beginning in the fifteenth century, the West developed six powerful new concepts, which served as unique instrumental tools that the "Rest" lacked. In such a dichotomous vision, those key concepts were competition, science, the rule of law, modern medicine, consumerism, and the work ethic. Using a new technologically influenced vocabulary, Ferguson defines them as "killer apps" that allowed the West to move forward faster and stronger than the "Rest". This led to the opening of global trade routes, the exploitation of new scientific knowledge, the political evolution of representative government, the increase in life expectancy, the industrial revolution, and, subsequently, a significant increase in human productivity. Adopting this dichotomous framework to represent history, Ferguson states that "Civilization" is a process demonstrating how a few Western empires came to control three-fifths of mankind and four-fifths of the world economy. Obviously, this position could eventually be historiographical faced adopting different perspective of analysis such as global history (Mazlish 1998; Berger 2003; Gruzinski 2006) post-colonial studies (Chakrabarty 2000), connected history (Subrahmanyan 1997, 2022; Douki and Minard 2007) among others, but what we really are interested in, here, is to consider that outcome as evidence of a recurrent tendency. A tendency that doesn't belong only to scholars, but it is shared in the largest areas of the societies, as it shows in 2011 a Tv British Documentary titled *Civilization: Is the West History?* Narrated in 6 episodes the Keys of the Western rise to the be the dominating area of the world, just a decade later, the Fear of the western people feel is to perceive having lost this ability of political, ideological, economical influence on the World, and the easier way to handle the Fear, as history tells, is projecting it and guilt of one's own failure onto the other.

The idea of decline or even of the "failure" of a Civilization, is not new and the interesting aspect of this series is of taking in account again the scholars' ideas on the decline of the west. The key concept, was already expressed by Sprengler in a research not completely accepted by historians (we were in the beginning of the Nazis ideology, and Sprengler was accused by socialists thinker to affinity with them) is that civilizations decay as an organism after his natural life cycle (Splenger 1918-1922). That could eventually allow historians to reconstruct the past and even predict "*the spiritual forms, duration, rhythm, meaning and product of the still unaccomplished stages of our Western history*". (Britannica and Spengler 2023).

Nevertheless, in the Past of Human Societies, of course we can find many of those that shows previous moments in which human societies have suffered moment of angst, fear, terror (Brogna 1997; Ginzburg 2015) even the clear perception of a serious risk of collective extinction (Vovelle 1984).

## 3. History and the politics of Fear

Fear has been used in many historical situations and human groups as an important leverage in constructing social and cultural consensus and social unity, to endorse policies, to strengthen power systems even to focus on an external enemy. It is not a coincidence that scholars are now back on the contribution of the German jurist Carl Schmitt (Schmitt 2012). Some categories he introduced as 'authoritarian democracy', 'absolute enemy and war', 'exceptional state', 'terrorism' are very much part of everyday political and mediatic debate in the last two decades. Such categories, as it's easy to understand, stress the radicalization in the public debates and increases social and individual anxiety, but at the same time are critical tools and legitimizing factor for regressive policies (Monod 2006; Mossa 2017).

The continuous perception of external and internal threats generating a widespread feeling of fear eventually prevails over other widespread social sentiments, to the detriment of constructive and shared political actions. In the age of increasing populism, fragmentation, and polarization, this fear is shared even in the richest countries. Based on the debate in recent literature and historiography, this contribution aims to focus on the emotional and cultural roots of fear not only the economic aspects – of our globalized modernity, highlighting what we truly have to dread: economic disparity, cultural impoverishment, environmental degradation, and a general perception of meaningless policies and individual actions. The pandemic has led to the emergence, as it has in the past, of a heightened sense of uncertainty. A secondary result of the pandemic, interacting with widespread use of social media and media, has been the growth of popular beliefs in conspiracies and power strategies, as well as attacks on the scientific system. We have once again witnessed penitential processions, the dissemination of miraculous potions, and the search for scapegoats (Prosperi 2021). These phenomena are evidence of a general lack of meaning and trust in collective or social ideas, political direction, and an alarming indicator of difficulties in giving meaning to the future (Sandel 1998). The world is changing so rapidly that what we are experiencing is more a metamorphosis than an evolution (Beck 2016). Such a pace makes it harder for human society and scientists to develop interpretations and suitable instruments of analysis. It's not just a matter of abandoning "all hope of totality, future as well as past" as we enter "the world of liquid modernity" (Bauman 2000), but also of a confusing loss of sense and meaning in both the public and private spheres (Ferraris 2019, 19-66).

In the last days of January 2024, just before the second anniversary of the Russian invasion of Ukraine, one of the most attentive and lucid thinkers of Western culture in recent decades, Edgar Morin, published a call to intellectuals and people of good sense to resist, calling it "The Resistance of the Spirit". Against ecological, economic, political, and social crises, he claims that Western societies need a bulwark. The idea is not new; we have many examples of such spiritual resistance, a cultural bulwark, and Morin himself cites examples from the fight against 20$^{th}$ century totalitarian regimes. Many times, the idea of resistance by a small group has led to a better future. The first example can be found in Herodotus' Histories, describing the feelings of the Westerners (in this case, the Greeks) facing what they perceived as a huge, overwhelming menace – the Persian Army of Cyrus. This was in the 5$^{th}$ century BCE. At the same time, Morin reminds the very dramatic allegiance between Molotov and Ribbentrop in 1939, that was just before the Poland invasion and division by soviet and Nazi's armies. The first January of such year, the former Russian revolutionary Victor Serge, published in France: *S'il est minuit dans le siècle* (Serge 1939). This book could be considered an earlier disenchanted denunciation by a political opponent to Stalinism, a warning to all the World. The same year was the outbreak of World War II. Morin does not hesitate to compare such highly dramatic historical moments to the one we are living nowadays.

Two wars are surrounding Europe, in Ukraine and in Palestine (he does not mention other important conflicts in other areas such Yemen,

Niger and so on). And both are involving a large scale of international interests, geopolitical matters. Consequences on world scale are already spreading: some more independence from the Western Countries in the South of the World and a strengthening in the relationship between China and Russia.

In the meanwhile, in the Middle East the Israelian military reaction against the terroristic Hamas attack on the 7$^{th}$ October 2023 is wide spreading a dissent and enforcing the crisis in the area, but Morin states there is not a easy strategy to stop that conflict, and he affirms at the moment: "thinking has become blind"!

His observations are touching with a great clarity the points that are connected with the potential causes of fear and we can observe that many of them are connected with threatens that human society perceived like them also in the past: wars, the environmental risks, struggles of power between greater actors in politics and economy in international level, the growing of control on every day and anyone life of the capitalism, and he uses the significant term of "policrisis". The crisis feed off each other in a kind of ever-growing ecological, economic, political, social and civilization polycrisis.

If we trust to Morin's words terrible clouds are standing around Europe and the west or even the entire Globalized society. Graziano affirmed that such «anxiety» depicted by Sandel and begun in 1970's, is now becoming a kind of Zeitgeist (Graziano 2021), with a series of threats and menaces that are overlapping one over the other increasing the situation of confusion. In the article of Morin this clearly confirmed (Morin 2024).

## 4. A step backward in the past: Plague and other pandemics

According to Beck, to deeply understand the metamorphosis of the world, it is necessary to see new possible beginnings. To do that, it is essential to "*focus on what is emerging from the old and seek to grasp future structures and norms in the turmoil of the present*" (Beck 2016).

Nevertheless, we are not aiming to reconstruct a history of fear as collective psychology here. However, we can draw a brief description of how fear has been part of many human societies at different times and how historians have analyzed this disturbing presence. Dealing with something entirely new can generate panic, but recognizing its presence and coexistence in other contexts can be helpful in facing it (Prosperi 2021).

When did those 'anxious times' begin? According to Sandel, it was in the second half of the last century, starting with the oil crisis of the 1970s. Undoubtedly, those were years of fear, loss of control, widespread dismay, and the search for shelter and protection, even spiritual. These years were also marked by the rise of religious fundamentalism (Sandel 1998, 3). The spread of a greater sense of precariousness and the end of unconditional faith in economic development contributed to revitalizing the spiritual quest and strengthening different religious groups, blocking the ongoing process of secularization and challenging the proclaimed 'death of God' in Western societies (Berger 1999).

The 1970s have being crucial years for the 'success of fear': as Daniel Gardner recalls in Science of Fear, many sociologists identify in that period the beginning of the obsession with risk, with security, with precaution. Frank Furedi defined Culture of Fear 1997 (Furedi 1997) this widespread sense of fear and examines the roots of this contemporary risk consciousness, arguing that it reflects an outlook of low expectation. Furedi explains that "*No doubt the tragic events of 11 September 2001 will make millions of people, Americans, and others, fearful of the world around them. But unfortunately, fear has been a big thing long before this terrible episode. Outwardly, the USA has presented a picture of confidence and optimism about the future. The image of massive skyscrapers, big cars, a dynamic popular culture, and energetic people has dominated the global imagination*" (Furedi 2018, VII) before that event. Now we have entered a time he defined "Culture of Fear" and he tried "*to explain what it is about society today that has encouraged such obsessive preoccupations about safety*" (Furedi 2018, VII).

If fear is not a matter that concerns only present time, basing on evidence and on the historiography, we can have an overlook that threats are something that human societies had always faced and experimented.

Recent Covid-19 SARS 2 Pandemic had nourished studies on analogue situation in History, so we can find examples in many pandemics and plagues along the past and in different areas. We can find mentioned cases of pestilences, and plagues in the Bible (e.g. *Deuteronomio*, 32.23-24), but one of the most relevant and ancient description by an Historians was by the Greek Historian Thucydides, in his War of the Peloponnesus (Thucydides and Canfora 2007). He describes the Plague of Athens, occurred in 430-429 BCE, that marked the dramatic end of what historian knows as the golden Age of Pericles and the democracy in Athens and the decline of the power of this city. We have description of epidemic in many ancient authors like Galen, Hippocrates, Aristoteles so we can imagine that was a recurrent phenomenon. Procopius of Caesarea (Procopius, *Storia delle guerre*, VII, 20) wrote that about ten centuries later, in 542 AC. Constantinople was hit by a plague which, after killing about 40% of the population, spread in throughout the Mediterranean in different waves, lasting centuries, until about the year 750. This plague caused 50 to 100 million deaths, for this reason, according to Naphy and Spicer it must be considered the first pandemic in history. (Naphy and Spicer 2006, p. 13). In this case has been discovered that some years before some huge Islandic Vulcanic eruption produced a cap that reduce the solar irradiation on earth for one year, causing a climate change, lasting one century, with a reduction of temperatures, called the Small Glacial Age in the Late Antiquity (Keller *et al.* 2019; McCormick 2019). Such discovery demonstrates a relation between the climate and the spreading of epidemics.

Nevertheless, this experience is not unique to Western societies; the Muslim world shared a similar situation. Starting from the Hegira, we have evidence of at least five plagues: the "plague of Shirawayh" (McCormick 2019, 627-628), the "plague of Amwas" (*ivi*, 638-639), the "violent plague" (*ivi*, 688-689), the "plague of virgins" (*ivi*, 706), and the "plague of notables" (*ivi*, 716-717) (Naphy and Spicer 2006; Cosmacini 2005).

Establishing a political or cultural divide between the West and "the Rest" is misleading when trying to understand such phenomena in the past. Perhaps the most significant plague in our knowledge originated in Mongolia and moved both southeast (China) and southwest (Syria, Anatolia). It then struck the Balkans (Greece in 1346), the Mediterranean (Egypt in 1346, Sicily in 1347, and Genoa in 1348), and spread through Switzerland in 1348 and across the Italian peninsula. From Switzerland, it spread to France and Spain, and then to England, Scotland, and Ireland in 1349. Historians call it the Black Death, although it is not certain what disease caused the plague. It wasn't until 1894 that the bacterium Yersinia pestis, probably transmitted from rats to humans by fleas, was isolated and considered the possible cause of the disease. The outbreak of the Black Death began to subside only around 1353.

We can estimate some important aspects. Firstly, that 50% of those affected by this epidemic died. Secondly, in Europe, it caused nearly 20 million deaths, a third of the European population at that time (Ujvari 2002; Vovelle 1984). Thirdly, this epidemic recurred on a smaller scale both in Europe and other areas (for the Islamic area, see Byrne 2008) for the following centuries, recurring until the $18^{th}$ century. The last plague epidemic struck Eastern Asia (China, India) until 1855 and even later in Australia in 1925.

It is easy to understand as such a broad and recurrent factor may be considered one of the prevalent threaten to Human societies almost everywhere, and since antiquity to modern times and with deep root in all the imaginaries (Prosperi 2021; Cosmacini 2005; Byrne 2008; Vovelle 1984, Delumeau 1995; Naphy and Spicer 2006).

## 5. What about wars, slavery, religious and political persecutions?

The recurrence of the plague and other pandemics from 1340 until 1855 justifies a sense of uncertainty about life and impotence in the face of the unknown, often interpreted as God's punishment (Delumeau 1995). Unexpected natural events like volcanic eruptions, earthquakes, and floods had similar effects, inspiring a sense of punishment and impotence in human societies from a superior metaphysical power (Nature, God, gods). Important evidence can be considered in the impact of the Lisbon earthquake in 1755 on the European intellectual society of the Enlightenment. *Candide*, written by Voltaire in 1759, can be considered a clear testament to this.

We can certainly mention other major threats that caused significant fear and were dreaded by almost all societies in the past. Among the most severe were slavery, religious persecution, and war. These factors acted in multiple historical events and periods, composing a terrifying combination of social disintegration and individual menace, as well as inspiring collective fear. The feeling of dread was nourished by wars, invasions, raids, conquests, and pillaging, even by religious wars among people of the same faith – Christians (Catholics, Calvinists, Lutherans, and others) as well as within Islam (Sunni and Shia Muslims). We know that in Asia, as well as in India and Latin America, these factors were also largely present.

Political, ideological, and religious persecutions last from antiquity to the present and often has been used has justification for wars. Numbers are sad and astonishing. We give just some examples from different events: the Emperor Charles called the Great and considered as father of Europe in a single day executed around 4,500 Saxons refusing conversion to Cristian faith; the Conquer and control of America by Europeans against natives (1492-1900) caused between 50 to 100 million deaths; Thirty Years war (1618-1648) caused only in the actual Germany around 20 million death; in the American Civil War it has been estimated around 600-750,000 victims; Holocaust in the 1938-1945 caused 17,000 millions of deaths in different groups (religious, social, ethnic, national…). We just stop this short list mentioning the World War II, the catastrophic military conflict which caused more victims in history. Between 1939-1945 has been estimated that between 70 to 85 million people have dead, about 3% of all human global population at that time (US-Census Bureau, 2023). Possibly the highest number of victims in a single event are the 200,000 deaths of Nuclear Bombing in Hiroshima and Nagasaki (1945).

This numbers are well known by scholars and not only, and even if some figure can be redefined, they are enough to give an idea of how much the uncertainty, sufferance and death can be spread in the past for reasons tied to human political behaviours and political and economic choices. As well, they clearly show the increasing numbers of the global phenomena, as could be wars in present times.

## 6. The new information eve

Today, we are still full of fears. Maybe because we have gone too far away (Harari 2011). The globalized society, the interconnected world, the financial markets, the network, the digital, far from offering us the certainties promised by a positivistic vision of linear progress, by considering a linear integration of markets and trade, of standardization and digitization, of hypertrophic communication and the by production of unseen flows of information and communication, is discovering that there are many uncontrollable variables (Berger 2003; Magatti 2009). We are (re)discovering that humanity is vulnerable. That our technology, our science, our security systems are vulnerable, our certainties are not standing any more against the uncertainty (Kumar 2000). In time of the pandemic Adriano Prosperi reminded us that being afraid is part of the human destiny (Prosperi 2021). The difficult times in which we are now (or what we perceive as them) also are part of this destiny. Therefore, this feeling of risks may immobilize us, like animals in the face of danger. But they just form part of the uncertainty, the impossibility of controlling any variable of the life as individuals, as groups, as nations, as "civilization", as humankind.

## 7. Fear it's not only in the West

The relationship with fear is certainly not unique to the historical moment we are experiencing (Vovelle 1984), nor is it a characteristic exclusive to Western societies, as we have seen. Tackling the subject of fear in the modern age cannot ignore certain fundamental references that represent milestones marking important steps along the historiographical path, which also reveal how our society is changing. For scholars and especially historians, fear can also be analyzed as a cultural aspect of a society (Vovelle 1984; Delumeau 1995; Prosperi 2021; Ginzburg 2015). Utilizing the concepts of diachronicity and synchronicity, as well as the approach of cultural history, allows for an investigation of fear as an aspect that changes over time and reveals certain characteristics of a human group and society.

From Delumeau's studies on fear in the West (Delumeau 1978), we know that fear has been a prevalent feeling in past societies. His analysis, both descriptive and conceptual, indicates that such fear was mainly linked to the dimensions of the unknown and the religious, as well as to guilt and sin. Even within this framework, we can find a large catalogue of fears, including fear of the spirits of the dead, of darkness, of storms, of ferocious beasts, and more. Additionally, there was fear of the female mystery, as well as a long range of fears related to natural and supernatural events, such as fear of misfortunes, famines, cataclysms, and epidemics. Above all, there was the great fear of the wrath of God.

In order to dominate such an ancestral anguish, Delumeau shows that fear, the most frequent social reaction, implies a need to identify someone to consider as responsible for these social fears and then to punish it, to extinguish such mood. For certain aspects, fear has indirectly ruled human history through the ages, affecting much of the cultural practices and patterns. At least in the pre-industrial society. The point for Delumeau is that fear is an essential device for escaping danger and temporarily for escaping death. So fear and death made a tied connection in the social imaginary. How to manage this ancestral anguish has been studied by Philippe Ariés, who analyzed also the different collective answers that have been developed in Western societies in different times to such terrible final challenge (Ariés 1975).

In most recent years, Todorov investigated on a different kind of fear perception, that manifest the greater concern the West is now suffering for geopolitical reasons tied to migration, feel like a new invasion. The changing of the previously known equilibrium leads the western societies to perceive a strong sense of menace that is not yet founded in the dichotomy West-East, neither in the opposition between North-South countries, but in countries dominated by rage, and by fear, by hostility. Todorov foreseen the increasing and wide spreading of the populistic, xenophobic, and nationalistic movement and opinions. The key for him is to retake and deepen the reflection on the relation with the "other", even basing on historical processes. Once more, a simplistic and dichotomic vision pushes to define such difference, such "otherness" with the incorrect term of "barbarian". Todorov argues that such "fear of the barbarians" is a feebleness for Europe nowadays (Todorov 2009).

## 8. Age of crisis and melancholy: war, pestilence, climatic change, revolutions, economic decline, international relationship in 17th century

The Italian Historian Aurelio Musi has recently published a study on the so called "Baroque melancholy", analysing different sources, from historical evidence to medical treaties, literacy, art, and reconstruct the imagine of a Century in which a diffuse sense of melancholy was spread in western societies.

In this century, we have simultaneously experienced many different causes of "anxiety" that can be evidenced historically: climatic changes, large-scale war, plague, poor harvests, economic crises, revolutions, religious wars, and the fall of the political international order (as known in the European cultural horizon). Most of these issues are the same ones that are causing anxiety today.

We know there was a minor glaciation that affected northern Europe, which, combined with the Thirty Years War, led to a decline in food production. During the same period, there was a strong resurgence of pestilence that affected populations: in Milan (1576-1577), in northern Italy again in 1630, in Seville (1647-1652). The Ottoman Empire was seriously affected in 1661. In Amsterdam, the plague killed around 35,000 people in 1663-1664. London was struck in 1665-1666, resulting in between 75,000 and 100,000 deaths (more than 20% of the population) (Naphy and Spicer 2006, 90-95). War, pestilence, insurrections, and economic crises led major European powers, particularly Spain, to collapse, lose their hegemony, and fragment into a series of revolutions (Portugal, Aragon, Naples, Flanders, etc.), as well as in other areas outside Spanish dominions, like Ukraine and France (Elliot 1963).

This period of global unrest and crisis has been called by Western historiography "The General Crisis" (Trevor Roper 1967). The 1640s are considered by many Western historians to be the most violent decade ever recorded in world history. Hobsbawm also highlights that this general crisis is related to the economic system changing from feudalism to capitalism (Hobsbawm 1954; Romano 1992; Elliot 1963).

## 9. A recent fear: climatic change

This breakdown is just adding to a general perception were broadly diffused on the media and social media of a strange new malaise, defined as "Ecoanxiety". "Many people report fearing for themselves, their children and future generations with deep feelings of loss, hopelessness, and anger as they witness the effects of climate change. It is important to understand the anxiety response evoked by the climate crisis, given its increased global awareness". (Coffeya *et al.* 2021)

The Climatic change is considered by Beck as crucial factor in reshaping our Concept of the World. For him "We live in a world that is increasingly difficult to understand. It is not just changing: it is metamorphosing.

Change implies that some things change while others remain the same; capitalism changes, but some aspects of capitalism remain as they always were. Metamorphosis implies a much more radical transformation in which the old certainties of modern society are falling away, and something quite new is emerging. Beck underlined that "*much of the debate about climate change has focused on whether or not it is really happening, and if it is, what we can do to stop or contain it*" (Beck 2016). Today, this debate is still open, but

> "*this emphasis on solutions blinds us to the fact that climate change is an agent of metamorphosis. It has already altered our way of being in the world – the way we live in the world, think about the world, and seek to act upon the world through our actions and politics. Rising sea levels are creating new landscapes of inequality, drawing new world maps whose key lines are not traditional boundaries between nation-states but elevations above sea level. It is creating an entirely different way of conceptualizing the world and our chances of survival within it*" (Beck 2016).

This aspect should not only be considered a reason for fear or anxiety; it "*goes beyond the theory of world risk society*" (Beck 2016), which, of course, has a connection with Furedi's ideas: "*it is not about the negative side effects of goods but the positive side effects of bads. They produce normative horizons of common goods and propel us beyond the national frame towards a cosmopolitan outlook*" (Beck 2016). Additionally, Morin points out that ecological degradation is causing social and economic divergences (Morin 2024). At the same time, it "*is widely recognized as one of the most serious global health threats of the 21st century, threatening public health worldwide, including the impacts of slow, gradual climate change and its effects on mental health, known as eco-anxiety*" (Coffeya *et al.* 2021).

It has to be stressed that this issue is not concerning only the Western Societies but the whole entire globe. Nevertheless, Climatic Change is not a condition that affects only the present, we know by different evidence, from literacy to biology, to chemistry, that Climate often has changed menacing the Human society. We have already saw in 17$^{th}$ century and in the 6$^{th}$ century historically recorded moments of climate changing to Coldest conditions, but a recent study on human population in the Pleistocene analysing human genomic sequence of 3,154 individuals reach an impressive result on those human ancestors. Between around 930,000 and 813,000 years ago, human had faced serious risks of extinction, loosing around the 98.7% of the estimated world human population. In that chronological arch, they suffered a severe population reduction to only 1280 breeding individuals. It took a long time to exit from this situation, about 117,000 years (Wangjie Hu *et al.* 2023).

## 10. The fear of losing the superabundance

On October 20th, 2023, the UN Secretary António Guterres wrote on Twitter from the Rafah Crossing:

> *"It's impossible to be at the Rafah crossing & not feel heartbroken. Behind these walls there are 2 million people in Gaza with no water, food, medicine, fuel. On this side, these trucks have what they need. We need to make them move – as soon as possible, as many as necessary".*

This is a significant metaphor of the Crisis of the western Globalized societies, not a need of resources, even an overabundance of them, but an incapability of use them adequately and to redistribute them properly. A feeling of a new perception of impotence, after century of leadership.

According to the historian Ferguson Western civilization's rise to global dominance is the single most important historical phenomenon of the past five centuries. Spread all around the world this model of culture and economic growth affects behaviours, dreams, and sentiments of a growing number of people with its influences. Ferguson questions how the West prevailed on its Eastern competitors and if the zenith of Western power has now passed (Ferguson 2018).

The debate on what may be defined as "Civilization" and the one on the peculiars characters of the West are both too large to be resumed here, even if they had been often tied, properly or not, between them. Anyway, this is not the place to go in it, because so many different aspects and disciplinary approaches should be considered in the evolution of the debate: such post-colonialist, philosophical, sociological, anthropological, and historical. Nevertheless, we can just record that a feeling of proudness and a feeling of losing a certain kind of supremacy has been recurrent in scholars. Notably in the 1920s of last Century Oswald Sprengler wrote on the Decline of Occident (Sprengler 1918-1922).

The Wester decline concept rose up in different terms and with different meaning during the post-World War II and the post-colonial time (Chakrabarty 2000).

Until, in the last decade of the 20th century, Samuel Huntington proposed to consider a different scenario, even more dramatic a "Clash of civilizations" that contrasted the optimistic analyses about the progress and the peaceful scenario of a globalization. He predicted a possible scenario of conflicts marked along cultural lines and especially after 9/11 2001 he has been considered to have predicted the conflict with the Islamic fundamentalism (Huntington 1996). The reaction among scholars and the public of this interpretation raised a debate on the relationship between the West and Islam and the changings in the world Order (Segura 2007).

Despite this binary and simplistic vision, more complex explanations are needed. As Morin recently observed, "*The hegemony of uncontrolled profit increases inequalities in every nation and across the planet. The qualities of our civilization have deteriorated, and its deficiencies have increased, particularly in the development of selfishness and the disappearance of traditional solidarities*". At the same time, possibly as a consequence of losing clarity of judgment or points of reference in the dialogue between institutions and citizens, and between representatives and the represented, one of the most characteristic achievements of the West – democracy – is in crisis. It is not a matter of "exporting democracy to other Asian or African areas, nor of expanding soft power". (Morin 2024) In almost all continents, democracy "*is increasingly being replaced by authoritarian regimes that, having computerized means of controlling populations and individuals, tend to create submissive societies that we could call neo-totalitarian. Globalization has not created any solidarity, and the United Nations is increasingly disunited*" (Morin 2024). Johanna Hoerning considers that, over the last decades, a significant part of the scientific effort in discussing and elaborating critical epistemologies that go beyond nationalism and Occidentalism has been affected by the "binary logic". Such binary categorization and analysis imply more fragmentary and eruptive results. For her, the outcome is a further division of the world (Hoerning 2024, 112-134). In such a metamorphically global change, appears like a paradox the fast and broad advance of technological and scientific progress, that is at the same "time the cause of the worst regressions of our century. It is this progress that has allowed the scientific organization of the Auschwitz extermination camp; it is this progress that has allowed the design and manufacture of the most destructive weapons, up to the first atomic bomb; it is this progress that makes wars more and more lethal; it is this progress that, driven by the thirst for profit, has created the ecological crisis on the planet". Morin, 2024). Progress, science, and knowledge "multiplying and separating them by creating barriers between disciplines, has led to a regression of thought, which has become blind. Bound to the dominance of calculation in an increasingly technocratic world, the progress of knowledge is incapable of conceiving the complexity of reality and in particular of human realities. The result is a return to dogmatism and fanaticism, and a crisis of morality as hatreds and idolatries run riot" (Morin 2024).

## 11. More than fifty years of concerns

At the time this volume is being produced, the world is being traversed by many serious alarms. Important issues are arising or increasing in social, political, ecological-environmental, military, international politics level and even war. A clear perception that there are phenomena of collective angst being witnessed. In the news, on internet sites and in the media world in general, there is a clear perception that there are some very strong reasons for widespread malaise, anxiety, anguish even collective fear.

Nevertheless, we could also look at it with other eyes, reminding us of what we really have to fear: a horizon of economic disparity, environmental plunder and cultural impoverishment. This is the real scourge (Prosperi 2021).

Fifty years before the Tv British Documentary Civilization: Is the West History? in 1961, A. Toynbee finished his research on genesis and growth of civilization. He considered that those were the results of opposing forces or challenges posed by humans and by nature, and the responses that the same Civilizations were capable to give to those challenges. His analysis considered a multiplicity of casual factor that may affect the decline or disintegration of civilizations such as luxury, internal fractures, and which could be the case of Fear, the "loss of spirit". He believed that a Western civilization decay would be the eventual result of its unwillingness or inability to respond adequately to future challenges.

In the same year, another British historian Edward. Carr, in his What is History? affirmed what was concerning him the most was not the fading faith in reason, but rather the loss of the deep sense that the world is in a perpetual becoming. That for him is the sense of History himself, of course, and affects Human societies. He argued that at first glance this seems paradoxical, because rarely there were heard so many opinions about the transformations taking place around him (Carr 1966, 165). The situation seems has not very much evolved.

As Morin argued, in the present day, we experience a similar sense of hopelessness, but the conditions are different from other past crucial moments. Morin considers the "*first resistance is that of the spirit, which must know how to resist the intimidation of all lies propagated as truth and the contagion of all collective intoxication*" (Morin 2024) For him it is evident the lesson from the past we must learn, especially the one we experienced in 1939-1945. We must avoid to "*give in to the delusion of the collective responsibility of a people or an ethnic group*" (Morin 2024, He also recalls "resist hatred and contempt". He demands the effort "*to understand the complexity of problems without ever giving in to a partial or one-sided view*"

(Morin 2024). For this kind of resistance, is vital the role of knowledge and for this purpose it's needed "*research, verification of information and acceptance of uncertainties*" (Morin 2024).

Human beings experience individually an impulse that we call fear, and which can be considered as a condition that predisposes to a reaction to the stimulus from unexpected and unpredictable circumstances and can be considered as a defensive factor, as such something to be managed, to be dealt with. Furedi observes that "*our personal experiences shape the imagination and our fears. However, today, many of our fears are often not based on personal experiences. Compared with the past, people living in Western societies have less familiarity with pain, suffering, debilitating disease and death than ever before. And yet, despite an unprecedented level of personal security, fear has become an ever-expanding part of our life. Western societies are increasingly dominated by a culture of fear. The defining feature of this culture is the belief that humanity is confronted by powerful destructive forces that threaten our everyday existence*" (Furedi 2018, VII).

Nevertheless, if history can be understood as a large series of events in the human past, we can find many instances where societies have suffered times of angst, fear, and terror (Borgna 1997; Ginzburg 2015), even the clear perception of a serious risk of collective extinction (Vovelle 1984). It is necessary to look beyond that and consider that even such difficult and dramatic events or times can offer a sort of consolation because knowledge can be a tool that helps humankind face even the hardest challenges (Prosperi 2021; Furedi 2018). It is crucial to recognize that fear is also a form of social domination, a kind of plague that affects the minds of individuals and societies (Borgna 1995), for which knowledge is possibly the only remedy (Prosperi 2021; Ferraris 2019, 155-158; Berger 2003).

A quick summary reminds us of the many uncertainties and risks we face every day: wars, a lack of political direction, ecological crises, risks to democracy, economic crises, and new technology challenges. And finally: Is the pandemic over? All of these are reasonable causes of fear and examples of possible unknown events. However, if we trust Toynbee's idea of what truly defines the decline or rise of a civilization (if we assume the Western as a civilization), it is its capability of being responsive (today we would say: resilient). We should learn from the lessons we have had in history and the ones we are currently experiencing. Fear is undoubtedly an important leverage and influences public opinion and political decisions, but we must consider, as Morin suggests, the importance of the complexity paradigm. This paradigm rejects the simplistic idea that a system can be explained as the simple sum of its parts, and that an open system continuously generates exchanges that are favorable to its adaptation and survival (Morin 2012).

## References

Antonelli, F. (2019). *Tecnocrazia e democrazia. L'egemonia al tempo della società digitale*. L'Asino d'Oro, Roma.

Ariés, P. (1975). *Essais sur l'histoire de la mort en occident: du Moyen Age à nos jours*. Seuil, Paris.

Armiero, M. (2021). *L'era degli scarti. Cronache dal Wasteocene, la discarica globale*. Einaudi, Torino.

Bauman, Z. (2000a). *Liquid Modernity*. Polity, Cambridge.

Bauman, Z. (2000b). *La Solitudine del cittadino globale*. Feltrinelli, Milano.

Bauman, Z. (2007). *Modus vivendi. Inferno e utopia del mondo liquido*. Laterza, Bari.

Beck, U. (2016). *The Metamorphosis of the World. How Climate Change is Transforming Our Concept of the World*. Polity, Cambridge (Kindle edition).

Berger, S. (2003). *Notre première mondialisation. Leçons d'un échec oublié*. Seuil, Paris.

Borgna, E. (1995). *Come se finisse il mondo. Il senso dell'esperienza schizofrenica*. Feltrinelli, Milano.

Borgna, E. (1997). *Le figure dell'ansia*. Feltrinelli, Milano.

Britannica, Editors of Encyclopaedia (2023). "Oswald Spengler". *Encyclopedia Britannica*, November 23, available at https://www.britannica.com/biography/Oswald-Spengler (accessed 24 January 2024).

Byrne, J.P. (2008). *Encyclopedia of Pestilence, Pandemics, and Plagues: A-M*. ABC-CLIO, Greenword Press, WestPort Connecticut.

Carr, E.H. (1966). *Sei lezioni sulla storia*. Einaudi, Torino, 165.

Catarci, M. *et al.* (2021). ""Non avere paura": prevenire le discriminazioni attraverso l'educazione interculturale". Educational *Reflective Practices*, Special Issue, 1, 21-39.

Chakrabarty, D. (2000). *Provincializing Europe. Postcolonial Thought and Historical Difference*. Princeton University Press, Princeton.

Chartier, R. (2001). "La Conscience de la globalité". *Annales HSS*, 56, 119-143.

Coffeya, Y. *et al.* (2021). "Understanding Eco-anxiety: A Systematic Scoping Review of Current Literature and Identified Knowledge Gaps". *The Journal of Climate Change and Health*, 3, 100047.

Cosmacini, G. (2005). *Storia della medicina e della sanità in Italia: dalla peste nera ai giorni nostri*. 1st ed. Laterza, Bari.

Delumeau, J. (1978; trad. it. 1979). *La peur en Occident (XIVe-XVIIIe siècles): une cité assiégée*. ed. or. Fayard, Paris, tr. it. Il Mulino, Bologna.

Delumeau, J. (1983; trad. it. 1987). *Le peché et la peur. La culpabilisation en*

*Occident (XIIIe-XVIIIe siècles).* ed. or. Paris, Fayard, tr. It. Il Mulino, Bologna.
Delumeau, J. (1989). *Rassurer et protéger.* Fayard, Paris.
Douki, C. and Minard, P. (2007). "Histoire globale, histoires connectées: un changement d'échelle historiographique? Introduction". *Revue d'histoire moderne & contemporaine*, 54-4, 5, 7-21.
Elliot, J.H. (1963). *The Revolt of the Catalans. A study on the decline of Spain 1598-1640.* Cambridge University Press, Cambridge.
Ferguson, N. (2011). *Civilization. The west and the Rest.* Penguin, New York.
Ferguson, N. (2018). *Civilization: Is the West history?,* Penguin, London.
Ferraris, M. (2019). *Post verità ed altri enigmi.* Il Mulino, Bologna.
Furedi, F. (2018). *Culture of Fear: Risk-Taking and the Morality of Low Expectation.* (1st ed., Cassel, London 1997) Continuum, London-New York.
Furedi, F. (2018). *How Fear Works.* Bloomsboory, London-New York.
Gardner, D. (2008). *The Science of Fear.* Dutton, New York.
Ginzburg, C. (2015). *Paura reverenza terrore.* Adelphi, Milano.
Gruzinski, S. (2015). *Les Quatre parties du monde. Histoire d'une mondialisation.* 2nd ed. Point-Seuil, Paris, 31-32.
Haller, P. *et al.* (2019). *Bridging Cultural Barriers: How to Overcome Preconceptions in Cross-Cultural Relationships*, Springer, Örebro.
Harari, Y.N. (2011). *From Animal to Gods: a Brief History of Humankind.* Kinneret, Zmora-Bitan, Dvir.
Harvey, C. (2011). "Civilisation: is the West History? Channel 4, Review". *The Daily Telegraph* (accessed 15 July 2014).
Hobsbawm, E.J. (1954). "The General Crisis of the European Economy in the 17th Century". *Past & Present*, 5, 1, 1 November, 33-53.
Huntington, S. (1996). *The Clash Of Civilizations: And The Remaking Of World Order.* Simon and Schuster, New York.
Keller, M. *et al.* (2019). "Ancient Yersinia pestis genomes from across Western Europe reveal early diversification during the First Pandemic (541-750)". *Proceedings of the National Academy of Sciences,* 116(25), 12363-72.
Khan, M., Serafeim, G. and Yoon, A. (2016). "Corporate Sustainability: First Evidence of Materiality". *Accounting Review*, 91, 6.
Kumar, K. (2000). *Le nuove teorie del mondo contemporaneo. Dalla società post-industriale alla società post-moderna.* Einaudi, Torino.
Magatti, M. (2009). *Libertà immaginaria. Le illusioni del capitalismo tecnonichilista.* Feltrinelli, Milano.
Mazlish, B. (1998a), "Comparing Global History to World History". *Journal of Interdisciplinary History*, 28, 385-95.

Mazlish, B. (1998b). "Crossing Boundaries: Ecumenical, World and Global History". *World History. Ideologies, Structures and Identities*, ed. by P. Pomper, R.H. Elphick and R.T. Vann. Blackwell, Oxford, 41-52.

McCormick, M. (2019). "Climates of History, Histories of Climate: From History to Archaeoscience". *Journal of Interdisciplinary History*, L:1 (Summer), 3-30.

Monod, J.C. (2006). *Penser l'ennemi, affronter l'exception: réflexions critiques sur l'actualité de Carl Schmitt*. Le Decouvérte, Paris.

Morin, E. (2012). *Pensare la complessità. Per un umanesimo planetario. Saggi critici e dialoghi di Edgar Morin con Gustavo Zagrebelsky e Gianni Vattimo*. Mimesis, Milano.

Morin, E. (2024). "La resistenza dello spirito". *La Repubblica*, 23 February 2024, available at https://www.repubblica.it/commenti/2024/01/23/news/resistenza_crisi_ambiente_politica_ecologia-421963146/.

Mossa, A. (2017). *Il nemico ritrovato. Carl Schmitt e gli Stati Uniti*. Accademia University Press, Torino.

Naphy, W. and Spicer, A. (2006). *La peste in Europa*. Il Mulino, Bologna.

Ostili, S.M. (2023). *Il Capitalismo Tecno-Nichilista. Modernità, tecnica e razionalità*, History Thesis, defended in University of Roma Tre, Rome, 30 Octber 2023.

Pellegrini, C.B. *et al.* (2020). *Valutazione d'azienda nel mondo ESG*. Egea, Milano.

Pomeranz, K. (2000). *The Great Divergence: Europe, China, and the Making of the Modern World Economy*. University Press Princeton, Princeton NJ.

Procopius from Cesarea (2005) *Storia delle guerre*, VII, 20, ed. by Domenico Comparetti. Garzanti, Milano.

Prosperi, A. (1996), *Tribunali della coscienza*. Il Mulino, Bologna

Prosperi, A. (2016), *Identità. L'altra faccia della storia*. Roma-Bari, Laterza

Prosperi, A. (2021). *Tremare è umano. Una breve storia della paura*. Solferino, Milano.

Revelli, M. (2019). *La politica senza politica. Perché la crisi ha fatto entrare il populismo nelle nostre vite*. Einaudi, Torino.

Rolli, R. (2020). *L'Impatto dei fattori ESG sull'impresa*. Il Mulino, Bologna.

Romano, R. (1992). *Opposte congiunture: la crisi del Seicento in Europa e in America*. Marsilio, Venezia.

Sandel, M.J. (1998). *Democracy's Discontent: America in Search of a Public Philosophy*. Harvard University Press, Cambridge.

Schmitt, C. (2012). *Il concetto di politica* (Begriff des Politischen, 1927). Meltemi, Milano-Udine.

Segura, A. (ed.) (2007). "El nuevo orden mundial y el mundo islámico". *AYER, Revista de Historia contemporánea*, 65(1), 11-213.

Serge, V. (1939). *S'il est minuit dans le siècle*. B. Grasset, Paris.

Sobrero, R. (2022). *Verde, Anzi Verdissimo*. Egea, Milano.

Sprengler, O. (1918-1922). *Der Untergang des Abendlandes*, 2 vol. *The Decline of the West*, Wien-Munich, tr. it. *Il tramonto dell'Occidente*, ed. by R. Calabrese Conte, M. Cottone and Furio Jesi; Introduction by S. Zecchi, Longanesi, Milano, 2008.

Subrahmanyam, S. (1997). "Connected Histories: Notes towards a Reconfiguration of Early Modern Eurasia". *Modern Asian Studies*, 31(3), 735-762.

Subrahmanyam, S. (2022). *Connected History: Essays and Arguments.* Verso, New York-London.

Tettamanzi, T. and Minutiello, E.V. (2022). *ESG: Bilanci di Sostenibilità e Integrated Reporting*. Ipsoa, Milano.

Todorov, T. (2009), *The fear of the barbarians. Beyond the clash of civilizations*. Garzanti, Milano.

Toynbee, A. (1922-1961). *A Study of History*, 12 volls. Oxfrod University Press, Oxford.

Trevor-Roper, H. (1967). *The Crisis of the Seventeenth Century*. Liberty Fund, Indianapolis.

Tucydides (1996). *La guerra del Peloponneso*, ed. e transl. by L. Canfora. Einaudi, Torino.

Ujvari, S.C. (2002). *Storia delle epidemie*. Odoya, Bologna.

US Census Bureau (2013). *International Programs – Historical Estimates of World Population*, March, https://www.census.gov/population/international/data/worldpop/table_history.php.

Voltaire, F. (1759). *Candide ou l'Optimisme*. S.n., Rouen.

Vovelle, M. (1984). *La morte e l'occidente. Dal 1300 ai nostri giorni*. Laterza, Roma.

Wangjie, H. *et al.* (2023). "Genomic inference of a severe human bottleneck during the Early to Middle Pleistocene transition". *Science*, 381, 979-984.

Chapter 2

# RELIGIOUS FEAR IN GREEK ANTIQUITY: PLUTARCH'S *ON SUPERSTITION*

**Massimo Giuseppetti**

ABSTRACT: *This chapter focuses on the role of fear in ancient Greek literary culture, focusing on religious fear and superstition during the Imperial age through the lens of Plutarch's treatise on superstition. This work presents a critical view of popular attitudes toward the divine, blending Greek religious and philosophical traditions. Plutarch's discussion illuminates the complexities of fear and superstition in ancient cultures are illuminated and sheds light on the intersection of emotions, beliefs, and power dynamics.*

SUMMARY: 1. Introduction: Research on emotions and the humanities. – 2. Greek fears: *Phobos* and *deisidaimonia*. – 3. Plutarch's *On Superstition*. – 4. Plutarch's superstition and/as atheism. – 5. Plutarch on the emotional and cognitive aspects of superstition. – 6. The politics of superstition. – 7. Concluding remarks. – References.

## 1. Introduction: Research on emotions and the humanities

Over the last decades emotions have played a key role in recent research in the humanities and social sciences. In different ways, scholars have developed a set of approaches to use emotions as a powerful insight to explore fields as varied as history, literature, and philosophy. But what is, exactly, an emotion? Although the problem of definition is far from settled, "*emotions are fundamentally event-like in structure, a feature often described in terms of 'scripts'*" (Cairns 2016). 'Script' is, in this context, a resolutely constructivist term that refers to emotions as concepts around which scenarios unfold. In this respect, emotions – both as a group and as specific emotions (shame, anger, fear, etc.) – are 'fuzzy' categories to which different labels and different effects and forms of agency can be attached. [1] Over the last decades emotions have increasingly represented for a large set of disciplines crucial affordances that allow scholars to explore how cultures simultaneously experience the world, share that experience, and act on it across a continuum that goes beyond the conventional polarities of reason and pas-

[1] On the prototypical nature of emotions see in particular Fehr and Russell 1984; Russell 1991; Russell 2003.

sion or cognition and affectivity. The humanities, with their large textual repositories and the various disciplines that takes on the task of investigating them, are a fundamental resource from which research on emotions can draw.

Philosophy and literature, for example, embody an invaluable archive for the study of emotions as social phenomena to be not only observed and recorded but also made into objects of reflection, for instance from the standpoint of ethics or politics. In the present contribution, I intend to use the emotion of fear as a lens through which literary and philosophical writing comes to terms with the complexity of the social and cultural world. As a student of ancient Greek literary culture, the case study I shall focus on concerns some aspects of the debate about religious fear and superstition in the Imperial age. In the early centuries AD the Greek world under Roman rule came in contact with a large number of different cultural and religious traditions. This prompted Greek thinkers and writers to reflect on both the value of their intellectual tradition within the framework of a Mediterranean empire dominated by Rome and the cultural diversity inherent in such a multiethnic empire. Emotions such as fear provided crucial dimensions through which they could carry out their investigations. [2]

## 2. Greek fears: *Phobos* and *deisidaimonia*

In the *Rhetoric* Aristotle (384-322 BCE) defines fear (*phobos*) as "*a kind of pain and trouble caused by the impression* (phantasia) *of an imminent evil that causes destruction or pain*". [3] By establishing here a connection between fear and the broader faculty of imagination (*phantasia*), Aristotle clearly envisages that, precisely qua emotion, fear has complex cognitive ramifications. People feel fear because they are capable of 'visualizing' and 'representing' threats in our mind; we are also capable of evaluating these threats by taking into account their scale and their temporal proximity. Considered in this light, fear provides important insights to explore cultural dynamics. For instance, to what extent do literary texts play on largely shared notions of fear or, rather, give local habitation to deeper forms of anxiety? How does politics manipulate or take advantage of such fears? How can the

---

[2] Cairns 2016 is a valuable introduction to the research into emotions from the point of view of Graeco-roman antiquity; see also Cairns 2008; Chaniotis 2012; Cairns and Nelis 2017. For a selection of studies on fear in Classics see Munteanu 2012; Coin-Longeray and Vallat 2015; Cairns 2017; De Poli 2018; Felton 2018; Estèves 2020; Konstan 2020; Beltrametti 2021; Craik 2022; Patera, Perentidis, and Wallensten 2023.

[3] Aristotle, *Rhetoric* 2.5, 1382a21-2 (transl. Freese 2020).

cognitive components of fear be used, for instance, to evaluate, discriminate, or control people? In order to approach the matter in a granular fashion, in the following pages I shall examine the cultural relevance of fear by focusing on the part it played in religious discourse. The first thing to note in this regard is that fear is involved in the very word that was used in the imperial age to indicate superstition, i.e. *deisidaimonia.* [4]

The English word 'superstition' derives from Latin *superstitio*, which has a notoriously problematic etymology of its own. [5] By contrast, Greek *deisidaimonia* is a compound which is perfectly clear from an etymological point of view: superstition is indeed a pervasive fear (*deisi-*, cf. the verb *deidō*) concerning the divine world (*-daimonia*, cf. the noun *daimōn*, 'demon', 'god'). [6] I have just felt the need to qualify such a fear as 'pervasive', but as a matter of fact *deisidaimonia* need not refer to superstition per se. The word has indeed a rather complex lexical history. The adjective *deisidaimōn* is attested for the first time in two works of Xenophon (*ca.* 430-*ca.* 353 BCE), in both instances (a) with the positive meaning of 'pious', 'religious' and, in a fairly broad sense, (b) in connection with the political sphere. [7] The relevance of politics appears more pronounced in Aristotle. In his treatise on the subject, he observes that the tyrant must appear fearful of the gods if he wants to stay in power. The passage is worth quoting in full (*Politics* 5.9, 1314b-1315a): [8]

> "*A tyrant should always be seen to be very zealous about matters concerning the gods, but without appearing foolish in the process. For people are less afraid of suffering illegal treatment at the hands of such people. And if they regard their ruler as a god-fearing man* (deisidaimona) *who pays heed to the gods, they plot against him less, since they think that he has the gods on his side*".

In this passage Aristotle uses different expressions for the same concept, i.e. having respect for the divine. We find here the only occurrence of *de-*

---

[4] For a historical overview of this concept in antiquity see the monograph by Koets 1929 and the more recent studies of Calderone 1972; Patera 2023. Lindner 2013 discusses relevant inscriptional evidence. See also Santaniello 2007, 27-34.

[5] *Superstitio* can of course be traced back to *supersto* ('to stand on top', 'to stand over'), but the semantic connection between the two words is far from obvious. On this see e.g. Ronca 1992.

[6] The noun *daimōn* may refer to a broad range of divine entities, from 'god' to 'semigod' and the general notion of one's 'lot' or 'fortune'; see François 1957; Greenbaum 2016.

[7] Xenophon, *Agesilaus* 11.8 and *Cyropaedia* 3.3.58.

[8] Translation by Reeve 1998.

*isidaimōn* in his works, but perhaps what really stands out about his discussion is the close connection with someone's else fear: if the tyrant appears to be fearful of the gods, his subjects will be less afraid (*phobountai*) to suffer illegal treatment at his hands. This is not to say, of course, that the tyrant will not resort to illegal means. Rather, what Aristotle suggests is that the appearance of piety in a tyrant alters the perception of his acts in the general population. There is thus an inverse correlation between the fear (of the gods) exhibited by the tyrant and the fear (*phobos*) of the tyrant experienced by his subjects. This is a remarkable example of how an emotional state such as fear can be considered from a philosophical point of view in its social ramification. Fear, especially in the moral and religious sense we have been discussing, amounts to a moral stance that can be merely displayed (this is the obvious implication in Aristotle's passage). Such display, in turn, inevitably affects the public, and precisely in their own capacity of experiencing a similar fear towards the divine (and the tyrant). From this point of view, then, politics also enacts strategies for the manipulation of collective emotions, which in turn provide behavioural 'scripts' that can be acted upon or, depending on the context, manipulated.[9]

Aristotle's pupil and successor as head of the Lyceum, Theophrastus (*ca.* 371-287 BCE), has left us a full-scale portrait of the superstitious man in his *Characters* (16).[10] In this very peculiar gallery of 'behavioural types'[11] the *deisidaimōn* is obsessed by fear of the supernatural and of impurity. In fact, what is distinctive of his attitude towards the divine is its compulsive nature: time and again Theophrastus portrays him as repeating his actions two or three times or as looking for alternative ways to appease his religious anxiety. He is convinced, for instance, that his house is haunted by Hecate; if a mouse nibbles through a bag of barley, he feels he needs to consult the expounder of sacred laws, and when the latter advises him to just have the bag repaired,[12] he disregards the suggestion and performs an apotropaic sacrifice. Theophrastus' portrayal implies a clear semantic shift. His *deisidaimōn* is not just a pious or devout man but an obsessively superstitious man. Still, this does not involve a negative moral stance towards him. Rather, his portrait is suffused with kindly irony. In this regard it may be interesting to consider that *Deisidaimōn* was also the title of a comedy by Me-

---

[9] See also below, n. 31.

[10] On Theophrastus' *Characters* see Ranocchia 2011 and the commentaries by Diggle 2004 and 2022; on the complex problems concerning its text see Diggle 2004, 17-27, who does not doubt the work's ultimate authenticity. More specifically on his *Superstitious Man* (16) see Bolkestein 1929.

[11] This is the original meaning of the title (Diggle 2022, 3).

[12] See Diggle 2004, 360.

nander.[13] This suggests that, for both the Athenian playwright and the philosopher, more than anything else the superstitious man was just someone to laugh at.

## 3. Plutarch's *On Superstition*

Things are rather different if we move on to consider the short treatise *On Superstition* (*Perì deisidaimonias*) written by Plutarch of Chaeronea (*ca.* 50 *ca.* 120 AD).[14] Plutarch was a prolific and versatile writer who, for the last thirty years of his life, held a priesthood in Delphi, one of the most ancient and venerable oracular shrines in the Greek world. A profound believer in the dialogue between Greek culture and Roman political power, Plutarch devoted a good portion of his intellectual efforts to rethinking Greek religious and philosophical culture from a perspective that combined his piety with a thoughtful study of its most venerable texts.[15] He contributed significantly to the revival of the Delphic sanctuary in the time of Trajan and Hadrian.

In contrast with Theophrastus' good-natured portrayal of the superstitious man, Plutarch's much later essay is a 'overheated tirade'.[16] *On Superstition*, which was possibly written between *ca.* 70 and 80 AD, belongs to a rather large group of treatises in which Plutarch explores themes of popular moral philosophy.[17] In this case the choice of the subject immediately evokes two distinct traditions. The first concerns the portrayal of popular attitudes towards the divine, a theme that, for Greek literature, was already familiar in Old Comedy. The second tradition is represented, of course, by the vast number of philosophical reflections on the nature of the gods, par-

---

[13] Only a few lines survive: see frr. 106-9 Kassel-Austin; see also his *Phasma* vv. 54-6.

[14] The treatise is no. 14 in the traditional order of the *Moralia* followed in modern editions; for a full catalogue see Russell 1993, xxiii-xxix. For the (notoriously slippery) chronology of Plutarch's works see e.g. Jones 1966. More in general on Plutarch see the recent synthesis provided by Roskam 2021.

[15] On Plutarch's attitude towards religion and the divine see e.g. Gallo 1996; Leão and Roig Lanzillotta 2019; Hirsch-Luipold and Roig Lanzillotta 2020; Brenk 2023.

[16] See Diggle 2004, 349.

[17] For a full commentary on this work see Santaniello 2007; for its dating, which remains rather problematic to establish, see Santaniello 2007, 24-5. It has often been assumed that *On Superstition* is an early work. Recent criticism, however, has stressed that its main themes are well represented in Plutarch's whole oeuvre (Roskam 2021, 150; see Berardi 1990). For a (selective) bibliography on Plutarch's *On Superstition* see Brenk 1977, especially 9-15, 65-84; Lozza 1980, 15-20; Berardi 1990; Baldassarri 1996; Lozza 1996; Pérez Jiménez 1996. In this paper I quote from the translation of *On Superstition* published by Russell 1993.

ticularly from the 4th century BCE onwards. In this specific respect, Plutarch's God was, essentially, the Demiurge of Plato's *Timaeus.*[18] For him God was the father and maker of all things, self-sufficient and perfectly good; his divine providence allowed him to bridge the divide between the intelligible world, where he confined himself to, and the corporeal world that we experience. From the point of view of morality and ethics, in his *On Superstition* Plutarch essentially followed an approach which can be traced back, in broad terms, to Aristotelian views. In such a perspective, human attitudes towards the divine fell within a spectrum marked by the two opposite extremes of atheism and superstition. The ideal 'mean' between them was piety and reverence (*eusebeia*).[19] Before looking more closely to how Plutarch treated that excess in matters religious that is superstition, a few remarks on the Greek word he used, *deisidaimonia*, are in order.

## 4. Plutarch's superstition and/as atheism

As we mentioned earlier, in his *On Superstition* Plutarch contrasts atheism and superstition as excesses, each of them negative in itself and far from the ideal mean of piety. As the title of the work suggests, however, he focuses on superstition and portrays it in stark tones. As a result, he makes it out to be a considerably more disturbing and problematic attitude than atheism. As he observes at the outset, ignorance and incomprehension of the gods are the primary causes for both atheism and superstition, but the latter is far worse in that it is accompanied by emotion (*pathos*)[20] whereas the former, on the contrary, stands out for the absence of emotion (*apathia*). If not believing in the existence of the gods results in having no fear of them,[21] believing that they can distress and harm human beings in irrational and unpredictable ways can only engender a state of terror and anxiety throughout one's life. From this point of view, for Plutarch 'Platonic metaphysics provides us with

[18] See in particular his *The Creation of the Soul in Plato's Timaeus* (68). More in general on Plutarch's religion see Russell 1973, 63-83.

[19] The key Aristotelian texts are *Nicomachean Ethics* 3.1115a4-1117b22 and *Eudemian Ethics* 3.1229b13-1230a8; see, among others, Berardi 1990. Cf. also e.g. Stobaeus, *Anthologium* 2.7.25 with Pötscher 1964, 127-128. Of course, defining the nature of what is precisely Aristotelian remains rather problematic, particularly in matters concerning morality: see the cautious remarks of Babut 1994, 517-518.

[20] *On Superstition* 1, 164e. Note how in this context superstition grows in 'tender characters' (*ēthesi... hapalois*) as if in soft soils.

[21] *On Superstition* 2, 165b.

a very important criterion for our attitude towards the gods', namely, 'the fundamental insight that they are benevolent and beneficent'.[22]

It must be kept in mind that atheism was a position that, in the time when Plutarch was writing, had gained full recognizability. Over the centuries, a distinctive philosophical tradition had emerged, leaving very important traces across the whole spectrum of literary production.[23] In a sense, then, there is something all too easy about accusing atheists of being impious. The real challenge, so Plutarch tells us, lies in highlighting that superstition involves, beneath the surface of reverence for the gods' powers, an even worse attitude from a moral and doctrinal standpoint (9, 169e-170a):

> "*If the unbeliever is unholy* (anosios)*, is not the man who holds views of the gods like those of the superstitious guilty of a much greater unholiness? I would much rather have men say that I do not exist, and there is no such person as Plutarch, than that Plutarch is unstable, unreliable, quick to anger, indiscriminately vindictive, and prone to take offence at trifles; or that, if you give a dinner and leave him out, or are too busy to call on him or speak to him, he will seize you and eat you up, or kidnap your baby and beat it to death, or let a wild animal loose on your crops and ruin your harvest*".

This passage makes very clear that, in Plutarch's perspective, superstition develops in and relies on wrong beliefs about the divine. These beliefs are also nourished by the representations offered by literary texts since the time of Homer. The thought of a wild animal threatening your harvest and sent as a divine punishment evokes, for instance, the myth of the Calydonian boar.[24] Traditional religion, particularly if grounded in unquestioned beliefs, is the main polemical target of Plutarch here. This becomes clear in the conclusion of this work, when Plutarch carries home the points that (a) the superstitious man is "an atheist in intention, but too cowardly to hold the opinion about the gods that he wishes to hold" (11, 170e), and that (b) superstition both gave rise to atheism and subsequently provided it with a defense (12, 171a).[25]

---

[22] Roskam 2021, 149. See *On Superstition* 4, 166d-e, and 5, 167d-e.

[23] On this tradition see Whitmarsh 2015.

[24] As Santaniello 2007, 205 notes, in the myth (e.g. Homer, *Iliad* 9.524-605; Ovid, *Metamorphoses* 8.260-444) it is Artemis who sent the boar – the same goddess Plutarch is about to mention in his discussion (quoting from Timotheus' hymn to the Artemis of Ephesus, fr. 778 (2b) Hordern).

[25] As Plutarch explains right after this, superstition spreads such malevolent portrayals of the gods that people rather wish that there were no gods at all.

## 5. Plutarch on the emotional and cognitive aspects of superstition

If we move onto a more general plane, what is remarkable about the way Plutarch frames superstition concerns its definition as a mistaken belief accompanied by emotion (*pathos*). This is particularly important from the point of view of the place that he assigns to emotions in general and especially to fear in his philosophical and rhetorical discourse. Superstition is, in this respect, a highly charged emotional state (6, 167e):

> "*Superstition is an excessive response* (polypatheia) *which views good as evil. The superstitious fear the gods, but take refuge with them. They flatter them, but abuse them. They pray to them, but blame them*".

'Excessive response' is *polypatheia*, that is, being emotionally overwhelmed to the point of having one's judgement clouded by it. From this point of view, the whole stance of Plutarch's essay is to counteract this condition with rhetorical *pathos*.

Let us consider, for instance, the passage in which he compares a rational approach to natural phenomena to one marked by superstition (8, 169a-b):

> "*There is nothing alarming about the interposition of the earth, nothing terrible about the conjunction of its shadow with the moon at the due point of the cycle; what is truly terrible is the power of the darkness of superstition to confuse and blind the intellect of the man who falls into it at the very moment when he most needs his intelligence*".

The rhetorical force of this passage lies in the contrast between the observable, 'material' darkness caused by an eclipse and the metaphorical darkness of superstition falling upon men:[26] the overwhelming sense of fear felt by the superstitious man is here contrasted with the one thing which is truly terrible, that is, frightful (*deinon*) – fear itself, as it takes the shape of superstition (*to tēs deisidaimonias skotos*).[27] It is very interesting to see how Plutarch reflects with great clarity on *deisidaimonia* as a deeply emotional way at looking at the world and at the interaction between daily life and the

---

[26] Plutarch often discusses eclipses as phenomena which trouble human being, especially in times of political or military conflict: see the cases discussed by Berardi 1990, 157-62.

[27] Note the assonance (and possible etymological association) between *deisidaimonia* and the adjective *deinos* ('terrible', 'frightful').

divine sphere. This crucial aspect is rejected on its own ground, so to speak: his arguments take often the shape, as in the passage we have just examined, of a reconfiguration of the very components of the 'emotional script' under scrutiny. His discursive approach, thus, does not rely on a stark polarity between reason and emotion. Rather, it deploys the rhetorical resources available to him to offer a vivid portrayal of how the superstitious man usually carries on his daily activities, particularly from an affective and emotional point of view, and to use that representation as a springboard for a radical criticism of a lifestyle, like that of the *deisidaimōn*, ultimately based on superficial or wrong ideas about the gods.

To take one remarkable example, in a passage which clearly has declamatory overtones Plutarch portrays superstition as an emotional state of terror (3.165d-e):

> "*The sleeping slave forgets his master, sleep lightens the prisoner's chains; suppurating wounds, savage ulcers, and gripping pains all vanish when we rest:*
> *O sleep's dear charm, that lightenest my disease,*
> *how sweet thy coming in my hour of need!*[28]
> *This is something superstition will never let you say. It alone makes no truce with sleep; it never lets the soul relax and regain courage in those hours by thrusting aside its bitter and depressing concept of god. On the contrary, it turns the sleep of the superstitious into a hell, rousing up terrifying visions, monstrous phantoms, and avenging spirits. It racks the wretched soul, and hounds it from its slumbers with nightmares; and that soul suffers torments of self-flagellation and self-chastisement in the belief that these are inflicted on it by another, and accepts the most dreadful and bizarre instructions. Nor, when he gets up, can the superstitious man set all this at naught or make fun of it, or feel pleased that none of the things that troubled him was real*".

Plutarch takes inspiration from the idealized image of a dream that brings refreshment to emphasize that this is exactly what the superstitious person cannot enjoy. They have no respite even in sleep. Instead, their situation is that of someone who has turned their existence into a hell. Indeed, the time of day that, for the average person, symbolizes detachment from daily life is, for the superstitious person, the moment when all their fears seem to take an even more tangible form. Not even waking up can help them, for it marks the return to the pervasive anxiety that characterizes them. It is evident that what Plutarch offers here is a portrait on the verge

[28] Euripides, *Orestes* 211.

of the paradoxical. From his perspective as a philosophical popularizer, however, it is an effective way to demonstrate that once the seed of a conception of deities as malevolent and the cause of pain is planted, man finds no rest, even when it would be most natural to do so. In a more general perspective, this passage is noteworthy because it seeks to focus on how an emotional dimension like fear takes its roots in experience. The detailed portrait that Plutarch paints here shows precisely how, at the moment when our reasoning abilities are less vigilant, fear takes over completely. All this establishes, once again, that religious beliefs cannot escape the scrutiny of reason, a reason that for Plutarch cannot but acknowledge the benevolence of God.

## 6. The politics of superstition

One last point deserves to be briefly discussed in this context. We saw above that, already in Aristotle, *deisidaimonia* can also be looked at from a political angle. After Aristotle this particular overtone surfaces again in historians like Polybius (*ca.* 200-*ca.* 118 BCE)[29] and also in the biographical writings of Plutarch himself.[30] This motif appears also in *On Superstition* but in a very peculiar fashion (8, 169c):[31]

> "*God is the hope of courage, not the excuse of cowardice. The Jews sat in their new clothes on the sabbath while the enemy set up their ladders*

[29] In his *Histories* (6.56.6-15) Polybius writes that it is 'the very thing which among other peoples is an object of reproach, I mean superstition (*deisidaimonian*), which maintains the cohesion of the Roman State', and that the Romans 'have adopted this course for the sake of the common people. It is a course which perhaps would not have been necessary had it been possible to form a state composed of wise men, but as every multitude is fickle, full of lawless desires, unreasoned passion, and violent anger, the multitude must be held in by invisible terrors (*tois adēlois phobois*) and suchlike pageantry (*tragōdiā*)' (translation by Paton 2011).

[30] On *deisidaimonia* as *instrumentum regni* see *Life of Sertorius* 11.2-4, *Life of Numa* 8.2 (see the anti-superstitious Galaxidorus in *On the Sign of Socrates*, 579f), *Life of Eumenes* 13.3, *On Isis and Osiris* 380a; see Berardi 1990, 148-51; Lozza 1996.

[31] See also above, note 9. In *On Superstition* Plutarch does mention political figures (amongst others, Tiribazos, Midas, Aristodemus and Nicias, 8, 168e-169a), but their exemplarity is to some extent as individuals and not as political figures who use popular superstition for pragmatic purposes, as it is in Aristotle's *Politics*. Besides, political tyranny can be fled by relocating to a new country, but if one considers the gods tyrants there is nowhere one can escape, as Plutarch observes in the case of Polycrates (4, 166c-d). By contrast, if there are figures that can take advantage of the superstitious, they are mostly individuals of lower social status who exploit religion for profit such as charlatans, wizards and old witches (3, 166a): see Santaniello 2007, 166-9, n. 43 *ad loc.*

*and seized the walls. They simply waited for them, trapped in the net of their superstition*".

This example comes last after several instances from authoritative Greek literary texts (Archilochus, Hesiod, Homer[32]) in which calling upon a god is always accompanied by the active effort of men, who cannot – and should not, Plutarch remarks – remain inert and leave all the initiative to the gods. The generalizing statement 'God is the hope of courage (*aretē*), not the excuse of cowardice' caps the series of Greek exempla and introduces the subsequent episode drawn from Jewish history. This brief mention makes it rather difficult to identify with precision its historical context.[33] Be that as it may, there is no doubting that here the Jews are discussed as an example of the dire consequences that superstition may have for whole political bodies.[34] Note also that, whereas Plutarch leaves undetermined the precise location in which this episode took place, he nevertheless emphasizes what their clothing was when they were attacked by the enemies: they "*sat in their new clothes on the sabbath*".[35] This detail clearly also serves to prepare the ground for the metaphorical phrase that follows next, "*trapped in the net of their superstition*". Here the verb (*syndedemenoi*, from *syndeō*, 'bind together') is particularly apt in that it is phonetically rather similar to *deisidaimonia* while also being a verb that may be applied to items of clothing.[36] It is noteworthy that in an essay essentially focused on superstition from the point of view of the individual, the one case where a collective body is mentioned essentially targets a culturally distant people such as the Jews. In this respect, Plutarch's treatise falls into the same contradictions as a large part of Greek ethnography does with its inclination to the 'othering' of what appears unfamiliar or foreign.[37]

---

[32] Archilochus, fr. 105 West; Hesiod, *Works and Days* 465; Homer, *Iliad* 7.186-213 and 2.382, 2.413-14.

[33] For a discussion of the several possibilities advanced by scholars see Santaniello 2007, 198 n. 112; Santaniello remarks that the vagueness of the passage makes it impossible to use it to date *On Superstition*.

[34] In a previous passage Plutarch has already mentioned in passing 'keeping sabbath' (*sabbatismous*) among other examples of bizzarre acts of devotion (3, 166a; R. Bentley proposed to emend *sabbatismous* – the reading in the medieval manuscripts – and write *baptismous*, 'immersions'; *contra* Santaniello 2007, 166, n. 42). On the theme of anti-Judaism in Plutarch see the bibliography cited by Santaniello 2007, 167-8.

[35] The passage about the clothings worn by the Jews is problematic in the original Greek text: for a full discussion see Santaniello 2007, 196-7 n. 111 *ad loc.*

[36] See e.g. Euripides, *Andromache* 832.

[37] For other instances in which Plutarch qualifies superstition as barbaric and foreign to the spirit of Greek religion see e.g. *Dialogue on Love* 756c, *Advice to Bride and*

## 7. Concluding remarks

The brief treatise that Plutarch dedicates to superstition, despite its brevity, is an attempt to combine philosophical reflection and religious tradition in a perspective that places the emotional components of this attitude towards the divine at the center. The complexity of the emotional dimension of this attitude justifies, for Plutarch, the use of arguments of various kinds, ranging from strictly logical discussion to the paradoxical and almost ridiculous portrayal of the excesses to which the superstitious person leads himself. In all this, the more general ambition to promote the Greek cultural heritage emerges very clearly, especially at a time when the latter is now measuring itself against other cultural and religious traditions. As we have seen, for Plutarch superstition is also an element that marks a profound difference between Greek culture and Jewish culture. In this, he clearly reflects an anti-Judaic prejudice that was not uncommon among Greek and Roman writers of the time. This also helps us understand the importance of the study of emotions. On one hand, Plutarch's writing appears as a defence of the epistemic vigilance that is necessitated by an 'excess of emotion', as can happen in the case of superstition. On the other hand, however, that same epistemic vigilance must also be extended to the judgment that Plutarch himself reserves for the 'Other', i.e. the non-Greek. For Aristotle, as we have seen, fear arises from our ability to imagine imminent suffering. This ability, however, can escalate to the point of becoming self-sustaining: it therefore requires our constant vigilance, even (or perhaps especially) in the study of cultures different from our own, whether ancient or not.[38]

## References

Babut, D. (1994). "Plutarque, Aristote, et l'aristotélisme". *Parerga. Choix d'articles de Daniel Babut (1974-1994)*. Maison de l'Orient, Lyon, 505-29.

Baldassarri, M. (1996). "Inquadramento filosofico del *De superstitione* plutarcheo", in I. Gallo (ed.). *Plutarco e la religione*. D'Auria, Napoli, 373-87.

---

*Groom* 140d, *Concerning the Face Which Appears in the Orb of the Moon* 935b, *Life of Sertorius* 11.6.

[38] I would like to warmly thank the editors of this volume for inviting me to participate in this project, which is deeply rooted in the diversity of the humanities. I am very grateful to Carlo Santaniello for reading a previous version of this contribution and for his generous comments; this does not mean, of course, that he necessarily shares the ideas discussed here. Any errors in the text remain solely my responsibility.

Beltrametti, A. (2021). *La più intelligente e la più stolta delle emozioni: la paura. Paure antiche e nuove paure.* Petite Plaisance, Pistoia.

Berardi, E. (1990). "Plutarco e la religione: l'εὐσέβεια come giusto mezzo fra δεισιδαιμονία e ἀθεότης". *Civiltà classica e cristiana*, 11, 142-70.

Bolkestein, H. (1929). *Theophrastos' Charakter der Deisidaimonia als religionsgeschichtliche Urkunde.* Töpelmann, Giessen.

Brenk, F.E. (2023). *Plutarch on Literature, Graeco-Roman Religion, Jews and Christians*, ed. by L. Roig Lanzillotta. Brill, Leiden-Boston.

Cairns, D. (2008). "Look both ways: studying emotion in ancient Greek". *Critical Quarterly*, 50.4, 43-62.

Cairns, D. (2016). "Emotions". *Oxford Classical Dictionary.* https://doi.org/10.1093/acrefore/9780199381135.013.7034.

Cairns, D.L. (2017), "Horror, Pity, and the Visual in Ancient Greek Aesthetics", in D.L. Cairns and D. Nelis (eds.). *Emotions in the Classical World: Methods, Approaches, and Directions.* Steiner, Stuttgart.

Cairns, D. and Nelis, D. (eds.) (2017). *Emotions in the Classical World: Methods, Approaches, and Directions.* Steiner, Stuttgart.

Calderone, S. (1972). "Superstitio", in H. Temporini (ed.). *Aufstieg und Niedergang der römischen Welt*, I 2. De Gruyter, Berlin-New York, 377-96.

Chaniotis, A. (2012). *Unveiling Emotions: Sources and Methods for the Study of Emotions in the Greek World.* Steiner, Stuttgart.

Coin-Longeray, S. and Vallat, D. (eds.) (2015). *Peurs antiques.* Publications de l'Université Saint-Étienne, Saint-Étienne.

Craik, E. (2022). "The Doctor's Dilemma: Addressing Irrational Fears", in G. Kazantzidis and D. Spatharas (eds.). *Medical Understandings of Emotions in Antiquity: Theory, Practice, Suffering. Ancient Emotions,* III. De Gruyter, Berlin-Boston, 117-22.

De Poli, M. (ed.) (2018). *Il teatro delle emozioni: la paura.* Padova University Press, Padova.

Diggle, J. (2004). *Theophrastus: Characters.* Cambridge University Press, Cambridge.

Diggle, J. (2022). *Theophrastus: Characters.* Cambridge University Press, Cambridge.

Estèves, A. (2020). *Poétique de l'horreur dans l'épopée et l'historiographie latines.* Ausonius, Bordeaux.

Fehr, B. and Russell, J.A. (1984). "Concept of emotion viewed from a prototype perspective". *Journal of Experimental Psychology: General*, 113.3, 464-86.

Felton, D. (ed.) (2018). *Landscapes of Dread in Classical Antiquity: Negative Emotion in Natural and Constructed Spaces.* Routledge, London-New York.

François, G., (1957). *Le polythéisme et l'emploi au singulier des mots* θεός, δαίμων *dans la littérature grecque d'Homère à Platon*. Les Belles Lettres, Paris.

Freese, J.H. (2020). *Aristotle: Art of Rhetoric*. Revised by G. Striker. Harvard University Press, Cambridge (MA)-London.

Gallo, I. (ed.) (1996). *Plutarco e la religione*. D'Auria, Napoli.

Greenbaum, D.G. (2016). *The Daimon in Hellenistic Astrology: Origins and Influence*. Brill, Leiden-Boston.

Guttenberger, G. (2009). "*Superstitio*. Facetten eines antik-religionstheoretischen Diskurses und die Genese des frühen Christentums als *religio*", in W. Kraus (ed.). *Beiträge zur urchristlichen Theologiegeschichte*. De Gruyter, Berlin-New York, 183-227.

Hirsch-Luipold, R. and Roig Lanzillotta, L. (eds.) (2020). *Plutarch's Religious Landscapes*. Brill, Leiden-Boston.

Hordern, J.H. (2002). *The Fragments of Timotheus of Miletus*. Oxford University Press, Oxford.

Jones, C.P. (1966). "Towards a chronology of Plutarch's works". *The Journal of Roman Studies*, 56, 61-74.

Koets, P. J. (1929). Δεισιδαιμονία*: A Contribution to the Knowledge of the Religious Terminology in Greek*. Muusses, Purmerend.

Konstan, D. (2020). "Fear and Anxiety: The View from Ancient Greece", in M. Liatsi (ed.). *Ethics in Ancient Greek Literature: Aspects of Ethical Reasoning from Homer to Aristotle and Beyond*. De Gruyter, Berlin-Boston, 179-90.

Leão, D. and Roig Lanzillotta, L. (eds.) (2019). *A Man of Many Interests: Plutarch on Religion, Myth, and Magic: Essays in Honor of Aurelio Pérez Jiménez*. Brill, Leiden-Boston.

Lindner, G. (2013). "Ein abergläubischer Schauspieler? Die Bedeutungsentwicklung von *deisidaimonia*". *Acta Classica Universitatis Scientiarum Debreceniensis*, 49, 191-202.

Lozza, G. (1980). *Plutarco: De superstitione*. Guerini, Milano.

Lozza, G. (1996). "Τυραννίς e δεισιδαιμονία in Plutarco", in I. Gallo (ed.). *Plutarco e la religione*. D'Auria, Napoli, 389-94.

Munteanu, D.L. (2012). *Tragic Pathos: Pity and Fear in Greek Philosophy and Tragedy*. Cambridge University Press, Cambridge.

Patera, M. (2023). "Représentations grecques de la «superstition»: gestes et concepts liés à la peur des dieux", in Patera, M., Perentidis, S. and Wallensten, J. (eds.). *La peur chez les Grecs. Usages et représentations de l'Antiquité à l'ère chrétienne*. Presses universitaires de Rennes, Rennes 131-42.

Patera, M., Perentidis, S. and Wallensten, J. (eds.) (2023). *La peur chez les*

*Grecs. Usages et représentations de l'Antiquité à l'ère chrétienne.* Presses universitaires de Rennes, Rennes.

Paton, W.R. (2011). *Polybius: The Histories.* Vol. III: *Books 5-8.* Revised by F.W. Walbank and C. Habicht. Harvard University Press, Cambridge (MA)-London.

Pérez Jiménez, A. (1996). "Δεισιδαιμονία: el miedo a los dioses en Plutarco", in L. Van der Stockt (ed.). *Plutarchea Lovaniensia: A Miscellany of Essays on Plutarch.* Peeters, Leuven, 195-225.

Pötscher, W. (1964). *Theophrastos:* Περὶ εὐσεβείας. Brill, Leiden.

Ranocchia, G. (2011). "Natura e fine dei *Caratteri* di Teofrasto. Storia di un enigma". *Philologus*, 155, 69-91.

Reeve, C.D.C. (1998) *Aristotle: Politics.* Hackett, Indianapolis-Cambridge.

Ronca, I. (1992). "What's in two names: old and new thoughts on the history and etymology of *religio* and *superstitio*". *Res Publica Litterarum*, 15, 43-60.

Roskam, G. (2021). *Plutarch.* Cambridge University Press, Cambridge.

Russell, D.A. (1973). *Plutarch.* Charles Scribner's Sons, New York.

Russell, D.A. (1993). *Plutarch: Selected Essays and Dialogues.* Oxford University Press, Oxford.

Russell, J.A. (1991). "Culture and the categorization of emotions". *Psychological Bulletin*, 110.3, 426-50.

Russell, J.A. (2003). "Core affect and the psychological construction of emotion". *Psychological Review*, 110.1, 145-72.

Santaniello, C. (2007). *Plutarco: La superstizione.* D'Auria, Napoli.

Whitmarsh, T. (2015). *Battling the Gods: Atheism in the Ancient World.* Knopf, New York.

# Chapter 3
# FEARFUL NEW WORLD


## Manlio Graziano



ABSTRACT: *The "Great Fear of 2020" has left an indelible mark on history, akin to a hurricane wreaking havoc on the global economic system and hastening the entropy of international politics. Even before the onset of the Covid-19 pandemic and the subsequent near-universal lockdowns, the world was grappling with a profound sense of disarray. This disarray is "great international disorder," set in motion by the collapse of the Yalta order and further compounded by the crisis of 2008 and 2020. The prevailing state of uncertainty, confusion, and apprehension experienced by populations across the world in disarray has come to define the prevailing* Zeitgeist, *the spirit of our age.*




"*The only thing we have to fear is fear itself*".
Franklin D. Roosevelt

Even prior to the Russian invasion of Ukraine and the war in Gaza, the "Great Fear of 2020" prompted by the spread of Covid-19 had struck history like a hurricane, buffeting the world economic system, and accelerating the entropy of international politics.

At that time, the world was already living in a state of "disarray," according to Richard Haass, the president of the Council on Foreign Relations, who used a term that signifies not only disorder but also "the state of being confused and having no organisation or of being untidy" (Cambridge dictionary). This disarray is the consequence of the "great international disorder", which was triggered by the collapse of the Yalta order, [1] and was further exacerbated by the crises of 2008, 2015, and 2020. The war in Ukraine has put the last touches on this dark picture, and in January 2023 the members of the Bulletin of the Atomic Scientists have reset to 90 sec-

---

[1] By "Yalta world order" we mean the system of international relations resulting from the Second World War, dominated by the United States and characterized bycollaboration/competition between Washington and Moscow. Although the "Cold War" began a few years after the Yalta and Potsdam agreements, the Yalta order is commonly identified with it.

onds before midnight the Doomsday Clock, the closest ever to a possible man-made global catastrophe.

The state of uncertainty, confusion and apprehension experienced by the populations living in the "world in disarray" had become the dominating *Zeitgeist*, or the spirit of the age.

## 1. Social fear

The action and interaction of the many factors that converge to determine the social – and thus political – life of a country, or of a group of countries, cannot be given once and for all. Obviously, some macrotrends – such as the rise and decline of great powers – impose themselves over the long run and are relatively simple to identify. For example, those who avoided the ideological trap of the Cold War and kept pace with developments in international relations by applying the analytical criterion of *uneven development* would easily have recognized the general trend, which first appeared in the 1950s, of the relative decline of the United States in the face of re-emerging then newly emerging powers and, therefore, the inevitable upsetting of international relations that had rested upon US hegemony.[2]

Major trends are, however, sped up or slowed down by many other conditioning factors. Some of them have directly to do with politics (one government in power rather than another, an international agreement, a local war), others concern the economy (a crisis, a boom, a technological revolution, a new power source), while still others regard social behavior (demography primarily), chance (a natural disaster, a pandemic) and, finally, the psychological repercussions of all these factors combined. No single factor works in isolation: all are correlated by intertwining actions and interactions which can only be untangled by placing them within the major current trend.

Social fear is one of these factors. It is one of the most important psychological effects of the shift of the world's geopolitical axis caused by uneven development, and, at the same time, one of the causes of the acceleration of this shift. This is why it deserves to be addressed from the point of view of geopolitical analysis.

---

[2] The analytical grid of uneven development is based on the axiom according to which single economic activities, various sectors, regions and countries grow at different rates and times, which in the long run results in upsetting international relations. In political science, this criterion was knowingly adopted, among others, by Thucydides (notoriously "rediscovered" by Xi Jinping in a speech in September 2015), Halford Mackinder, Lenin, Robert Gilpin, Paul Kennedy and Richard Haass.

But does such a thing as the geopolitics of fear exist? In 2009, the French political scientist Dominique Moïsi published a book entitled *The Geopolitics of Emotion: How Cultures of Fear, Humiliation, and Hope Are Reshaping the World.* This was a first: emotions explicitly daring to set foot in the holy precincts of geopolitics, hitherto guarded by the sullen temple guards who see geopolitics only as the relationship between power and territory. Moïsi himself deemed it necessary to state that the title of his book could seem an "oxymoron," because geopolitics is "*about rationality, about objective data such as frontiers, economic resources, military might and the cold political calculus of interests*" whereas "*emotions are essentially subjective, if not purely irrational*". And yet, he wrote, "*one cannot comprehend the world in which we live without examining the emotions that help to shape it*" (Moïsi 2009, X-XI).

Moïsi was right: to separate emotions from politics is to violate the nature of things, and it can only lead to a hermeneutic dead end. Just think about fear: its use in politics – in particular the stimulation and manipulation of this emotion for a specific purpose – has been examined, and even prescribed, by Thucydides, Aristotle, Machiavelli, Hobbes and others. Machiavelli, in particular, advised the Prince to take proper account of the fact that human beings are a tangle of feelings and emotions: "*They are ungrateful, fickle, false, cowardly, covetous*"; and his conclusion seems to describe today's state of affairs perfectly: "*As long as you succeed, they are yours entirely; they will offer you their blood, property, life and children [...] when the need is far distant; but when it approaches they turn against you*"; therefore, for the Prince "*it is much safer to be feared than loved, when, of the two, either must be dispensed with*". (Machiavelli 1908, 134). Thus, this first modern political scientist well knew that "the cold political calculus of interests" cannot and must not ignore feelings and emotions.

If one intends to use geopolitics as a tool for the analysis of political phenomena, one must take into consideration all the factors that determine it. Not only material factors – geography, economy, demography, military strength, infrastructure, institutions, and alliances – but also immaterial ones, such as historical heritage, traditions, ideologies, religions and, finally, social psychology. These factors must, of course, be placed within specific realities, because they differ for every country, carry different weights and combine in different ways depending on space and time.

Those who might endeavour, for example, to undertake a geopolitical analysis of the United States while ignoring the importance of the Mississippi basin would not go very far; but nor would those who may try to perform a geopolitical analysis of the US (let alone govern the country) while ignoring the importance of social psychology, traditions and ideologies. In the first pages of his book *Diplomacy*, Henry Kissinger writes that Woodrow Wilson succeeded where Theodore Roosevelt had failed – that is, to bring the country to war in order to consolidate the conditions for its world leadership – because, although Roosevelt had a clear understanding of the cold relations of force on the international level, Wilson was able to mobilize the deep feelings of his fellow citizens.

From Paris and Menelaus to the 2003 "war on terror," including all the religious wars and the two world wars in between, passions have been a driving force of utmost importance. One does not have to be familiar with Clausewitz's work to understand how moral and psychological factors in war (which is, notoriously, politics by other means) can overturn the "objective" weight of material factors: suffice it to recall the unstoppable impetus of the French revolutionary armies after 1789, the Confederates' tough resistance to the Unionists, and the "impossible" victory of Israel's newly created army in 1948. In some cases, like those just mentioned, the role of moral and psychological factors proved decisive, in some others it was important and in yet others almost irrelevant. However, leaving them aside means getting an incomplete, and therefore distorted, picture of the situation under analysis. In a nutshell, feelings and emotions fully belong to conditioning political factors.

## 2. "Selfish and Proud"

Fear has accompanied mankind throughout its prehistory and history. But here we are focusing on social fear as a constant emotional substratum in the age of capitalism. This emotional substratum began to take shape when social roles in the pre-capitalist era, which were relatively stable, were progressively replaced by their permanent mobility in the capitalist era. Simultaneously, the safety nets of feudal society were dismantled, and individuals found themselves alone and isolated in the face of blind market forces. At the same time, the religions' ethical and normative framework that had justified and explained fear was replaced with a Promethean illusion that man is *faber fortunæ suæ* (the maker of his own fortune).

Social fear has intensified over the last half century. This state of concern crept in during the second half of the 1970s with the beginning of what later would be called "globalisation," was accentuated at the end of the Yalta order, spread widely during the period of terror attacks and, finally, became a veritable *Zeitgeist* after the 2008 crisis, even before the Covid pandemic and the wars in Ukraine and in Gaza (which, of course, did not help heal it). This concern fed on a pervasive sense of fragility in the face of all possible dangers. Both large and small, these concerns regarded everyday life, but they also involved imaginary catastrophes (from environmental apocalypse to the death of Western civilization), possible real catastrophes (contagion by a deadly plague or nuclear Armageddon), and often intertwined to bring about a growing demand – as confused as much as exigent – for protection.

Even before 2008, globalization, terrorism, immigrants, Muslims, global warming and epidemics – you name it – were indicated as main threats to be protected against. Following the 2008 subprime mortgage crisis, the slow recovery of the following years, and, finally, the 2015 massive exodus of refugees and migrants, the fear of those threats skyrocketed, and the political fallout was massive. It included not only Brexit and the election of Donald Trump, but also the rise of populism, the discovery of sovereignism and the petty-bourgeois *jacqueries* whose paradigmatic quintessence was France's Yellow Vest movement. The coronavirus pandemic in the spring of 2020 and the subsequent quarantines imposed on the global productive and commercial systems unavoidably took that social fear to unprecedented heights, both in intensity and reach, thus contributing to an aggravation of tensions at local and international levels. The war in Ukraine was another huge step, and certainly not the final step: German Chancellor Olaf Scholz labelled it as a *Zeitenwende*, an epochal turning point; but the world had been experiencing a series of dramatic *Zeitenwenden* for at least fifty years before it.

After having for years criticized Donald Trump for his isolationist instincts, nearly all countries threw themselves headlong into the most uninhibited of economic nationalism. The dread of interrupting the supply chain loosened tongues: in addition to repatriating the production of masks and disinfectant gel, almost all governments have begun to suggest repatriating the production of those semi-finished products and components that suddenly disappeared when China was locked down; in the same way, the old distrust of globalization and free trade has become the conventional wisdom, accompanied by paeans of national production, local consumption, short supply chains, zero-mile food, Victory gardens and backyard orchards. As a (psycho)logical sequence, "my-country-first" could only lead to "my-region-first," then "my-city-first," "my-neighborhood-first," "my-family-first" and, finally, "me-first" in a backwards motion which brings to mind the state of nature described by Hobbes.

One American anti-lockdown protester was immortalized by the sign he carried saying "Selfish and proud"; moralists were scandalized, but they failed to notice the direction in which almost all governments of the world – whether right or left, liberal or conservative – were moving: "ourselves first". Once again, as after 2015, political decisions driven by fear could only produce even more frightening conditions (as Brexit), fueling a vicious circle that seemed impossible to escape.

## 3. The search for a scapegoat

Traditionally, political scientists have addressed the role of fear in politics as a tool used by the ruling class to condition the behavior of the masses; today, it seems that things are going the other way around: it is the fear experienced by the masses (a social fear) that conditions the behavior of the political class and tends to become an open revolt – including street riots – against politics.

The notion of "social fear" descends from that of "social psychology," which Antonio Labriola introduced to political thought in 1899: "*the specific consciousness of people in given social condition*" (Labriola 1903, 112). Here, "consciousness" should not be confused with "awareness" (besides, to Marx, "consciousness" in the sense of "awareness" is the prerogative of the party, not of the masses) because it is precisely in the context of social fear that awareness is lacking. Labriola also warned against "*those attempts at generalization... the general idea of which is to transport and apply to a subject which is called social consciousness the known categories and forms of individual psychology*" (Labriola 1903, 111). Paraphrasing Émile Durkheim, society is not the mere sum of individuals, because the form that social life takes depends on how individuals combine and interact.

In the same way, social fear is not the mere sum of individual fears; it is their particular combination, which varies in time and space. Of course, individual and social fear have some features in common, one of the most important being that neither individuals nor masses are able to distinguish between perceived and actual risk. The search for a scapegoat, i.e., somebody to blame for social anxiety and tension, built up in the aftermath of the 2008 crisis in the older industrialized countries, proves that the failure to understand actual threats creates the need for imaginary threats. Individuals who are incapable of distinguishing between actual and perceived risk end up harming themselves; when this incapacity extends to the social level, it harms the entire society. For example, the blaming of immigrants for our social anxieties not only proves that there is no relationship between perceived and actual risk, it also rules out the possibility of dealing with one of the most serious, and potentially fatal, problems of our society: the demographic deficit. And creating conditions for not being able to deal with demographic deficit automatically means increasing social fears and tensions. Thus, we have another vicious circle, with no way out.

## 4. The Great Fear of 2008

The last decade of the twentieth century seemed to have marked the definitive victory of capitalism, not only because of the miserable failure of what had been presented as an alternative economic model – the Soviet Union – but most importantly because new "economic miracles" seemed to be looming on the horizon. In the 1990s, the United States (momentarily) reversed the trend of its relative economic decline, partly due to the disappearance of the USSR and partly due to the adoption of vigorous deregulation measures under the Reagan administration, later extended by the Clinton administration; Americans recovered from the demoralization of the Vietnam War and celebrated the return to a placid era of growing prosperity.

In that same decade, Europe started its process of continental integration, creating a political union and, most importantly, a federal currency, symbol of a momentum that seemed difficult to resist (to the point that the British government was planning for the country to possibly join the euro). Asia's economic rise allowed American, European and Japanese companies to make huge profits without *yet* creating new competitors on world markets with their investments. Finally, an awed and enchanted world was entering the digital age with all its fabulous promises. Before the turn of the century, what was beginning to be called "globalization" was generally viewed favourably. In the older industrialized countries, those years were characterized by a general optimism.

The new century, however, dealt a series of fatal blows to the rosy expectations of the previous decade: the bursting of the dot-com bubble in 2000; the carnage of September 11, 2001, followed by the interminable wars in Afghanistan and Iraq; the great financial crisis in 2008; and finally, in 2015, the exodus of millions of migrants and refugees to Europe, the birth of the "Islamic State" in Syria and Iraq, and the terror attacks in Paris (not to mention the periodic arrival of potential new pandemics: SARS, avian flu, swine flu and Ebola, to name the best known).

Of all these events, however, it is the financial crisis of 2008 – the "great recession" – that represented the true turning point, the beginning of a new era in which the "anxiety" described by Sandel in 1998 was transformed in the *Zeitgeist* of our age, affecting national political cycles and, consequently, international political cycle.

In *The Wealth of Nations*, Adam Smith affirms that the periods of economic growth determine "*the cheerful and the hearty state to all the different orders of society*"; the "*stationary state*", or stagnation, "*is dull*", while decline is "*melancholy*" (Campbell and Skinner 1979, 99). British economist Stephen Daryl King, commenting on this passage, writes: "*The 'sta-*

*tionary state' – where there is no growth – is not just dull but also full of uncertainties... And the 'declining state' is one in which the vast majority of people are likely to end up worse off, an outcome that, at the very least, is melancholy*". And he adds: "*It is also a reflection of our fear of losing what we already have*" (King 2013, 40).

The "great fear" of losing what we have is probably the most important psychological legacy of the 2008 crisis. For many, the "great recession" had immediate, disastrous consequences: in the United States alone, it wiped out eight million jobs and about $2 trillion in income, devalued real estate assets by 18% (the largest loss of wealth in fifty years) and led to the foreclosure of 5% of all homes. Ten years later, that is, on the eve of the next crisis, Americans had not yet fully recovered: while the median household income had regained some ground and gone up to 6% higher than that of 2007,[3] the net asset loss amounted to –8.7%, and to –13.6% of financial assets alone.[4]

Individual losses must obviously be added to collective losses, that is, those concerning social services. In the US health sector alone, 55,000 jobs were lost (a quarter of the total); between 2008 and 2015, 34 US States cut their budgets for primary and secondary education, 43 for higher education (universities and colleges), 31 for healthcare and 29 for elderly care, according to the Center on Budget and Policy Priorities.

Thus, on average the losses were only partly recovered. When, due to a crisis, something is lost – a job or a home, for example – the immediate response to the trauma is acute and the situation is often desperate; so desperate that, one could say, there is no time for fear because all the energy is channeled towards finding a solution; fear comes later, when the solution proves unsatisfactory or elusive, or when even a satisfactory solution is not a shield against future setbacks. Anxiety and fear are dominant feelings among both those who have not lost anything but *are afraid* of losing it, and those who *have lost* and are afraid of not being able to recover. The fragility and slowness of recovery in the years following the 2008 crisis prolonged the anxiety for the former and increased it for the latter. In the medium to long term, when a robust and prolonged recovery is lacking, the loss is felt as definitive, even by those who have not lost anything and those who have managed to recover their losses.

Therefore, in the older industrialized countries, even prior to the catastrophic impact of the following crises, there was little chance of reacquir-

---

[3] https://www.statista.com/statistics/200838/median-household-income-in-the-united-states/ (accessed on 12 September 2024).

[4] OECD data for assets and financial assets.

ing serenity and confidence – due first to the new pace of development: in 2013, the economist Robert J. Samuelson forecast future growth for the United States of just over 2% annually, almost 1/3 less than the average had been since 1950. And that, indeed, is what happened: between 2010 and 2018, average growth was 2.25% (according to the World Bank data). Structurally, a steady decline in growth by nearly a third means that in the medium to long term the United States could afford about one third less than it could afford before 2008. This reduction of economic potential was, according to Samuelson, the "*new economic norm [that] threatens to upend our political and social order*" (Samuelson 2013). Three years after Samuelson's article came out, Americans elected Donald Trump to the White House. And a similar slowdown in growth took place, but to a much greater extent, in all the other older industrialized countries: the *average* annual growth in Japan went from 2.8% in the period 1975-2007 to 0.5% in the period 2008-2018; in Germany, from 2.2 to 1.3; in France, from 2.4 to 0.9; in the UK, from 2.7 to 1.2; and in Italy, from 2.2 to negative territory: -0.4%.[5]

Secondarily, the chances of returning to the pre-crisis state of affairs and of reacquiring serenity and confidence were slim because the "recovery" had been achieved in part not thanks to production (declining everywhere, as we have seen), but by increasing public debt, that is, using money that did not exist, or in other words, by mortgaging the future goods and services of citizens. The public debt of the six aforementioned countries increased sharply between 2008 and 2018: in the UK, it grew by 77.5% over these eleven years, in France by 47.5%, and in the United States, Japan and Italy by just over 30%.[6] The example of Germany, where public debt declined (albeit slightly, from 70.6% to 70.4%) shows that it was not inevitable.

Although the public money that flooded into companies in response to the coronavirus crisis would seem to justify the reasoning of advocates of deficit spending *ad libitum* (according to whom a state can borrow money indefinitely), the reality is that all debts come due sooner or later; and when this happens, everyone is required to pay. And since capitalism can continue to thrive only if there are investments, the higher one's rank is on the social ladder (that is, the more one is a potential investor), the less one is called to pay; and, vice versa, the lower one's rank is, the more one pays (directly and in terms of reduced services). Thus, the banks that were responsible for the 2008 crisis received billions of dollars, euros or pounds

---

[5] Data World Bank, constant USD 2010.

[6] OECD data.

from the state, while the debtors paid up to the last cent. It seems absurd and unjust, and in fact it is; but no one in good faith would claim that capitalism is sensible and fair.

A political problem arises from the fact that those on the lower or even middle rungs of the social ladder do not eagerly accept the ineluctability of injustice. And when injustice hits them directly, or they feel that it does, they demand compensation: every social group, every profession, every guild and, finally, every individual claims more money; little does it matter if money is lacking, or if it is lacking for others: "my guild first!" (ultimately, "me first!") has become the rallying cry of all those who have benefited for decades from the generosity of the welfare state and are sure that if the cornucopia becomes jammed, the fault lies with the ill will or ineptitude or iniquity or mere wickedness of someone else, easily identifiable.

## 5. Fear and anger

"*There is no generally applicable dynamic relationship between perceived and actual risk*," two American researchers assert in an article on the processes of psychological mediation between the severity of a problem and its social perception. Of course, the authors added, "*some types of risks evoke a measured and proportionate response*"; however, most of the time, this is not true (Loewenstein and Mather 1990, 155-175). In the case of social fear, the relationship between actual threats and their perception is muddled by the fact that those who feel threatened are unaware of the real causes of their anxiety. Therefore, they try to find these threats elsewhere, in phenomena and especially in groups of people that *seem* threatening, but in reality are not, or are much less threatening than they are subjectively perceived to be. These perceived threats can even be a potential resource to partially address some of the real threats.

In "advanced" countries, social fear – *average* social fear – is caused by the concern of losing what one possesses or of not being able to rely on a continuous improvement in one's standard of living. Of course, this is an actual threat inasmuch as these countries can no longer guarantee their populations all the benefits and privileges that they had been able to guarantee when they monopolized the world market. But their populations, having neither knowledge nor awareness of the dynamics of international relations, cannot "recognize" the origins of their anxieties; it could also be said that they *do not want to recognize them* because, if they did, they would deprive themselves of outlets to release their anxiety.

Those who fear that their social status might be jeopardized *sense* the actual threat hanging over their heads, but they attribute it to the most diverse of causes: the ill will of politicians, the rapacity of the "élites," the "deep state," Brussels bureaucrats, Wall Street wolves, the Chinese, the immigrants, the Muslims, the Jews – as you please. In our social organization, everyone is perpetually exposed to the uncertainties of markets, uncertainties that rise in periods of crisis, of slow recovery and of uncontrolled public debt. But blaming the "market" is unsatisfactory because it is an impersonal force, and as such cannot be identified, blackmailed or punished; it is known that, in order to give relief and consolation to the victim of an injustice (true, alleged, or just feared), it is necessary to finger a flesh-and-blood culprit from whom to demand compensation.

The populations of the "advanced" countries *feel* the decline – albeit relative – of their societies but refuse to admit it, and, therefore, to face it. The Swiss-American psychologist Elisabeth Kübler-Ross considered denial as the first of the five psychological stages a terminal patient goes through; the other four are anger, bargaining, depression and, finally, acceptance of the inevitable. From the second decade of the 21st century, the populations of the countries that dominated world markets in the past have been swinging between denial, anger and a particular form of bargaining, tormented by the fear of losing their privileges or having to share them with populations who were used to having no privileges at all.

Denial of the rise of new powers consists precisely in not recognizing the shift in the world's economic balance, that is, in refusing to deal with the reality of decline, albeit relative. The direct expression of this denial is the determination to continue to live as before, even when a country is no longer able to afford it.

According to Kübler-Ross, the next psychological stage – anger – is fuelled by a sense of dispossession and a feeling of injustice that comes with it:

> "*Maybe we too would be angry if all our life activities were interrupted so prematurely… if we had put some hard-earned money aside to enjoy a few years of rest and enjoyment, only to be confronted with the fact that "this is not for me". What else would we do with our anger, but let it out on the people who are most likely to enjoy all these things?*".

The expression of this fear in individual and in social reactions is similar in this case too: "*This anger is displaced in all directions and projected onto the environment at times almost random*", but it "*has originally nothing or little to do with the people who become the target of the anger*" (Kubler-Ross 1997, 64, 65). A patient's anger is taken out on doctors, nurses and even relatives and friends, whereas social anger targets all those who, for one reason or another, are identified as potential dispossessors.

After the 2008 crisis, in the collective imaginary, what was once condescendingly called the "Third World" has become the source of all attacks on our living standards: the main cause of global warming, the cluster of pandemics, the hotbed of unfair competition, the receptacle of hostile and dangerous religions, the homeland of masses of miserable people who, instead of staying where nature (or Providence) had placed them, have proffered the "absurd" claim to live like Europeans, Americans and Japanese. Anger had found its outlets.

Kübler-Ross points out that, once a dying patient realizes that nothing has been achieved through anger, he changes his attitude. He begins to hope that "*there is a slim chance that he may be rewarded for good behavior and be granted a wish for special services*" (Kubler-Ross 1997, 94): this is the stage of bargaining. In a society, teachers present their role as essential for the proper functioning of the community, and therefore feel authorized to request an increase in the education budget. But so do nurses, electric utility employees, tram drivers, mail carriers and garbage collectors; similarly, a worker of a company that has gone out of business feels entitled to demand that the government intervene to ensure his job and wages. Just like a terminally ill patient, everyone is right in wanting to survive, and many are right in considering their social role as essential; but the numbers just do not add up. Everyone demands protection, and everyone demands money. Some regard the exponential growth of public debt with suspicion because they fear that the government may use up the resources that they are claiming; yet all are convinced that it is the others who must make sacrifices to save public finances and therefore save their jobs and their salaries.

The patient can only bargain with one possible interlocutor – a charlatan who may be selling magic potions. The analogy works in this case too: a whole range of self-proclaimed good Samaritans come to the social bargaining table claiming to have the solution to all problems. These sellers of political magic potions take full advantage of social anxieties to obtain electoral support: they exploit, fuel and propagate them, and sometimes they even create them, in a classic mercantile relationship of supply and demand. Politics has always tried to leverage emotions, and fear in particular, to assert or consolidate control over society; yet, although this ruse is as old as politics itself, its effectiveness in space and time has proved very inconsistent. The success or the failure of this or that message depends not so much on the message itself (the supply) as on the need of its recipients to find an answer, whatever it may be, to their anxieties (the demand). In a nutshell, fear must become pervasive and on a mass level in order for scaremongering vote-hunters to be successful; similarly, charlatans can only sell their potions if there is a disease – or fear of one. The German National

Socialist Party obtained 2.6% of the vote in the May 1928 election, which rose to 18.3% in September 1930 and 37.8% in July 1932. The supply was more or less the same, but the demand had changed.

Scaremongers respond to the demand for protection and compensation with the so-called "get 'em sick, get 'em well" tactics: they stir up anxieties and then present themselves as bearers of solutions ("Only I can fix it"). If anxieties are attributed to migration and crime, the recipe to follow is to exaggerate the risks that migrants and crime pose to society and then propose the solution: the closure of borders and the imposition of more draconian "law and order" measures. But anxieties necessarily precede purveyors of tranquilizers; those purveyors obviously have every interest in preserving and spreading anxieties, but they cannot create them themselves.

## 6. Suicide for fear of dying

As has often happened since fear became the *Zeitgeist* of our age, decisions based on this emotion have led to a dead end: the race for protection "at any cost" has accelerated, and every country believes it can protect itself better by turning inward, toward isolation and an embrace of that which is closest to it, as always happens after an economic crisis. In the immediate aftermath of the 2008 crisis, the heads of state and government of the G20 countries decided to meet for the first time in an attempt to limit the damage to the global system as much as possible, with the shared feeling that the health of each country depended on the health of all (and vice versa). In the final communiqué of their second meeting, there was a meaningful statement: "*We will not repeat the historic mistake of protectionism of previous eras*". It was "historic" because that very mistake aggravated the crisis and triggered a domino effect that would lead to the outbreak of the global conflict ten years later.

This declaration shows that every government knows that isolation and protectionism can only aggravate the situation, both economically and politically, but every government seems to be carried away by a fatal repetition compulsion. "We the people" demand protection, and governments obediently bow to the will of the people. Thus, every corner of the world becomes a fortress that feels besieged; and inside the fortress, the battle for the best way to defend itself rages on.

Since historical analogies are in vogue, we allow ourselves a quick intrusion of the Roman Empire. Around 150 CE, writes Peter Brown, it was possible for a young student, Tatian, to pass from the eastern, Syrian, fringe of the Roman empire to Rome, speaking Greek all the way and participating in a uniform Greek philosophical culture… To humbler men, [the peace of the Empire] meant wider horizons and unprecedented opportunities for travel; it meant the erosion of local differences through trade and emigration; and the weakening of ancient barriers before new wealth and new criteria of status.

But only a century later, in the western part of the Empire "*there was a gradual reversion to small-scale, hand-to-mouth craftsmanship, producing for the local market and for specific orders in the vicinity… the splitting-up of a single oecumenical trade system into a number of provincial blocks*" (Wallbank 1946, 38 and 51). Sounds familiar. And we know how that turned out.

## References

Brown, P. (1971). *The World of Late Antiquity: AD 150-750.* Thames & Hudson, London.

Campbell, R.H. and Skinner, A.S. (1979). *The Glasgow Edition of the Works and Correspondence of Adam Smith*, vol. II. Clarendon Press, Oxford.

King, S.D. (2013). *When the Money Runs Out: The End of Western Affluence.* Yale, New Haven.

Kübler-Ross, E. (1997). *On Death and Dying.* Scribner, New York (or. ed. Macmillan, New York, 1969).

Labriola, A. (1903). *Essays on the Materialistic Conception of History*, transl. by C.H. Kerr. Monthly Review Press, New York.

Loewenstein, G. and Mather, J. (1990). "Dynamic Processes in Risk Perception". *Journal of Risk and Uncertainty*, 3.

Machiavelli, N. (1908). *The Prince*, transl. by W.K. Marriott. J.M. Dent & Son, London-Toronto.

Moïsi, D. (2009). *The Geopolitics of Emotion: How Cultures of Fear, Humiliation, and Hope are Reshaping the World.* Doubleday, New York.

Samuelson, R.J. (2013). "The Shutdown Heralds a New Economic Norm". *The Washington Post*, October 14.

Walbank, F.W. (1946). *The Decline of the Roman Empire in the West.* H. Schuman, New York.

Chapter 4

# FROM LAMPEDUSA TO KASSEL: MIGRATION, ART AND THE RUINS OF EUROPE

**Iain Chambers**

ABSTRACT: *This essay embarks on a transformative journey, proposing to shift the migration question from an isolated object of academic study to the dynamic practice of thinking with migration. This shift, which inevitably disrupts national and disciplinary boundaries, holds the potential to dismantle a colonial mindset, its philosophical presumptions, and Occidental lineage, and brings the racial constitution of modernity into sharper focus. The limited application of rights and the borders of European humanism are then starkly exposed to promote other horizons of understanding.*

*Such a perspective is pursued through the author's personal experience of the art event documenta 15 at Kassel in 2022. There, accusations of antisemitism and the putting in jeopardy of the public configuration of German identity with the state of Israel went on to reveal a deeper racism directed against the non-Occidental world and its challenge to European control of aesthetic and ethical parameters. Only local German authority was allowed to speak on the question, only Europe had custody of the definitions of genocide and racism, and the ex-colonial world was expected to listen and learn.*

*Art, as the unauthorized exploration and elaboration of 'our' languages, particularly in its postcolonial and decolonial articulations, fractured this archive and apparatuses of power. Artists from elsewhere displaced the certainties of the canon, its institutions, and practices.*

*Unacknowledged narratives disturbed the premises of historical temporality and led to the past being reworked in future becomings. This is what happened at Kassel. Caliban took over and, in a profoundly pedagogical and political set of practices, temporarily proposed an open and more democratic laboratory of modernity.*



> "*…the hyperbolic presentation of drowning refugees and orphaned children as an elemental threat is so peculiar, so neurotic and so duplicitous that it demands uncomfortable answers to the question of what the local variety of civilization might now entail?*"
>
> (Gilroy 2018, 15).

> *"The global world is organised around the ordering of bodies-bodies that are expendable: black bodies, transgender bodies, Roma bodies, 'white trash' bodies, migrants; bodies that are collateral 'damage', as can be seen from the so-called human rights practiced in the EU which leave the refugees dispossessed, discriminated against, ghettoised and incarcerated (that is, captivated). Financialised bio- and necro-political structures produce uncontrollable violence as the only aesthetic intensity that profoundly reorders space and time.*
> *Consequently, it is possible to state the following: if the body of the refugee is taken as the ultimate political figure of necrocapitalism, the emergent necroaesthetic parameters are: a) hyperviolence, b) the body as corpse and c) hyperimmobilisation, all of which are predicated on the erasure of history".*
>
> (Grzinić 2018, 28-29).

## 1. On the beach

In Isaac Julien's prescient three-screen video installation *Western Union Small Boats* (2007), silver body bags lie near bathers on a southern Italian beach. In another sequence, a dance of migrant death is transposed from the waters of the Mediterranean to the exquisitely tiled floor of Palazzo Gangi in Palermo, the exact location used for the ballroom sequence in Luchino Visconti's film *The Leopard* (1963). In the repetition of the European cinematic and aesthetic canon, the hidden histories of the uninvited guest disturb the scene. The terrible beauty of Julien's installation releases an unauthorised telling of European culture. The social relations of a planetary economy, the Occidental colonisation and appropriation of resources and non-white lives interrupt the customary narrative of European progress. Dead black bodies in the pleasure zones of Europe not only emphasise the negated destined for anonymous cancellation under racial capitalism in the Black Mediterranean (Robinson 1983; Di Maio 2012; Proglio 2018). They also focus on a world that exceeds the categories we Europeans have prepared for it. The question is not of migration; after all, Europeans have been doing it for centuries. The question is of rights. For concentrated in these images lies the history of the modern world attendant on justice.

A beach is a liminal space. It lies between the presumed certainties of land and the ambiguous openness of the sea. On the shoreline, we register a limit, a frontier. It is where we can feel our grip on the world slipping away. Today, on the northern shore of the Mediterranean, with the arrival of modern migrants and refugees, we are increasingly reminded of this threat and associated fears. So, Europe turns its back on the sea, transforming it into a barrier and deadly passage. Moving from Giorgio Agamben's noted evocation of 'bare life', the migrant acquires the exceptional state of being that exposes the limits of European humanism and its vaunted universal rights. She takes us to the lip of the abyss… and beyond Agamben and much of modern philosophy. The migrant, even if mute and lifeless, strips the political and philosophical paradigm of Europe and the West of its authority. Her presence interrogates our framing of the world. According to Article 13 of the Declaration of Human Rights (1948), everyone has the right to migrate. No one is inherently illegal. Yet, migration has been made illegal, transformed into a death-defying process by those who assume they have the authority to confine and define the world. In the water and on the beach, there are not only the bodies of migrants who failed to cross the sea. There is also the wreck of a particular idea of Europe, progress and the West.

Aimé Césaire and Frantz Fanon famously pointed out this discrepancy in their scathing critique of the universal claims of European humanism. Both exposed the hypocrisies and self-serving premises of its procedures. The limits of this humanism were fully brought home in the shock of racist colonial practices exercised on European soil against a part of its population in the Holocaust. We will return to that moment, referring to events in Kassel in the summer of 2022 at the documenta 15 art exhibition, critically to undo its continuing hold on public discourse in Germany and the Occident. Today, the migrant, crossing from North Africa and Asia or trudging through the Balkans and amassing on the borders of Eastern Europe, reiterates Fanon's request of demanding human behaviour from the other. We are that other.

Migration persists and insists. It questions the idea of the nation-state and exclusive citizenship. It reintroduces worldly forces that interrupt the local logic of political control and legal confines. The migrant subverts the nation's norm as the unique unit of identification for rights and recognition. As the Italian philosopher Donatella Di Cesare puts it:

> "*The migrant is atopos – without a place, out of place – just as much as the alien, or rather more so. For the migrant is placed at the frontier, in the attempt to cross it. The migrant is neither citizen nor alien. Unwelcome everywhere, she is an intruder who blows up barriers, wipes out boundaries and provokes embarrassment. Therein lies the difficulty in thinking about her. Unless, that is, the world's agreed boundaries are put back into discussion, and we revisit the centuries-long foundations of the city and citizenship, and alter the entrenched pillars of the state, sovereignty and the nation*" (Di Cesare 2020, 16-17).

Underlying historical processes invariably push against the narrow grain of nationalist and autochthonous reasoning. We are alerted to the restrictive prescriptions of European political philosophy, historically secured in the profitable regime of property, the authority of the state and the ontological privilege of individual sovereignty.

Suppose we were to think *with* migration, the sea, and the Mediterranean. Thinking with the histories and archives they sustain we might begin to break away from the objectification of the world that serves only to confirm our subjectivity. We would then need to reach beyond our narcissism. That would mean acknowledging and disbanding the continuing constitution of modernity exclusively through our political and philosophical colonialisms. If, as many presume, philosophy is the autobiography of Europe and the West, then we will have to turn philosophy against itself and subsequently puncture the inbred positivism of our social sciences. We will have to look beneath superficial labels and distinctions; for example, between the civil and secular West set against the religious and barbaric other. Here, we could tap into more complex intersections and acknowledge a form of urbane secularism that is Christianity pretending to be universalist and a hegemonic moral order. It would be to dub Occidental history and its narrative of disinterested progress with the violence and repression of its darker side. Insisting with the Fourteenth-century thinker Ibn Khaldûn that history "*is firmly rooted in philosophy*" produces a breach in the Occidental custody of *logos* and proposes modes of reasoning irreducible to a unique or unilateral rationality.

Modern European philosophy is centred on the sovereignty of the individual and premised on the idea that the world and its objects (including non-European subjects) can be rendered transparent to its rationalism. In her book *Towards a Global Idea of Race*, Denise Ferreira da Silva incisively illustrates how elevating the European individual to the source and centre of history and knowledge secretes a racial disposition. It brings us to understand "*how the knowledge arsenal, which now governs the global (juridic, economic, and moral) configuration, institutes racial subjection as it presupposes and postulates that the elimination of its 'others' is necessary for the realization of the subject's exclusive ethical attribute, namely, self-determination*". (Ferreira da Silva 2007, Kindle Edition). In other words, the problem is not what Occidental philosophy can identify and resolve but a deeper one: the problem is philosophy itself and the disciplines and languages it endorses and sustains.

Rather than the hierarchical organisation of the modern world, seemingly emanating outwards from its home in Europe, further understandings begin to take shape. Contra knowledge formations disciplined in a European lineage, other chartings of modernity, in their subaltern and unequal power relations, pose more complicated and heterogeneous procedures. The latter leads not simply to redrawing the inherited map and adjusting existing accounts of time and place. Rather, they fold and interrupt the usual north-south, Europe and the rest, dichotomies to traverse Mediterranean landscapes with histories of belonging that precede and exceed their Europeanisation, nationalisation and modern bleaching by white hegemony (Greenberg and Hamilakis 2022).

As an in-between zone between three continents with multiple histories and cultures, the Mediterranean Sea is an anarchic space that escapes ready capture in the political confines of property. It is where a terrestrial order, or *nomos*, dissolves in an extra-juridical area: origins are disturbed in the currents of creolisation. The fear of alterity is not simply associated with anxiety embodied in the migrant or Muslim. It is also, more profoundly, a fear of the migrant and Muslim within ourselves, a fear of the complex composition of a refused past breaking in to disturb the sought uniformity of the present. As Frantz Fanon and Cedric Robinson point out, it was in Europe, and certainly not in Africa, that the 'Negro' was invented: "*a being that was biologically, intellectually, and culturally predetermined by his irreducible difference*" (Mbembe 2017, 73). The world that is othered and shunned through diverse skin pigmentation, religious adherence, and cultural custom is also a world constructed by the psychic fear of heterogeneity. The continuing attempt to discipline and control such historical vibrancy releases the ghosts of modernity – from the deeper histories of Islam and Arabic culture *within* the formation of Europe to the after-life of slavery and half-hearted confrontations with genocidal modernity and the Holocaust – that rattle the chains of Occidental security. Seeking solutions that distance discomfort and disruption, the West, even in its most liberal extension, continues to propose a lexicon in which only it (and those who successfully mimic its language) can speak. The others are objects, fundamentally mute and absent. Or else they exist in the incomprehensible noise that provides a background to the reasoning of hegemony.

To insist on the significance of the historical and political interruption posed by the modern migrant is not only to de-centre the Western's presumed autonomy and propose more complex cultural and political consequences. Seemingly timeless guarantees of blood, soil and tradition are now deviated by the pressure of historical processes arriving from the sea and elsewhere. The timeless referents of the nation and the myths of tradition turn out to be sites of transit, transformation and translation. Other coordinates emerge with which to navigate the African-Asian-European matrix of the Mediterranean. Refusing to reduce the world to a single inventory of time encourages us to adopt a more ironic relation to origins while encountering further genealogies that do not simply reflect a European will to power. What has once rendered separate and distant becomes both proximate and potentially disruptive. The flat taxonomy of time, where everything is allotted its chronological and cultural place, is interrupted and fractured, ready for another assemblage of comprehension (Chambers and Cariello, 2022). The historical formation of the purportedly objective languages of the social sciences is challenged. While Occidental research paradigms and political powers mesh in the execution of their 'superior' explanation and management of the globe, their universality and purported neutrality betray the historical particularities of methodological racism. Ultimately, this arrives at a "*colonial technology of life and premature death built on ideologies of whiteness and white supremacy*" (Rutazibwa, 2020).

## 2. Art and the fractured archive

This cutting and interrupting of time reminds us that the past does not simply pass. Time accumulates. Rather than a closed chapter, we are pulled into a spiral of historical processes where different cultures and temporalities intersect and overlap in the stratified sediments of the present. We now find ourselves under wider and wilder skies by the sea. The persistence of colonialism, which repeatedly returns in the racism that produces the violent grammar of contemporary inhospitality, is inscribed most directly on the body of the modern migrant. Until recently, the Mediterranean was a colonial lake ruled by London, Paris, and Rome. Today, the apparent independence of its African and Asian shores is still subject to the economic and political prerogatives of the northern coast. The colonial relationship continues. The migrant is a recursive reminder of this repressed history. How can we disrupt the ongoing colonial appropriation of the world to bring that past into play and give it critical authority? What we might call postcolonial art, that is, the crossing of Western aesthetics by uninvited guests, who are often second or third-generation residents (when does one stop being a migrant, a foreigner?), does not simply lead to stylistic innovation and novelty. It also produces a critical language capable of proposing other narratives of spacetime.

In modernity, understood in more mobile and migratory terms, black and brown lives remain reified on dispossessing seas and punishing perimeters. They are exposed to all the violence of Europe's political and juridical borders. Between the Black Atlantic, the Black Mediterranean, and the Balkans, the epistemic foundations of Western democracy and philosophy are now adrift. Those on the water, the damned of the sea, like those who trudge through the fields, forests, and roads from Anatolia to Eastern Europe, cannot find their identity in the nation-state's territory. They are without rights. They have no social or human validity. They have no place in the world. Yet, puncturing the existing map, they sustain holes of concentrated historical and cultural energy that exist and endure. They provoke the end of one particular political and philosophical settlement and the inauguration of another. They interrupt a specific understanding of modernity, cut through its languages, and reshuffle its coordinates to produce a ragged opening, an untidy series of interrogations.

Insisting on the incalculable, on what escapes the meshes of omnipresent positivism and faith in the truth of Western social sciences means discovering that we do not know what we thought we knew. To sow critical language with inconclusiveness and uncertainty is what Afro-Brazilian philosopher Denise Ferreira da Silva calls a knowing without being imprisoned in the categories of modernity. In Achille Mbembe's words, it is to begin to respond and take responsibility for the becoming black of the world. In subaltern formations, underground histories and fugitive cultures, we encounter other knowledge, practices and politics elaborating an emerging planetary formation without immediate resolution or repair.

To think and work in this manner of receiving and reworking the archive as a living and continuous site of critical elaboration and redistribution of responsibilities for the future, as Derrida would have put it, and not as a mausoleum, a catalogue of documents, or a museum technology that narrates the nation, is not only to retrieve from the rubble of the past means to conceive of a diverse today and tomorrow. It also interrupts a precise understanding of the present provided by a national (and disciplinary) identity. New circuits of connections and arrangements emerge to interrupt the teleology of history as if the latter was simply the linear passage of progress through empty time and space. Here, certain art practices suggest another direction, employing coordinates that do not respond to a single rhythm or score. Repetition, recovery, and the search for a repressed and denied past lead to a radical reworking and renewal. What has been inherited and transmitted in the multiplicities of planetary modernity is translated and transformed. Here, contemporary postcolonial art suggests an altogether broader and unfinished activity. In their ambivalence, images, sounds, and words provoke holes in existing maps and explanations as they punctuate the pretensions of a single narrative.

We understand the past through the lens and language of the present. This means comprehending that we and our historiography are always anachronistic to our sources. Configuring the past always means thinking about the how and now of the present (Portanova 2022). Walter Benjamin defined origins as "*that which emerges from the process of becoming and disappearing, where there is no stable source but rather a 'whirlpool in the river of becoming*'" (Benjamin 1985, 45). We are constantly working with a past that is intrinsically cast loose from any single measure of time or place.

Here, the recent output of artists and critics, often from subaltern and once-invisible histories, provides us with a broader and more dynamic critical script. Sharp distinctions between the factual and the fictional evaporate in a critical narrative willing to reward the imagination that gives the contemporary moment a more complex sense of the unfinished past, the open present, and possible futures. Necessarily incomplete and ambiguous, this produces another analytical and political grammar. Bringing to our attention such practices and procedures – directly, obliquely, ironically, or in bitter tones – the archive is traversed and translated in such a way as to be untethered from a single authority: history, the museum, the nation-state. As a result, historical temporality is freed from the single measure of 'progress' and its version of the world. We are left gathering from the debris of the past discontinuous elements to assemble the present and insist on histories beside and beyond the existing version.

If this archive arrives from the future – given that its histories are still to be recognised and recorded – then the past is neither over nor concluded. This critical freedom has probably been most fruitfully elaborated in contemporary postcolonial art. The names and works that can be evoked at this point are many. There are so many that perhaps we should speak of a 'postcolonial turn' in modern art, literature, and poetics. This reappraisal of the archive and its documentation of time and place proposes a critical discontinuity within current art practices, curating and art history, and the teleological formation of modern knowledge. Through sensory and bodily engagement, contemporary postcolonial art and its decolonising imperative seek a reconfiguration of signs and meaning in which both ethics and aesthetics, past and present, become inseparable. They register the repressed, reworking and reissuing what conventional history cannot recognise.

By emphasising temporal and spatial diversity as essential to the violent and ambiguous making of modernity an understanding of the production of time and space, history and geography, as processes and unfinished business come to the fore. We are talking neither of a neutral experience nor merely an aesthetic act. Revisiting and reworking the artistic and political lexicons of the canon, another sense of time and space emerges to affect our aesthetic and ethical understanding of the making of the present.

Here, we can move from considering the work of art as a limited object of art history to registering it as a critical apparatus and practice. In inviting us to look and think anew, a supplement emerges that charges the circulation of art with an anachronism: the present shot through and reconfigured by a denied past that we can never fully recover nor know. Here, despite the overwhelming consensus imposed by capital and the neoliberal order that insists on the absence of alternatives, postcolonial art persistently operates the gap and sustains the contradictions that render its language critical. Such art, pushing against the seemingly neutral white walls of the modern museum and art gallery, certainly does not escape capture within the institutional framework and circuits of commerce. Nevertheless, it disturbs its premises. Precisely through its insistence on a past yet to come, such art projects us into another history of the present.

Considering art as the index and signature of this unsolicited cut takes us toward what we have been unable to see, record, and feel. To walk this line is to follow the rift between the enlightenment of Western modernity and the darkness that sustains and concentrates its power. While speaking of the past, to ask whose time we are referring to is to interrupt the continuum; it is to split time from itself and force its abstract universality to take root and acknowledge a place. There, we can register other configurations that come to us from a world we may not have the authorised but which exists, persists, and endures.

## 3. Chaos at Kassel

The phrase 'Chaos at Kassel', attributed to the German Minister for Culture, Claudia Roth, emerged in the initial storm of accusations of antisemitism at the international art event documenta fifteen (18 June-25 September 2022) that takes place every five years in Kassel. A world-renowned exhibition of the contemporary arts, for the fifteenth edition, the artistic direction was entrusted to the Indonesian collective ruangrupa. Accusations began brewing even before the official opening. The presence of the Palestinian collective 'The Question of Funding' was signalled out for attention in a country where a recent law outlaws any criticism of the state of Israel, turning support for the Palestinian cause and the peaceful Boycott Disinvestment Sanctions (BDS) campaign into a federal crime. Subsequently, a caricatural antisemitic figure of a Jewish male, reminiscent of the stereotypes circulating in Europe in the early Twentieth century, and most notably in Nazi Germany, was identified in one of the painted banners of the Indonesian collective Taring Padi. It was withdrawn and led to an apology by the group. A further accusation later arrived from the depiction of an Israeli soldier mistreating a Palestinian child in a comic illustration by the well-known Palestinian artist Naji Al-Ali (1937-87) in the space devoted to

Archives des luttes des femmes en Algérie. Finally, in September, just weeks before closing, the Subversive Film collective installation of films on the Palestinian struggles in the 1970s was also singled out for censure and attempted closure.

It led to talk of vetting all the works for antisemitism under the tutelage of a scientific committee. However, like the removal of books and uncomfortable topics such as slavery from school curriculums presently being pursued in parts of the United States, the desire to cleanse the archive of troubling material that disturbs the consensual narrative is ultimately about censorship. Whether one likes it or not, such politically sensitive issues open up far deeper vaults, posing questions of their management, definition, and control. Ultimately, we are left asking who has the right to narrate, which, put more starkly and to evoke Hannah Arendt's noted phrase, means who has the right to have rights. Art, aesthetics, and racism combined into a critical configuration that transformed documenta fifteen into a significant political event.

From the cracks in the facade at Kassel also emerged further issues involving homophobia, Islamophobia, and a generalised intolerance for non-normative lifestyles. The public discussion and highly restricted debate on antisemitism consistently maintained a distance from other forms of racism that would necessarily include the histories of black, brown, and... Palestinian bodies. Altogether, a somewhat perverse limitation in what is, and was most strikingly the case with documenta fifteen, a global art event. Insisting exclusively on Germany's responsibility for the Holocaust, it became a local question directed and decreed by white Europeans. The aesthetics were colonised. Other racisms, other genocides, and their centrality to the colonial constitution of Occidental modernity were excluded from consideration, most immediately, earlier German colonialism in sub-Saharan Africa. The opportunity for a radical re-examination of the histories that the scandal exposed was deliberately shunned. Too much national authority had been invested in curating the question of antisemitism in exclusively German terms for it to be questioned. Where national identity is seemingly bound up in unconditional support for the state of Israel as atonement for the Holocaust, we encounter a political and cultural failure in German and Occidental public life. Once again, a totalising solution is proposed to the 'Jewish Question'.

Meanwhile, eminent German art critics, intellectuals and philosophers stepped into the fray and inadvertently (or perhaps not) fuelled the suspicion that this was all about defending the colonising cultural authority of Occidental culture, German identity and white supremacy. As Michael Rothberg, an important critical voice on Holocaust memory (Rothberg

2009), has put it: "*Germany is haunted by the specter of comparison*" (Rothberg 2022). To close down discussion in the name of a national sense of moral righteousness leads us down a well-trodden path. Europe is full of the remains of those savage dreams. So, an incident of antisemitism that also drew on other historical contexts and colonial memories in Indonesia in the case of a banner by the collective Taring Padi (while reminding ourselves that for most of the world, Europe and modernity have meant only one thing: colonialism) transformed documenta fifteen into truly planetary significance. Art and politics, or aesthetics and ethics to echo Wittgenstein, became one and suggested a discussion that should certainly not have been limited to only Occidental concerns.

Through inviting collectives rather than internationally recognised individual artists (there were some, but nearly always associated with the multiple souths of the world), ruangrupa insisted on the interaction of collective practices to create a *lumbung*. Lumbung is an Indonesian concept that indicates the rice barn for shared communal distribution. The encouragement of artistic and aesthetic excess and redistribution raised profound interrogations. These decisively interrupt the institutional consensus presently directing the modern art world. The guests remain and wish to propose their recipes and agendas.

The artistic collectives, primarily from non-Occidental localities, provided dynamic and expanded ecosystems that brought others to participate and share resources. The ongoing harvesting of practices, events and processes was never static. Workshops, discussions, debates, cooking, dance, printing, sauna, free coffee from Vietnam, and listening to music arriving from the banks of the Niger meant that documenta was constantly in movement. A tentacular network emerged, stretching well beyond the buildings and events of Kassel, Europe, and the Occidental management of contemporary art. Archives des luttes des femmes en Algérie were next to the Black Archives from the Netherlands. Walking the underground passages in central Kassel, sounds and signs from Black Quantum Futurism invited us to cut up and redistribute time in the temporalities of social and historical justice. Meanwhile, the possibility, or better impossibility, of contemporary art in Baghdad was caught in the harsh light of the videos of Sada (regroup). It went on and on and involved more than 50 collectives and their outreach in a remarkable breakdown, interruption, and redistribution of artistic practices that breached the gallery walls, the curatorial regimes, and the fetishism of artistic objects in both the museum and the market.

The idea of collective art practices and the removal of an individual signature struck at the very core of the political economy of the modern art system. The liberal imbrication of the individual and property, of names and capital, unwound. Of course, there may still be products or art objects coming out of the process, but the premises for evaluation were radically stunted. The existing global system of the modern art world becomes vulnerable to other questions and practices not automatically authorised by capital and the market. All of this explains the lukewarm, even hostile, response of curators, gallerists, and many renowned artists to the collectivising or lumbung procedures proposed by the Jakarta art collective ruangrupa.

> "*What makes a "real" artist? For many of the collectives invited to Documenta this year, making a living selling art is not an easy or particularly urgent task. Their practices are wound up in creative living and community building, rather than producing collectible objects*" (Brown 2022).

The Artist disappears into the artistry of the collective; the individual – the source of the artwork's inspiration and authenticity – into the anonymity of shared networks and socialised production. As a result, a whole aesthetic and commercial apparatus was threatened, and the modern Occidental formation of taste and value was exposed to more worldly concerns. Does that mean the end of Art as we know it? Not necessarily. But it certainly opens up a potential discussion and critical friction between that art history and others. Perhaps the former, hegemonic variant, to remain ethically significant and not merely a collectible value in the market, would do well to practice this undoing and displacement through listening and learning to live in a ruin called Europe and the West.

## 4. Europe, race, and a ruined order

David Lloyd has suggested: "*Aesthetic philosophy arises out of the necessity to forestall the revolutionary claims of its epoch and to substitute for the immediacy of political demands and practices an aesthetic formation of the disinterested and 'liberal' subject*" (Lloyd 2019, Kindle edition). The authorisation of such procedures by an abstract universality appropriating the planet was sharply exposed under the skies of northern Germany in the summer of 2022. To continue listening to Lloyd and his disassembling of Occidental aesthetics: "*The terms put in play by aesthetics establish the set of discriminations and distributions by which the Savage comes to be distinguished from the civil subject, the partial and particular human from the universal Subject, and the 'pathological' or suffering, needing, desiring human from the ethical human Subject*". The conclusion is that: "*Race is not… exorbitant to the aesthetic. It is not some historically contingent matter that contaminates the transcendental foundations of pure thought; it is essential to the very possibility of positing a 'common sense' on which the subjective but universal claims of the aesthetic could be based*" (Lloyd 2019). As Frantz Fanon would have put it, the necessary abandonment of Europe and its limited humanism is precisely an interrogation of the former's universalist pretensions, and not only in artistic terms.

The storm over antisemitism was initially stirred up by right-wing groups (who these days are all pro-Israel, having moved their hatred to Muslims and Islam) and then uncritically amplified in the German press and carried forward into the German parliament from both the left and the right. Yet, if we return to the artistic practices at work at Kassel, these provide another route into the debate. The question, which was too big for documenta fifteen to answer on its own (and why should it?), lies most obviously in the charred history bequeathed to Germany and Europe by the Shoah. Centuries of Occidental antisemitism, transformed into industrialised genocide under the Nazis, have been dumped on the Middle East. Initially sustained by the British, the post-1945 world has subsequently allowed Germany and the West to consider the 'Jewish Question' resolved through unconditional support of the state of Israel. The absolute statute of this resolution, recalling other absolutisms and solutions, is highly troubling. Of course, it has resolved nothing, and certainly not the racist hierarchies essential to the colonial fashioning of Occidental modernity, both at home and abroad.

The Israeli historian Ilan Pappe has recently argued that you cannot answer the 'Jewish Question' and antisemitism through a totalising response, whether in the murderous rationalisation of the death camp or unconditional support for the state of Israel (Pappe 2022). Such an approach to antisemitism disturbingly suggests a failure to acknowledge totalitarian tendencies in one's own historical and cultural formation. If insisting that the right to have rights also includes Palestinians leads to accusations of antisemitism, then the concept has been emptied and become the symptom of narcissistic paranoia (Micaeli 2021). It speaks only to a censured and poorly elaborated understanding of the German and European past. Proposing a politics whose confident labelling ensures the smug assurance of one's grip on memory, history, and justice is to lose your hold on the cruel complexities of the modern world. In a further paradox in the national narrative and its self-assured political mediation, such practices reveal the contemporary consistency of what, many decades ago, the Frankfurt School would have identified as the authoritarian personality.

The drive for confident universal verification also emerged in the proposal by documenta's management for a scientific committee or advisory board to oversee the artworks for antisemitism and avoid the scandal of unauthorised voices and counter-narratives. The appeal to 'science' in this proposed authority betrayed the belief of capturing the complexity of social and historical processes and rendering them transparent, hence fully knowable and controllable. This colonial certitude is the stuff of Nineteenth-century positivism and a historical moment when, during the division and colonising of the rest of the planet, a triumphant Europe proposed scientific theories of race, nation and civilisation that morally constituted the historical necessity of the white man's burden: whether it was the British in India, the French in Algeria, the Belgians in the Congo, the Americans on the frontier, in the Caribbean, the Pacific and the Philippines or the Germans in East and Southwest Africa. Subsequently transferred to European soil and the configuration of European Jews and Romani people as non-white, foreign populations to be eliminated, such a connection is studiously avoided. Until it confronts the colonial constitution of its present – from carving up Africa with other European empires in Berlin in 1884-5 to massacring colonial populations in what today are Namibia, Tanzania and Cameroon – the official German position on antisemitism and its choking entanglement with the state of Israel comes across as a tired ideological pantomime. Its rhetoric, which the historian Enzo Traverso has called a perverted form of civil religion (Traverso 2022), has little to do with contesting the racial disposition of power upon which it and the rest of Europe have historically depended for their 'progress'.

The investment in Israel as a historical solution to national guilt and shame veils these deeper connections of European antisemitism to violent colonial management and racial discrimination organised through what were then considered scientific categories. Such protocols are always destined to fail. Their unilateral rationalisation, or 'science', can never capture the historical processes and cultural relations they pretend to explain. In its limits and uncertainties, a genuinely rigorous social and historical analysis inevitably registers the opacities its language fails to reduce to a uniform perspective and point of view. That could also be a definition of art.

In the swirl of accusations of antisemitism that marked documenta 15 from the very first day, twenty films presented by Subversive Film documenting Palestinian struggle in the 1960s and 1970s led in the final weeks to a call for their withdrawal owing to their 'anti-Semitic and terrorist violence'. These films are, first and foremost, an archive. No doubt, it is an uncomfortable and disturbing one that suggests that Palestinians also have rights, including the right to resist their elimination from the territory and the narrative. The 1960s and 1970s were the years of armed anti-colonial struggle in Cuba, Algeria, Vietnam, South Africa, Angola, Mozambique,

Palestine and many other countries worldwide. These were also the years in which Jean-Luc Godard formed the Dziga Vertov Group to pursue militant cinema. At that moment, anti-colonial struggle and film sharply underlined what Walter Benjamin called the communicative democracy of cinema. The embarrassing attempt at censorship displayed a fundamental failure to engage with the challenge these films pose: both as alternative narratives and histories of Palestine-Israel and, above all, as a challenge to the status quo of a complacent image economy. Such films liberate us from the conclusive narration of the nation and the illusory coherence of balance and neutrality sustained by CNN and the BBC. Instead, these images reveal the asymmetrical relations of power that structure the world. Returning to Benjamin again: "*There is no document of civilisation which is not at the same time a document of barbarism*". When I cited this phrase in a short article in the leftist German daily *taz,* apart from the vitriolic feedback I received, the Benjamin quote significantly enough disappeared (Chambers 2022).

Unruly archives overflow the past and reopen history to another telling of time and place. They forcibly remind us that behind German and European guilt for the Holocaust lie a more profound series of responsibilities for planetary genocide – from the Americas to Africa and Asia – and their centrality, as Arendt, Césaire, and Fanon all insisted, to the colonial constitution of Occidental modernity. To castigate these films as antisemitic is to remain caught in a provincial thicket. Their images explode that particular telling of time with responsibility for a spacetime that is not only ours. It is the concept of responsibility that should substitute the category of guilt. A critical undoing of the absolute authority of antisemitism over the national narrative in Germany would have to respond not only to the Holocaust as a specific historical event but also to the global colonial conditions out of which it emerged in the heart of Europe. In *Origins of Totalitarianism*, Hannah Arendt insists most forcibly on this connection. More than policing antisemitism, this requires, as a Jewish philosopher from the Maghreb – Jacques Derrida – has taught us, a willingness to take responsibility for a past still to be registered and worked through; that is, a history still to come. To take responsibility for Europe's heart of darkness requires breaking present indifference to all forms of racism, counter-narratives, subaltern formations, and the suffering of others, including Palestinians.

Taking this on, which was undoubtedly at work in many artistic practices at documenta fifteen, involves turning the table around. It means, commencing from antisemitism, entering an altogether deeper and vaster space that is not only policed by Occidental concerns. In its artistic and aesthetic manifestation, drawn from practices and languages developed in the multiple 'souths' of the planet, what occurred at documenta fifteen clogged the colonial clock with unauthorised grit, forcing its time out of joint. The linearity of liberal 'progress' deviated towards registering racism as a planetary apparatus of power rather than simply a local pathology requiring a home cure. The burning fuse of aesthetics and ethics acquired an energetic urgency in the potential of planetary combustion. The embarrassed and failed response to this challenge, leading to attempted censure by governing bodies and public authorities, is revealing, and not only for Germany.

This brings us back to the beach, the body bags, migrants, and the necropolitics of the modern world. From sunlit Mediterranean shores to the green hills of northern Europe, the refusal to confront the insistence of the past in its complex constitution of the present leads to both moral amnesia and political violence. It guarantees the asymmetrical relations of power that ensure the reproduction of the status quo and the existing planetary order. It blocks the request for social and historical justice. The neat linearity of liberal progress and democracy is a fragile home, dependent on exclusion and refusal. However, the past that is dispatched to oblivion insists and persists. The storm raging outside the door continues. It suggests that other coordinates are required: ones that alienate me from my narcissism and immediate concerns. Our language and manner of explanation, the disciplines that construct our objects of study, are all punctured by these interrogations. Neutrality and 'scientific' credentials are stripped of local scholarly control. Contemporary migration and contemporary art are not merely posing problems and issues to be identified, objectified, and explained. They trouble our sovereignty by refuting the drive for transparency. They promote other perspectives and premises for our being and becoming in the world. In the run-up to documenta fifteen, with hostility and accusations of antisemitism already brewing, ruangrupa set up an online conversation series entitled 'We Need To Talk!'. Symptomatically, it had to be cancelled.

Iain Chambers has taught cultural, postcolonial, and Mediterranean studies at the University of Naples, Orientale for many years. Among his publications are *Migrancy Culture Identity* (1994), *Mediterranean Crossings* (2008), *Postcolonial Interruptions, Unauthorised Modernities* (2017), *Mediterraneo Blues* (2020), "It's about time: notes on quantum history", *Postcolonial Studies*, 26, 4 (2023), and with Marta Cariello, *The Mediterranean Question* (2025). He participated in documenta 15 (2022) as a member of the collective «Jimmie Durham & A Stick in the Forest by the Side of the Road».

## References

Benjamin, W. (1985). *The Origin of German Tragic Drama*. Verso, London.

Brown, K. (2022). "Documenta Presents an Invigorating Alternative to a Market-Driven Art World. Maybe That's Why the Industry's Establishment Has Largely Dismissed It". *Art Net News*, available at https://news.artnet.com/market/documenta-art-market-2135862 (accessed 27 July 2024).

Chambers, I. (2022). "Unbequeme Archive", available at https://taz.de/Umstrittene-Documenta-Filme/!5877650/ (accessed 27 July 2024).

Chambers, I. and Cariello, M. (2025). *The Mediterranean Question*. Punctum Books, Santa Barbara.

Di Cesare, D. (2020). *Resident Foreigners*. Polity Press, London.

Di Maio, A. (2021). "The Black Mediterranean: A View from Sicily". *Transition,* 132, 34-53.

Ferreira da Silva, D. (2007). *Toward a Global Idea of Race*. University of Minnesota Press, Minneapolis.

Gilroy, P. (2018). "'Where every breeze speaks of courage and liberty': Offshore Humanism and Marine Xenology, or, Racism and the Problem of Critique at Sea Level". *Antipode*, 50, 1. DOI: 10.1111/anti.12333.

Greenberg, R. and Hamilakis, Y. (2022). *Archaeology, Nation and Race: Confronting the Past, Decolonising the Future in Greece and Israel*. Cambridge University Press, Cambridge.

Grzinić, M. (2018). "What Is the Aesthetics of Necropolitics?", in N. Lushetich (eds.). *The Aesthetics of Necropolitics*. Rowman & Littlefield, London.

Ibn Khaldūn (2005). *The Muqaddimah: An Introduction to History*. Translated by F. Rosenthal. Princeton University Press, Princeton.

Lloyd, D. (2019). *Under Representation: The Racial Regime of Aesthetics*, Fordham University Press, New York.

Mbembe, A. (2017). *Critique of Black Reason*. Duke University Press, Durham.

Micaeli, I. (2021). "Why Germany gets it wrong about antisemitism and Palestine". *Open Democracy*, available at https://www.opendemocracy.net/en/north-africa-west-asia/why-germany-gets-it-wrong-about-antisemitism-and-palestine/ (accessed 27 July 2024).

Pappe, I. (2022). "Germany's Position on Palestine: Twice on the Wrong Side of History?". *Palestine Responds*, available at https://www.palestinechronicle.com/germany-and-palestine-twice-on-the-wrong-side-of-history/ (accessed 27 July 2024).

Portanova, S. (2022). *Whose Time Is It? Asocial Robots, Syncolonialism, and Artificial Chronological Intelligence.* Sternberg Press, London.

Proglio, G. (2018). "Is the Mediterranean a White Italian-European Sea? The multiplication of borders in the production of historical subjectivity". *Interventions.* DOI:10.1080/1369801X.2017.1421025.

Robinson, C. (1983). *Black Marxism. The Making of the Black Radical Tradition.* Zed Press, London.

Rothberg, M. (2009). *Multidirectional Memory: Remembering the Holocaust in the Age of Decolonization.* Stanford University Press, Stanford.

Rothberg, M. (2020). "The Specters of Comparison", available at https://www.goethe.de/prj/zei/en/art/21864662.html (accessed 27 July 2024).

Rutazibwa, O.U. (2020). "Why Is Mainstream International Relations Blind to Racism?". *Foreign Policy*, available at https://foreignpolicy.com/author/olivia-u-rutazibwa/ (accessed 27 July 2024).

Traverso, E. (2022). "No, Post-Nazi Germany Isn't A Model of Atoning for the Past". *Jacobin*, available at https://jacobin.com/2022/06/post-nazi-germany-colonialism-holocaust-israel-atonement (accessed 27 July 2024).

Chapter 5

# WHITE MYTHOLOGIES IN THE MEDITERRANEAN: MOBILITY AS A TOOL FOR DISMANTLING EUROCENTRIC STATIC GEOGRAPHIES

**Gabriele Proglio**

ABSTRACT: *This contribution is devoted to discussing white mythologies in the Mediterranean using some colonial food advertisements in order to analyse the Eurocentric perspectives on the Sea. Introducing the idea of mobility as a lens for dismantling this "imaginative geography", the contribution deals with the history of couscous and its ongoing process of reshaping the recipe. This example, then, is used for proposing some theoretical interpretations on visual effects concerning the stories of otherness by the hegemonic narratives. The final part proposes some suggestions on practices and approaches for decentring the Eurocentric gaze on the Mediterranean.*



## 1. Introduction

This Chapter aims to analyse from a historical perspective some mobilities of food and people in the Mediterranean to dismantle a white-European imaginary in the area. *Is the Mediterranean a White Italian-European Sea?*: in this contribution, published in 2018, I tried to show, on the one hand, the persistence of racialized imaginaries in the Mediterranean, from colonialism to the present day. On the other hand, I pointed out that the role of racialized subjects was and is pivotal in forcing and breaking down borders as well as the Eurocentric production of knowledge in disciplines. As Edward Said proposed, there is a close relationship between culture and power in the definition of both geographies of a place and history of people (Said 1993).

In the first part of the writing, I will examine white mythologies in the Mediterranean starting with the analysis of some food advertisements. A second part will follow: it is dedicated to a specific case study, namely *couscous* and its many interconnected and overlapping Mediterranean stories. In the last part of the chapter the above-mentioned case study will be problematized from the perspective of both white mythologies and diversities. A final section, then, will close the contribution: it will be devoted to proposing some possible approaches to de-centring Europe (see Chakrabarty 2008) and the Eurocentric gaze on the Mediterranean.

## 2. Impressions of continuity and homogeneity

This piece aims to continue my research path, focusing on another aspect connected to the previous ones: how the study of different mobilities of people in the Mediterranean can be useful to understand what Iain Chambers called interruptions (2017), namely *signs or emblems* of fractured modernities. Specifically, in the case of the Mediterranean, this chapter aims to analyse many different interruptions that have marked its history so far. They are the outcome of spontaneous effects based, for thousands of people, on the need to find a new place for living after conflicts, ejections, and migrations. In other cases, these interruptions follow a series of structural factors (i.e., economy, society, pollution, climate change, etc.) leading to major changes in the configuration of both geography and society.

In this framework, mobility will be approached through the lens of food history (see Bender and Cinotto 2023). From right wing politics to part of popular culture, food has often been used to create a national identity, imaginary and cultural homogeneity in a society or part of it. Or, at least, to make people believe that this uniformity and unity existed. Literature, music, art, and language were used to reinforce the belief in being part of an imagined community (Anderson 1983). Similarly, food played a significant role in constructing cultural and racial boundaries, often reinforcing the Eurocentric imaginary of the Mediterranean. In this sense, it is possible to mention the Mediterranean trio (grape, olive, and wheat), which is often considered the Holy Trinity of Mediterranean food and closely associated with a specific identity. UNESCO, after Ancel Keys' invention of the Mediterranean diet, used this trio to promote the concept of intangible cultural heritage, which is often tied to nation-states and a fixed idea of identity. [1]

[1] Watch the video "Mediterranean Diet. Intangible Cultural Heritage UNESCO", which was realized for the inscription of Mediterranean Diet on the Intangible Cultural Heritage List of Unesco, available at https://www.youtube.com/watch?v=oYsqldG3kxM (latest accessed 13 April 2024).

Moving from a supranational to a national level of analysis, it is possible to find the use of the trio in national propaganda in support of colonial conquests of the other shore of the Mediterranean. It is the case of Italy and its colonial campaign in Libya: the North African country was imagined as the granary of the Mediterranean, re-evoking an ancient imaginary of the Roman Empire (see Labanca 2012; Proglio 2016). Nationalist Enrico Corradini and many other politicians and journalists promoted the idea of *Mare Nostrum*, conveying the idea that Italy had an inherent right to control the entire Mediterranean Sea because the geographical area was under the control of its supposed ancient ancestors, namely Romans. The other shore was depicted as barbaric and in need of civilization: only Italy, through the war as fertile violence (Filippo Tommaso Marinetti) against the oblivion of the other shore's civilization, could bring progress and modernity in the Northern African country. According to this rhetoric, bringing Libya back to food prosperity means offering a direct solution to poverty in the Italian countryside and Southern areas as well as a possibility to get back home for thousands of Italian families who emigrated to the Americas and other parts of the world.

This typology of propaganda serves as a clear example of how food has been utilized to construct and reinforce nationalist and colonialist ideologies. Furthermore, it was not merely a piece of news. Paris first used this narrative, representing the colonialist nation both as a female goodness (*Le petit Journal*) and masculine soldier (*L'Algérie 1830-1930*) and depicting local communities as primitive, poor, and barbaric. In some instances, the plow symbolized impending change; in others, food as a direct product of colonization was represented as a metaphor for the unequal relationship between white colonizers and several racialized natives, or as a direct result of modernization – the man in red who is pouring olive oil onto the Tunisian map (*L'Huile d'Olive de Tunisie*).

Figure 1. Le Petit Journal, November 10, 1911

Source: © Ministry of Culture, National University Library of Turin. Reproduction prohibited.

Figure 2. Advertisement about Tunisian Olive Oil, made by Damour Publicité, Paris

Source: © Archives Nationales d'outre-mer, Aix-en-Provence.

Figure 3. Advertisement about agricultural production in Algeria, from 1830 to 1930, made by Henri Dormoy for the French Republic

Source: © Archives Nationales d'outre-mer, Aix-en-Provence.

A white European superiority and a desire to dominate and control the entire Mediterranean region are clear in these visual representations. Some mythical pasts were invoked to propose and legitimise conquests through food advertising. The diversity and otherness of the Mediterranean were depicted by European writers in different ways, ranging from barbarism to civilised natives. It was essential to affirm the "need" for European intervention and to justify colonisation as an act of bringing civilization and progress. Setting aside the background of how violence was legitimated, it is important to focus on how a common narrative around food and agriculture has been used, from the first colonisation to the current age of globalisation, to reinforce and justify unequal power relations. This use of the same rhetoric across different contexts (Libya, Tunisia, Algeria, Morocco) and time periods (the end of the 19th century, the 20-30-40s, and even after the fall of Empires) was deliberately adopted to support various colonial projects. From another perspective, this recurrence of the same narrative can be approached through the lens of the colonial archive[2] (see Stoler 2002).

[2] For a clear description of the historical debate on the archive, please read: A.L. Stoler. "Colonial Archives and the Arts of Governance". *Archival Science*, 2, 2002, 87-109.

In the first case, the movement of representations was theorised by Edward Said on the European continent through the concept of circularity:

> "*representations of what lay beyond insular or metropolitan boundaries came, almost from the start, to confirm European power. There is an impressive circularity here: we are dominant because we have the power (industrial, technological, military, moral), and they don't, because of which they are not dominant; they are inferior, we are superior*" (Said 1993, 106).

In the second case, the archive becomes a site where a defined set of records – signs, symbols, words, myths, etc. – converges to support colonial powers and, consequently, the mobilities of European institutions and subjects beyond the national and European borders. This twofold movement creates a sort of optical illusion: Europe appears to be omnipresent due to this repetitive, linear, smooth, continuous, and homogeneous historical narrative. The Mediterranean is one of the symbolic spaces for this optical illusion, where white mythologies bear the narrative.

From this point, I will explore certain food mobilities in the Mediterranean – focusing specifically on the Italian Peninsula – to challenge narratives on gastro-nationalism and problematize the issue of diversity through not-Eurocentric geographies. Examining food through the lens of interconnectivity and migration flows between various micro-regions of the area – as proposed by Peregrine Horden and Nicholas Purcell (2000) – will serve as a key focus to demonstrate the impact of interruptions on European modernity.

## 3. Rethinking diversity through couscous

In approaching white mythologies in the Mediterranean, it is important to first define what white mythology is. From Jacques Derrida to Robert Young, the concept of white mythology has been to highlight the overlap between logocentrism and European/Western ethnocentrism.[3] Gloria Wekker, in her *White Innocence*, adopts a different perspective. She is interested in

---

[3] See the review of Young's volume by Matthew Sparke in *Environment and Planning D Society and Space*, 12, 1, 1994, 105-123.

*"a satisfying way of being in the world [...] a dominant way in which the Dutch think of themselves, as being a small, but just, ethical nation; colour-blind, thus free of racism; as being inherently on the moral and ethical high ground, thus a guiding light to other folks and nations"* (Wekker 2016, 2).

My use of white mythologies draws on both of the perspectives quoted above, blending them into a new one. In the text below, the concept of white mythology will be used to demonstrate how the construction of history generates different types of visual effects on individual and communities. Sometimes, the myth of origin (state-nations, religions, common pasts, heroes, etc.) is hyper-visible, reinforcing a homogeneity of narratives in terms of race, gender, beliefs, and values. All these factors appear in a coherent discourse, seemingly interconnected, to affirm a shared, 'autentic' past – a kind of unique, living root for a community. We might say that the true aim is to harmonize representations of the past, fostering an imagined community (Anderson, 1983) based on shared cultural traits that define national identity. The other visual effect, by contrast, works to render the 'other' and otherness invisible. The combination of these two effects in shaping the narrative about the past makes history appear homogeneous and standardized. The pattern is often the same: a rhetoric of a common, shared past or, alternatively, a narrative that positions someone or something in opposition to national identity (i.e. Arabs, Muslims, Jews; thieves, migrants, etc.).

From this theoretical yet practical standpoint, we can now turn to a specific case study involving the Mediterranean and food. In 2016, the far-right, xenophobic, and racist Lega Nord party in Italy launched a campaign to promote "100% Italian" food, using the slogan "*Defend our traditions from foreign invasions*". Couscous was at central to Lega Nord's attack, viewed as a foreign, Muslim, Islamic, and Arab food that threatened Italian identity and tradition. The campaign poster, featuring a plate of polenta beside the Lega Nord logo, included the words: "*sì alla polenta, no al cous-cous. Orgogliosi delle nostre tradizioni*" (yes to polenta, no to cous-cous. Proud of our traditions). As described in the white mythology framework during colonialisms, Lega Nord's campaign hyper-visibilized the myth of origin surrounding Northern Italian cuisine (polenta) and how it "should" to be. At the same time, it rendered invisible the role of couscous (the diversity element) in reshaping both Italian and Mediterranean cuisines.

Figure 4. Lega Nord advertising, 2001

Source: Lega Nord website. Please visit https://www.leganord.org.

Lega Nord's campaign crafted an imagined community based on a standardized and false representation of Italian culinary "tradition". In fact, historical sources show that many Italian cities have had, and continue to have, special couscous dishes. In Livorno and Palermo, for example, one can find delicious couscous dishes that have been present in these regions for centuries. It is clear that campaigns like the one spearheaded by Lega Nord perpetuate harmful stereotypes and contribute to a culture of exclusion. Therefore, it is crucial to recognize the cultural diversities – plural is important – which have shaped the Mediterranean region and to embrace them as part of a shared cultural heritage.

This attack by the Lega Nord party is a clear example of how nationalist campaigns can distort historical facts and demonize diversities. It is important to recognize that culinary traditions can serve as a lens of cultural diversities and should be examined in all their complexity, rather than being used for exclusionist purposes. Food, like music, art, literature, and popular culture in general, is deeply interconnected with cultural expression. The "right to represent" can be explored through the lens of postcolonial interruptions, shedding light on how the supposed homogeneity at the heart of Eurocentric thinking is, in fact, a constructed invention. This doesn't mean that it is not real: on the contrary, it becomes real! If many people come to believe that couscous is only an African/Muslim/Islamic dish, the diversity associated with it is seen as "otherness", a narrative unauthorized to be part of a common national or European identity. These unauthorized stories, as Iain Chambers highlights, offer a powerful point of observation from which to understand the persistence of a "*structural distribution of power*" (Chambers 2022, 22) and to reveal the fractures within European modernity.

Couscous can be used as a tool to explore some Mediterranean interruptions. We can begin by examining the term 'couscous' which comes from the Hamazig word *seksu*, meaning 'well rolled'. Another interpretation suggests it derives from the Arabic word *kaskasa,* meaning 'to pound until the particles are tiny'. Couscous is a dish made from crushed wheat semolina dumplings that are steamed. In its "traditional" preparation, it is cooked in a *couscoussier, allowing* the grains to expand and become softer. However, many variants of couscous can be found throughout the Mediterranean. In Tunisian cuisine, medium-sized couscous semolina is used, while in Morocco, larger fragrant grains are preferred. In Algeria, fine semolina grains are rolled in fermented butter. Different sauces add flavour to couscous: *harissa* is common in Tunisia and Morocco, while in Algeria a white broth made from vegetables and meat is used. Regarding meat, Tunisian couscous is served with tripe, whereas Algerian and Moroccan recipes typically include lamb and chicken. The choice of vegetables also varies: in Tunisia, zucchini, potatoes, carrots, and turnips are common; in Algeria, squash or pumpkin is added; and in Morocco, a dish known as the "seven vegetables" is used. Each region also has its own specific spices: Tunisian couscous features *ras el hanout*; Algerian couscous includes cinnamon, pinches of pepper, cumin, and paprika; and in Morocco, ginger, saffron, cumin, turmeric, peppers, cilantro are common.

In addition, the name used for each type of couscous reveals further distinctions. For instance, there are at least six different typologies of couscous. Tunisian couscous is served in a large deep dish with meat and chickpeas in the centre, in a sort of well, typically with three ladles of stock added. As mentioned earlier, it is served with curd and harissa. While Tunisian couscous reflects as a peasant's economy, Algerian couscous is closely tied to *Hamazig* culture. Semolina is served with loose, with meat and vegetables placed in the center. This dish is traditionally accompanied by *Lben*, a fermented milk found in many countries across North Africa, the Levant, and Arabia. Interestingly, the interruptions of modernity – not only the European modernity, but also those concerning Arab nationalisms and cultural identities – are evident here. Ashkenazi Jews in the Ottoman Palestine began producing a variant of the *Lben* called *Leben*. In Israel, during *tzena*-austerity period (1947-1953), Leben become part of the state's rationing system. Another variety, Royal couscous, was prepared and eaten by *pieds-noires* in North Africa and, after the fall of the empire, in France. Al least, two types of meats – lamb and chicken – are used, served with merguez sauce (a mix of lamb and beef with cumin, harissa, sumac, fennel, and garlic). Israeli Couscous, known as "ptitim" (also called Ben-Gurion rice), is made from toasted pasta in tiny balls (wheat flour and toasted in an oven). It was created by Osem food company in 1953, during the aforementioned austerity period in Israel.

As mentioned earlier, it is possible to identify at least two different typologies of historical couscous in Italy. The first, Trapanese or Pantese couscous, reflects the presence, connections, and heritage of Arabs in Sicily. It is typically served with fresh fish caught in the Mediterranean Sea, using a fish broth made by simmering the fish with peeled onion, celery and bay leaves. It is cooked in a terracotta bowl decorated with floral patterns, known as a tagine or the 'pignatta di cùscu-su'. Livorno Couscous is linked to the Sephardic Jews in Pisa and later in Livorno. This community began calling couscous 'cuscussù' in the XVI century. They fled Spain after the Reconquista, where they were forced to either convert to Catholicism or face expulsion. Ferdinando de Medici, Grand Duke of Tuscany, issued a charter in 1597 allowing foreigners to settle in Livorno, and in 1603, they were permitted to build a synagogue. For religious reasons, in Livorno couscous, mutton or lamb were replaced by veal, and no cheese is used in the preparation of the meatballs, while the bread is not softened in milk. Egg is used to form the micro-granules of semolina, a method practiced by Jews of Libyan origin.

The diverse histories and cultural influences behind couscous dishes illustrate the complexity of food culture and its mobility across the Mediterranean. According to anthropologist Luis da Cámara Cascudo (1983), Brazilian couscous arrived in the Portuguese colony in the 16$^{th}$ century, influenced by both Portuguese and African slave food traditions. The two varieties – *cuscuz paulista* and *cuscus nordestino* – were prepared in different regions, from Rio Grande to São Paolo. He wrote: "*couscous, kuz-kuz, alcuz-cuz, is the national dish of the Moors in North Africa, from Egypt to Morocco. Initially made by rice, wheat flour, millet, sorghum, it became American when corn spread throughout the world during the 16th century*" (ivi, 204). This evidence suggests that couscous is more than just a food culture. While xenophobic, racist, and gastro-nationalist voices consider couscous solely an Arab, Muslim, and Islamic food, its mobilities and the reshaping of its recipes reveal a complex geography and history. Marranos and Berbers, French colonizers and new migrants, slaves and afro-descendants, Muslims, Christians and Jews, colonizers and natives: the range of people involved in the preparation and consumption of cous-cous is vast. Similarly, there is no single "authentic" recipe of couscous. Many communities, groups, identities have re-interpreted and continue to reshape the "original", "typical", and "traditional" recipe. By the end of this process – driven by oral traditions and intersubjectivity – is becomes impossible to define "first" recipe, or what can be considered "traditional", "typical", or "original". Is couscous a Southern Mediterranean dish? Given the multitude of recipes, it seems reductive to label it as merely transnational. The global dimension seems too narrow for this dish, as it fails to capture how specific variations of couscous express a combination of historical facts, cultural identities, conditions of hegemony and subalternity, and unequal scales of power based on gender, race and class. It also reflects a sense of belonging to imagined communities and established orders. It is essential to remember, as Montanari (2004) points out, that food is culture because it combines both symbolism and materiality. In this sense, it is possible to state that the flavours of couscous reveal a complex relationship between subjects of and subjectivities, as well as the nexus of space and time. Iain Chambers postulates that geographies and histories of "*subalterns and subordinated elements do not simply constitute a potential counter-hegemony in the dialectic of historical becoming and political understanding*" (ivi, 7). He argues: "*although they cannot replace hegemony with a complete or utopian alternative, they can transform and rework its rationality through other forms of reasoning*" (ibidem). Chambers emphasizes that undoing the premises of a social and political order does not to erase history or heritage. On the contrary, these perspectives highlight the role of the time/space superstructure in defining an accepted, shared, and common vision of the world, reproduced through national languages, which establishes distinctions between North and South, East and West; who is white and who is black, who is a citizen and who is a migrant.

## 4. White mythologies and diversities

Building on this case study, we can critically examine the role of white mythologies in the Mediterranean and their relationship to diversity. The couscous case is representative of how nationalist narratives contribute to shaping an imaginary of Mediterranean whiteness in collective memory. As Maurice Halbwachs pointed out, collective memory is formed by the shared views of a social group (see Halbwachs 1925). It is important to identify the key factors and mechanisms that reinforce these white mythologies in the minds and consciousnesses of many Europeans and, consequently, in the organization of Mediterranean space through borders and boundaries.

1. White, masculine, heteronormative, with roots in Greco-Roman Classical antiquity: this is the repertory evoked when a body, language, sign, practice, music, or taste coming from outside the European borders of the Mediterranean comes into contact – either symbolically or in really – with European national ideologies. Since the boundary between the symbolic and real is often blurred, it is crucial to analyse and challenge this process, as it perpetuates a narrow and exclusionary view of the Mediterranean. The danger of a unique history is twofold: it standardizes the time/space nexus in the region, allowing European states and subjects to impose their role as arbiters of what is significant or valuable for the future of the entire area. Thus, anything that does not fit this one-dimensional, linear, and continuous vision of the Mediterranean is ontologically understood as "diversity". Belonging to this group is defined in opposition to the mythical origin of the European canon in the Mediterranean, characterized by "not-being" and "being only something different". In this sense, couscous has been portrayed as not part of European history but as the story of non-European people.

2. The relationship of difference/otherness between the history evoked by the myth and those arising from the intertwined relationships between multiple subjectivities in the Mediterranean can be articulated through the lens of fixity/mobility. A singular, fixed history, to remain truthful and credible to a group of people, requires a set of selective 'a priori'. That is, the history of the Mediterranean, seen through the lens of European colonization of the maritime space and the Middle East and North Africa, relies on the 'not-being' and 'being just something different', of those not considered part of the imagined community. These 'a-priori' are selective because, to ensure that the myth remains omnipresent and unchallenged, the subjects of diversity must be portrayed with many facets, ambivalent values, and meanings. Their mobilities exists only in the discourse of those who speak about them. The ongoing effort to maintain the centrality of European language, therefore, requires multiple meanings to define what and who is considered part of this diversity.

3. As a result of this work at the edge of the historical subject's context, mobility and static could change their meanings in the perception of some Europeans. What is static – such as the gastro-nationalist rhetoric proposed by the Lega Nord party and Matteo Salvini – appears dynamic and multi-oriented, encompassing both the past (mythical history) and future (modernity, progress, evolution, civilization, etc.). Conversely, those who have experienced mobility are perceived as fixed and unchanging: they are seen

as exiting outside of history, unable to occupy the central position of a historical subject, as framed by xenophobic rhetoric. This reversal of reference points reflects a theme often explored in critical theory and history – such as the relationship between North and South; Europe and its Orients; modernity, progress, and civilization on one hand, and barbarism on the other. Clearly, the static/mobility relationship is central to this debate.

4. To uncover the role of diversity in the Mediterranean, then, it is necessary to challenge and crack – both symbolically and materially – the boundaries of national and European history; to engage with the historical context, identifying all "a-priori" assumptions that sustain Eurocentric views of the Mediterranean world. Mobility should be used as a methodological tool as well as a historical lens to highlight the multiple and multifaceted connections among people, objects, ideas in the Mediterranean. Replacing a unique history with numerous stories reveals unauthorized forms of time/space in the Eurocentric vision of the Mediterranean.

## 5. Diversity: A matter of approach

In a historical moment during which, on the one hand, every topic seems to be approached through the lens of decolonization practices and, on the other, new and old forms of racism, xenophobia, Islamophobia, and nationalistic rhetoric spread across Europe, it is crucial to reconsider what diversity means and how to approach it in the Mediterranean. Historical categories, such as the static vs mobile dichotomy, need to be re-evaluated to challenge Eurocentric views and to better understand the complex dynamics of the Mediterranean region. Clearly, this kind of reassessment requires a shift in perspective and a willingness to explore narratives, traces, and signs by unauthorized subjects, going beyond the traditional framework.

Hence, how is it possible to scrutinize the past and its traces to make visible the marginalized stories of the Mediterranean region? Approaching and analysing sources from various types of archives (physical, images, practices, etc.) will provide scholars with a set of information that can shed light on historical subjects. In this sense, if we truly want to understand the diversity of the Mediterranean and challenge Eurocentric views, it is essential to adopt a multidimensional approach. Simply deconstructing a single or a group of historical sources will not be enough. In fact, the ultimate outcome of this process involves examining the power relations between hegemonic and unauthorized subjects. When we propose a critique of Eurocentric views of the Mediterranean, are we seriously thinking of creating an open space for the study of the past? Where 'open' simply means that in this space it is allowed to embrace multiple perspectives and challenge the hegemonic Eurocentric lens. Or, conversely, are we satisfied with perpetuating the same Eurocentric narratives that have dominated our understanding of the Mediterranean for so long, merely adopting a new facet or angle for dealing with the same genealogy of power?

Other words, practices and processes are necessary if we would like to consider the term 'diversity' in ways that diverge from the norm. These ways should not be limited to embracing different subjectivities and cultures within the Mediterranean context; they should also encompass a re-evaluation of historical narratives, power dynamics, and marginalized stories. These ways are not 'inclusion' or 'assimilation' as proposed by the UK and French governments, but rather about truly engaging with the complexities of the Mediterranean region in a way that enables a more comprehensive understanding of its diverse stories and experiences. Dualities such as the exotic and the oriental, the unmodern and the savage: these canons appear whenever narratives about otherness are made to appear homogeneous and coherent. Conversely, as hypothesized by Aimé Césaire, it is precisely through this cultural process – played onto the skin of the other – that Europe and every Western nation have found ways for inventing themselves. A historical analysis, as in the case of couscous, is open to complexity, ambiguities, double or multiple meanings, and highlights all facets of cultural resignifications. In this sense, the fear of the other is the outcome of a shared narrative that creates boundaries where, according to history, one can instead find multiple points of contact and countless examples of mobility.

If every transformation revolutionizes the horizon of vision and the idea of history, we are currently in a state of waiting, where we continue to hope for change while referring to those arriving from the Mediterranean Sea on European shores as 'migrants'. They are always 'migrants'; sometimes they are a singular 'migrant'; but rarely they are Rashid, Hamed, Kalid, and Amina. They never are Amina Hassam, with a personal story. The limit of this process is obvious: the European system is so violent that it does not generate any other words beyond the familiar ones. Supporting the subjectivities that daily force and crack the order of the European discourse in the Mediterranean requires an ongoing reformulation of cultural, intellectual, and epistemological practices. This does not mean inventing new critical thinking, but rather discerning the critical shortcomings of Eurocentric thought in what and who remains invisible and inaudible within the historical sources of each archive. It involves rethinking the context – which is the symbolic place of significance for history and every discipline in the field of humanities and social sciences – by questioning the spatial and temporal nexus, their relationship to the historical source, and revealing the conventions accepted by historiography to write the history of Europe in the Mediterranean. Furthermore, geographies and histories of unauthorized subjectivities – such as those relating to the Black Mediterranean (Proglio, Hawthorne and Danewid 2021; Proglio 2019; Hawthorne 2022) – can challenge the historical forms and structures of European modernity. Alternatively, one can approach diversity not by describing it directly, but by working on the folds of official narratives – I am thinking of Hartman's wonderful volumes (2019 and 2006) – or by analysing the historical fact not by seeking to account every action, every moment, every space crossed by a subject, but by giving relevance to the Glissant's notion of right to opacity: a way for protecting cultures from the Eurocentric gaze that translates everything. Another method is the backlight approach (Proglio, 2023), which examines the power relations between the subjects that constitute archives and those described by historical sources.

## References

Anderson, B. (1983). *Imagined Communities: Reflections on the Origin and Spread of Nationalism*. Verso, London.

Bender, D.E. and Cinotto, S. (2023). *Food Mobilities: Making World Cuisines*. University of Toronto Press, Toronto.

Chakrabarty, D. (2008). *Provincializing Europe. Postcolonial Thought and Historical Difference.* Princeton University Press, Princeton.

Chambers, I. (2017). *Postcolonial Interruptions, Unauthorized Modernities.* Rowman & Littlefield, London-New York.

Chambes, I. and Cariello, M. (2022). "At History's Edge: The Mediterranean Question". *New Formations*, 6-24.

da Câmara Cascudo, L. (1983). *História da Alimentação no Brasil.* 2 vols. Editora da Universidade de São Paulo, São Paulo.

Hartman, S. (2006). *Lose Your Mother*. Macmillan Publishers, New York.

Hartman, S. (2019). *Wayward Lives, Beautiful Experiments*. Serpent's Tail, New York.

Hawthorne, C. (2022). *Contesting Race and Citizenship: Youth Politics in the Black Mediterranean*. Cornell University Press, Ithaca.

Horden, P. and Purcell, N. (2000). *The Corrupting Sea: A Study of Mediterranean History*. Blackwell Publishers, London.

Labanca, N. (2012). *La guerra italiana per la Libia. 1911-1931*. Il Mulino, Bologna.

Montanari, M. (2004). *Il cibo come cultura*. Laterza, Roma-Bari.

Proglio, G. (2016). *Libia 1911-1912. Immaginari coloniali e italianità*. Mondadori Le Monnier, Milano-Firenze.
Proglio, G. (2019). *Mediterraneo Nero. Archivio, memorie, corpi*. Manifesto Libri, Roma.
Proglio, G. (2024). "Food, Land and Resistances across the Black Mediterranean. Toward a History of Disobedience in Backlight", in K.P. Suvi A.A. Amenkeng and M. Seikkula (eds.). *Race, Bordering and Disobedient Knowledge?*. Manchester University Press, Manchester, 204-225.
Proglio, G., Hawthorne, C., Danewid, I. *et al.* (eds.) (2021). *The Black Mediterranean: Bodies, Borders and Citizenship*. Palgrave, London-New York.
Said, E. (1993). *Culture and Imperialism*. Vintage Books, New York.
Stoler, A.L. (2002). "Colonial Archives and the Arts of Governance". *Archival Science*, 2, 87-109.
Wekker, G. (2016). *White Innocence: Paradoxes of Colonialism and Race*. Duke University Press, Durham.

Chapter 6

# MIGRATION, ISLAM, AND DEMOGRAPHIC FEARS: THE NARRATIVE OF REPLACEMENT IN ITALIAN POLITICS

**Alberta Giorgi**

ABSTRACT: *This chapter focuses on how the fear of the religion of people who are members of different religions or cultures plays out in the political sphere by analysing the narrative of replacement in Italian politics. First, it introduces the populist "politics of fear" and the concept of demographic fear. Then, it presents an analysis of the discourse of an Italian far-right populist party showing how the authority of science is discursively mobilized – three mechanisms are explored, in particular: the reference to "numbers" (either producing or referring to data); enlisting experts and academics; repurposing scientific theories. The discursive mobilization of science is meant to legitimize and normalize fringe narratives and fears.*



## 1. Introduction: Politics of othering, politics of fear

The academic conversation around the othering of Islam often refers to the "Muslim Question" (MQ), which is the constructions of Muslim and Islam as something problematic. As Selby and Beaman (2016, 8-9) point out: "In this way, ''Islam'' as a singular object is positioned as wholly divergent from (or ''clashing'' with) the social and cultural norms of the similarly constructed West". The Muslim Question essentializes Islam as a homogeneous actor, fundamentally different from "the West", and normalises and naturalises this difference.

The normalisation of difference is often politically weaponized: in 2015, Ruth Wodak published a book titled *The politics of fear: What right-wing populist discourses mean*, in which she provided detailed illustration of the discourse of far-right and right-wing populism, and argued that "*all right-wing populist parties instrumentalize some kind of ethnic/religious/linguistic/political minority as a scapegoat for most if not all current woes and subsequently con-*

*strue the respective group as dangerous and a threat 'to us', to 'our' nation; this phenomenon manifests itself as a 'politics of fear'*" (Wodak 2015, 23).

Among the many fears evoked and the minorities targeted by right-wing populist parties, Islam is particularly relevant: it came to represent the 'absolute other', and this 'otherness' is discursively grounded on allegedly incompatible values – particularly on the supposed conflation between religion and politics in Islamic thought, opposing European secularism, and on the allegedly discriminatory treatment of women and sexual minorities, opposing European gender equality (Giorgi *et al.* 2023).

This discourse assumes the overlap of secularism with gender equality and presents the European culture as a champion of both, echoing the same articulation of Europeanness, gender equality and religion put forward by the colonial discourse (Scott 2018). In this sense, European secularism is conceived of as 'sexual secularism', to use an expression of Fassin (2010, 513), "*insofar as it pertains to women and sexuality, rather than the separation of church and state*". Furthermore, Islam is implicitly depicted as an 'alien', something that does not belong, thus disregarding Muslim presence in Europe – including, for example, Bosnia-Herzegovina – and positing Europe as white and Christian (Bracke and Hernández Aguilar 2020).

In addition, this discourse constructs the 'other' as homogeneously cisgender and heterosexual, invisibilizing Muslim sexual minorities (Korteweg 2020), and depicts Muslim women as in need of being 'saved' from their culture (Bracke 2012). This 'rescue narrative', in turn, grounds on the broad vernacular discourse of 'masculinities in crisis', applied to the Middle Eastern context. As Amar (2011, 40) puts it:

> "*Moralized, criminalized, racialized, colonized masculinities in the Middle East are some of the most popular subjects of modern geopolitical hypervisibility, twinned with their fetishized Others or victims – the supposedly suppressed traditionalized veiled woman and the supposedly Occidentally-identified modernized gay man*".

In other words, the 'othering' processes combine gender, religious, and ethnic dimensions in complex identity assemblages of 'us' and 'them' (Norocel and Giorgi 2021) – the unpacking of which would require an intersectional approach (Singh and Féron 2021).

Against this broad background, a particularly relevant illustration of this intersectional practice of othering is the politics of fear surrounding Muslim demography in Europe, that combines the concerns related to Islam and immigration, and Muslims' birth rates, in a narrative of 'replacement' according to which Muslims will 'replace' Christians. In the following, I will explore one Italian iteration of the narrative of replacement by focusing on how it is articulated by the First report on Islamization of Europe, published in 2019 by the Foundation Farefuturo (*Doing Future*), a think tank connected to Fratelli d'Italia (FDI, Brothers of Italy), which at the time was a minor actor in the Italian political sphere and is currently (2022) the leading party in the Italian government.

The chapter is structured as follows: the next section will discuss the narrative of replacement and the demographic fears, while section three presents the case study and the methodology, section four analyses the results, and section five discusses the outcomes and draws some conclusions.

## 2. Demographic fears

Recently, Bracke and Hernández Aguilar (2020) have reconstructed the rise of the discourse of 'replacement', showing how each iteration has added new layers and arguments to the narrative. The core of the narrative focuses on:

> "*the migration of non-Europeans to Europe – migrants who allegedly have higher birth rates compared to Europeans, and who are considered to inaugurate a process which will eventually lead to a deleterious transformation of the social, political, cultural, and "racial" make up of European societies*" (Bracke and Hernández Aguilar 2020, 683).

First, migration is framed as an 'invasion' from the outside: migrants are not European. Second, this 'invasion' will lead to a transformation of Europe, which in turn will have nefarious consequences. The narrative evokes the trope of hypersexualized (and, for this, threatening) 'other', who will conquer the actual as well as the metaphorical motherland, materialized in women's bodies, through their sexual power. Non-European – and, sometimes, European – women would be complicit in this 'invasion', which occurs through their bodies.

This core narrative is articulated with the addition of various elements, depending on actors and circumstances. Often, the role of the European élite is pointed out, and framed as either incapable or unwilling to 'stop the invasion', or even to recognize and acknowledge the situation and the threat it poses. This element is particularly resonant with the populist discursive logic of differentiation between the 'people' and the 'elite' (see, for example, Wodak 2015).

Another popular element is the understanding of 'replacement' as a conscious strategy of warfare: in this vision, Muslims, or Muslim leaders, would invite Muslim migrating to Europe to reproduce, in order to conquer the European future. The warfare trope is often expressed through concepts such as 'Eurabia', a term that indicates the 'Arabization' – and Islamization – of Europe through immigration; the term has been popularized by the Italian journalist and writer Oriana Fallaci (Cousin and Vitale 2014). Another popular concept in this frame is that of 'Demographic Jihad', 'Baby Jihad' (Hudson 2022), or 'Love Jihad', particularly spread in the Indian context to warn against the marriages between Muslim men and Indian women, and which focuses the attention on women's alleged vulnerability:

> "*The young men apparently waging war through love – through the capture of innocent Hindu women – are also referred to as 'Love Romeos'. Given credence by the courts and police in some states, it is argued that the proponents of Love Jihad see this as a strategy by Muslim fundamentalists to lure Hindu and Christian girls literally into their arms, thus swelling their numbers in an ongoing demographic war*" (Rao 2011, 425).

More broadly, the narrative of demographic threat focusing on Muslims' strategies uses the language of war to discuss the issue at stake. The element of demographic warfare is often connected to more conspiratorial utterances, such as the 'Kalergi plan', a conspiracy theory popularized by the Japanese-Austrian politician Coudenhove-Kalergi in the 1920s and relaunched by contemporary alt-right, according to which there is an ongoing plan for a 'genocide' of the 'whites' (or 'whites' identity') by mixing them with other populations via immigration (De Bruin 2022). Different from strategic warfare, still connected to the language of war, is the element of terrorism, which is sometimes connected to the core narrative: this element focuses the attention on European Muslims' youth and points out that they are extremely vulnerable to radicalization, and becoming either internal terrorists or foreign fighters, leaving Europe to join, for example, Daesh.

Finally, the reference to the nation is another prominent element, which focuses the attention on those invaded rather than on the 'others', and it is usually expressed by differentiating the concepts of nation and state, or territory (differentiation which revives the long-term debate over the concept of nation – see for example Anderson 1983). In this frame, one can be formally a citizen, without, however, being part of 'the nation' – that is, without sharing values and attitudes, the national spirit, which is reserved to those born and bred in the country. The culturalization of difference is illustrated, for example, by the reference to a clash of civilization (Hungtington 1991; for a discussion, see Brubacker 2017) which sometimes becomes fully-fledged cultural racism (see Froio 2018).

The discursive genres that articulate the demographic threat allegedly posed by Muslims in Europe range from fiction to newspaper editorials, political manifestos, posters and memes (see on this Hernández Aguilar 2023), to make only some examples. What is particularly interesting is the translation of the narrative into scientific discourses, which is often grounded on statistics, supposedly conveying 'hard facts', rather than opinion (Bracke and Hernández Aguilar 2020). In this way, the narrative of demographic threat is normalized, and de-politicized, as it would be based in fact on science and 'objective data' rather than emotional and political stances. The use of arguments based on science is an illustration of how 'uncivil' stances can be normalized, shifting the boundaries of what can be said in the political sphere (see Ekman and Krzyzanowski 2021; Ekman 2022).

In different contexts and in relation to different actors bringing forward the narrative, the main elements can be variously articulated and more or less emphasized. Broadly speaking, Bracke and Hernández Aguilar (2020) differentiate between a mainstream discourse, which focuses on warnings, and a 'fringe' discourse, more related to far-right extremism, which combines warnings with 'solutions', including for example selective (discriminatory) immigration policies.

Even though it is overwhelmingly associated with Islam, the 'threat of demography' narrative has been put forward in relation to different populations, such as Jews or sexual minorities. In this latter case, for example, the 'anti-gender ideology' discourse would warn against 'indoctrination' that would result from teaching students about nondiscrimination and sexual education (see for example Khuar and Zobec 2017).

## 3. An illustration: Italy, right-wing populism, Islam

Italy is an interesting case in which to explore the politics of difference. Considering survey data, Italians are largely hostile towards migrants (Angelucci *et al.* 2021). Among the minorities to which population is more hostile are Roma, and Muslims.[1] Monitoring activities on social media show how hate speech, Islamophobia, and hostility against immigrants and LGBT+ people have been increasing – see for example Amnesty Barometer of Hate 2021,[2] the Maps of Hate by Vox – Italian Observatory on Rights,[3]

[1]See data from the European Union Agency for Fundamental Rights - https://fra.europa.eu/en (accessed 26 March 2024).

[2]Available at https://www.amnesty.it/barometro-dellodio-intolleranza-pandemica/ (accessed 26 March 2024).

Contro l'Odio – BIT 2021.[4] Hostility is related to the topic salience in the public and political discourse.

The topic of immigration in Italy has risen to prominence in the 1990s: public visibility took the form of 'moral panic' in the mass media (Maneri, 2001). Broadly speaking, research on media framing in Europe points out that migrants are usually referenced to through collective names (e.g. Muslims) and negative labeling, and that are portrayed as either victims or threat (Giorgi and Vitale 2017): monitoring activities on Italian mass media and journalism show that only recently the negative connotations of migrants – through labeling and framing – are decreasing (Osservatorio Carta di Roma 2021).

Since the 1990s, the politicization of immigration has been one of the key issues in political campaigns. In the 2000s, as a result of a combination of internal and external factors, concerns over Islam began to be raised particularly by anti-immigration political parties. Lega Nord (now Lega), for example, started to praise Christianity as one of the main tenets of national identity against Islam, in a frame of civilizational opposition between Islam and 'the West' (McDonnel 2016; Ozzano 2013). The political narrative conflates Islam and migration, combining religious, ethnic-racial background, and the status of migrants (Evolvi 2019).

Many studies have focused on the anti-Islam political discourses in Italy, particularly exploring right-wing and far-right populists parties (Caiani and Carvalho 2021; Farris and Scrinzi 2018; Evolvi 2019; Giorgi 2021; Giorgi 2023; Marchetti *et al.* 2022; Ozzano 2020; Ruzza; 2018; Vitullo 2021) which also resulted in the firm inclusion of topics related to immigration and Islam also in the political agenda of the centre-left (see for example Ozzano and Giorgi 2016). Overall, studies demonstrate how right-wing and far-right political parties capitalize on raising fears related to immigration and, particularly, Islam.

Here, I focus on one specific aspect of this politics of fear: the alleged 'demographic threat' posed by Muslims in Europe, through the analysis of the 'First report on the Islamization in Europe' published by the Foundation Farefuturo, FDI think tank. The website explains that the think tank was founded in 2007 to "*with ideas, projects and conferences in order to define programs and forming the new ruling class*" of the centre-right and

[3] Available at http://www.voxdiritti.it/ecco-le-mappe-di-vox-contro-lintolleranza/ (accessed 26 March 2024).

[4] Website: https://controlodio.it/ (latest accessed: 26/93/2024; data and comments available at https://benvenutiinitalia.it/wp-content/uploads/2021/06/quaderno151.pdf (accessed: 26 March 2024).

right-wing parties in Italy, to promote "*the culture and values of the Nation, avoiding the pervasive 'presentism'*, believing that we need the maximum effort to design the future of Italy in the context of a Homelands' Europe. The foundation operates in Rome and in different territorial realities with conferences, seminars, training courses, publishing activities and research programs".[5] The title of the Dossier immediately sets the tone of the publication and establishes 'islamization' as a fact.

Methodology is based on quantitative content analysis and thematic analysis. I applied a flexible coding technique to the dossier, focusing on the elements outlined in section two and at the same time identifying emerging themes and topics (Deterting and Waters 2018). The analytical strategies included an attention to argumentative structure and boundary-work – how boundaries are created, on what is grounded the process of 'othering' of Islam, what are the material and symbolic elements that work as anchorage for the discursive categorization of ingroup and outgroup (see Lamont and Molnár 2002).

## 4. "First report on the Islamization in Europe". Demography and fear

The Dossier, titled 'First report on the Islamization in Europe' is 184 pages long and it is divided in three parts, plus a Foreword, 'Our Identity, Guarantee for the Future', authored by Giorgia Meloni as the leader of Fratelli d'Italia (FDI, Brothers of Italy), and an Introduction, 'Neither Discrimination nor Submission', by Adolfo Urso, President of the Foundation Farefuturo (Doing future).

The first section presents the result of a 2019 survey commissioned by the society AnalisiPolitica with the aim of understanding "*the perception and assessment of some aspects related to the growing presence of the population of Islamic faith on the national territory*" (Fondazione Farefuturo 2019, 24).[6] Respondents are a representative sample of the Italian population (800 individuals) and the questions covered knowledge about Islam, the Quran, sharia laws, and general history, as well as opinions about the possibility of Muslims' integration in Italy.[7] The survey often uses leading questions: for example, the first question reads 'Let's talk about the diverse nationalities/ethnic groups living in Italy and that sometimes raise prob-

---

[5] https://farefuturofondazione.it/la-fondazione/ (access 20 April 2024).

[6] All the translations from the Dossier are by the author.

[7] It is unclear if the survey was CAWI or CATI.

lems for security and public order. Which ones do you fear the most, among those listed? Max. 2 responses'. The question is not only leading, but, also, loaded, since it immediately frames the 'others' in terms of nationality and as trouble-makers, who create problems for national security, and it assumes that respondents 'fear' these 'others': it is not possible to answer 'None', only 'I do not know'. Moreover, the answering options are profoundly racialized: for example, Africans are divided, along the line of colour, between North Africans and Black Africans. Moreover, the options include 'Gypsies' (Zingari), a word that has a profound derogatory connotation, in Italy. Furthermore, the formulation of the questions often includes other common survey mistakes, among which double-barreled questions, such as: "Can you tell us you if agree or disagree with this statement that we have heard from others: 'Muslims should be double-checked, including those having lived here for years'". This question includes two different elements: whether Muslims should be double-checked, and whether this double-checking should also include those having lived in Italy for a long time. In addition to the detailed comment on the data by the President of Analisi Politica, the section also includes a contribution, by a scholar of Arab literature, about the pitfalls of the concept of Islamophobia, both in theoretical terms and in relation to survey results.

The second section is titled 'A threat to Europe. Analysis' and includes contributions from scholars (in sociology, psychiatry, political sciences and philosophy), an ambassador and former Minister of Foreign Affairs and International Cooperation, and an MP, who discuss, articulate and detail the various elements of the Islamic threat, and suggest courses of action.

The third section presents 'Frontier Line. Case studies', which variously articulate the demographic narrative. The first case study concerns demography in its plain meaning, and it is analysed by Camilla Trombetti, who is presented as an 'Expert on International Relations and Public Policies'. The second case study, analysed by an MP, concerns the Western Balkans and points out the risks of this 'internal Islam' which, the author argues, is radical and extremely conservative, as a result of the Balkan wars: in this sense, the threat here is represented by Muslims who will become European citizens if Bosnia-Herzegovina completes the process of membership. The other case studies focus instead on the strategies that Middle Eastern Islam would use to culturally colonise and influence Muslim communities in Europe and, at the same time, present MENA states as reliable economic and political partners. One case study focuses on the media strategy of Isis and is authored by a scholar collaborating with a couple of Italian Universities and a centre study of CNRS in France. Another case study, presented by the head of FDI press office, focuses on the demographic threat with a twist: it pays attention to the implications of appointing Qatar as host for the male soccer world cup in 2022, and it warns against Qatar's soft power. Other case studies are analysed by the Study Center Averroè and its President, Suad Sbai, and focus on the radicalization of inmates, warning against the risks of promiscuity and advocating for specific measures, and the financial penetration of Qatar and the Muslim Brotherhood in Europe through funding activities that would favour the most intransigent and conservative Islam. The last case study discusses the Austrian legislation concerning foreign funding for Mosques and whether it would be possible to apply similar controls in Italy – this contribution, authored by a PhD candidate, was later published in the online section of an Italian scientific journal.

The lineup of authors is particularly interesting, and it includes two groups. The first group includes FDI politicians, such as Giorgia Meloni, and their staff. Trombetti, for example, has collaborated with Giorgia Meloni for a long time, while also writing for the online website 'The Voice of the Patriot'. The second group includes sympathetic study centres and scholars who, in some cases, also served as MPs. Souad Sbai, for example, in addition of being the President of the study centre Averroè, participated to the Committee for Islam in Italy, was an MP for the right-wing coalition Popolo delle Libertà (People of Freedom), and is the founder of the Association of Maroquin women in Italy. Her first book, 'The deceit. Victims of multiculturalism', published in 2010, argued that Muslim women in Europe are the victims of multicultural policies incapable of protecting individual rights and save them from their culture (somehow answering, while repurposing, Okin's question 'Is Multiculturalism Bad for Women?', see Okin 1999). Some of the scholars are close to radical and fringe milieus – for example, the psychiatrist Alessandro Meluzzi is supposedly a follower of QAnon.[8]

Even though the voices are diverse, and the positions nuanced, the dossier can be analysed as producing its own discourse through the juxtaposition of contributions. Overall, the Dossier relies on the authors and the survey to set a tone of scientificity to its contents. In the following, I will explore the narrative of demographic threat and the presence of the main elements outlined in section one.

[8] QAnon is a conspiracy theory developed in the USA around 'drops' launched by the anonymous account 'Q' on the bulletin board 4chan (and, then, on 8chan). On QAnon in Italy, see Murru 2022.

## 5. Discursive articulations

The demographic threat constitutes the backbone of the Dossier, and the narrative is reiterated in all the contributions. The text starts with a quotation from *Soumission*, the well-known and controversial[9] fiction by Michael Houellebecq in which the author imagines a dystopic future in which an Islamist and patriarchal party gains the presidential elections in France with the support of the Socialist Party. The quotation opening the Dossier reads 'Whoever controls the children controls the future'. The reference immediately evokes the core elements of the narrative: the threat of invasion through demography.

Europe is described as a "*dying continent, demographically speaking*" (Farefuturo 2019, 11). The frame of doom (see Norocel and Pettersson, 2022) is variously present in the dossier, for example "*Future will not be our problem, simply because we will not be there*" (Farefuturo 2019, 12), or "*in 2100, Muslims could account for half of the Italian population*" (Farefuturo 2019, 117). The discursive positioning is that of alarm-raisers, urging the audience and the governments to deal with the problem (see Chateauraynaud and Torny 2005)

The "risk of replacement" (Farefuturo 2019, 60) is presented as a fact, primarily because of Muslims' birth rates, both in their homeland, and in Europe. Broadly speaking, raising birth rates are in fact recorded in poor countries, and in Muslim-majority countries in particular, it is argued. One contribution specifically focuses on the analysis of PEW research centre, which traces three scenarios of 2050 demography: Muslim population would be 7.5% of Europeans in the case of 'zero immigration', 11,2% in the case of 'regular migration' (excluding asylum seekers), and 14% in case of 'massive' migration – with high differences among the European countries, and a general decreasing of non-Muslim Europeans. Data projections also point out that immigrants' fertility rates would adjust in time, however, the contribution argues, that would not be particularly relevant because Muslim population is generally younger and migration in Italy started later than in other European countries (Farefuturo 2019, 79).

While the discourse on demography is based on data, in some cases data are only evoked, as an entity legitimising the narrative by virtue of their mere existence. For example: "*what does the data say? That a Muslim woman, here in Europe, has a higher fertility rate, twice that of a non-Muslim woman*" (Farefuturo 2019, 8). Here, no specific data source is mentioned:

[9] In addition to the controversy on its contents, the day of the book release the Charlie Hebdo attack occurred, and the book inadvertently contributed to the debate.

still, data works as an argument of authority legitimising the statement.[10]

The demographic threat combines birth rates with migration – and, more specifically, with what is labelled as 'illegal migration':

> "*When analysing legal [migration], for example, it turns out that if the European nations were only interested in this [...] there would not be a pervasive process of Islamization of Europe (46% of legal migrants are of Islamic religion). However, the numbers also tell us another thing: that as regards illegal immigration, however, this in recent years has been largely of Islamic origin (78% of asylum seekers are Muslims). Yet Christians are the first persecuted religious minority in the world*" (Farefuturo 2019, 12).

The quotation hints at the fact that Europe should become a sanctuary for persecuted Christians among the world. In this sense, migration is not problematic per se, but only insofar as it concerns non-Christian migrants whom, the narrative implies, would have the priority over non-Christians. Also, the quotation sets a connection between Islam and 'illegal' migration, which is variously reinforced throughout the text. Illegal migration is suspicious because it is mostly masculine, and because those who migrate, it is said, are those who could afford it: if they are not economically desperate, the reasoning goes, what reason would they have to leave? This kind of suspicion is illustrated, for example, by the following quotation (which is also an example of dehumanisation of migrants – see Giuliani 2020):

> "*Migrationism is financed today by someone who wants to change the European ethnicity to create a Eurafrica or a Eurasia. Furthermore, we welcome individuals who are already criminals before leaving and who vent their monstrous inclination in our country*". (Farefuturo 2019, 58).

The quotation also articulates the trope of migration as an act of strategic warfare, by alluding to some unknown forces behind people's mobility.[11] Contributions are rather explicit in speaking about an "Islamic strategy" (Farefuturo 2019, 72) that would be confirmed by statements allegedly attributed to relevant Muslim figures (even though these statements are sometimes fabricated – see Bracke and Hernández Aguilar, 2020) and a more general ambition toward the conquest of Europe attributed to Muslims. The following quotation illustrates the point:

---

[10] The same discursive function is played by the many references to study, scholars, well known opinion-leaders or public figures.

[11] In the same contribution 'Kalergi' is also mentioned.

> "*Islamic attention to demographic growth in relation to other peoples and in particular in relation to Europe, the object of ancestral longing of Muslim leaders of every era, is ancient and expresses a generalised aspiration throughout the Islamic world*" (Farefuturo 2019, 74).

That Muslim migration is an act of warfare is also argued with reference to the financial support to Islam in Europe by allegedly traditionalist and integralist 'branches' of Islam, including Muslim Brotherhood. In this situation, European Muslims in favour of "*a Western approach, [...] run the risk of being branded traitors [...] Paradoxically, moderate Islam is more likely in Muslim countries such as Morocco, rather than in Europe*" (Farefuturo 2019, 63). Also, it is said, Muslims have patience, they can wait.

The demographic discourse is variously gendered. While men are conquerors, the portrayal of 'Muslim woman' is more nuanced: "*the main victim of fundamentalism and at the same time as the main actor of an integration policy*" (Farefuturo 2019, 20). This exotic figure is a victim if "*do[es]n't wear the veil, dress[es] in Western style, [has] Christian friends, get[s] divorced, [is] too "independent"*" (Farefuturo 2019, 88). Also, Muslim women are seen as accomplices of Muslim men in the conquest of Europe, not only because of their role as 'wombs', giving birth to Muslims, but also because their role is increasing in terrorist attacks (Farefuturo 2019, 95). Moreover, Muslim women rising to political power in Europe would be mostly related to traditionalist Islam, thus working as door-opening for Islam fundamentalism in European politics (Farefuturo 2019, 159).

The othering discourse points out the familiar tropes already outlined by research: the alleged overlapping of religious and political sphere, the incompatible culture, values and history, and the condition of women (polygamy is also mentioned). On occasion, to illustrate Muslims' difference contributions also point out the existence of 'Islamic enclaves', such as the neighborhoods of "Rosengård, Nørrebro, Molenbeek" (Farefuturo 2019, 74), or other places in Europe, that constitute an internal danger: "*entire metropolitan and rural areas where the English police don't even enter, because everything is governed by native militias*" (Farefuturo 2019, 62). Also, the absence of a leading unitary religious figure is said to complicate the relationships with Islam.

Broadly speaking, it emerges the idea that no integration would be possible, only assimilation. The results of the survey are put forward to underline that Italians are not culturally racist, but strong defenders of Italian laws, culture and traditions, that the 'incomings' should respect for successful co-existence. Culture and traditions are the backbone of the nation, a concept variously raised in the dossier, which warns that Italy is an endangered nation, or making reference to western civilization – "*Survival of a civilization is linked first of all to the birth rate, and to the system of values that thanks to this it manages to transmit*" (Farefuturo 2019, 7). Intergenerational transmission of values is a key mechanism for keeping nationhood alive. In this sense, it is assumed that the boundaries between European and Muslims will overcome generational change: the narrative of demographic threat is grounded on intergenerational boundaries and othering processes, as well as on the reification of culture.

Broadly speaking, many contributions point out that Europe is not only a territory: it is a civilization as well as a way of life, it shares Judeo-Christian roots, faith in liberal democracies and human rights, values and cultural identity, a 'European spirit' that is based on the "dialogue between faith and reason" and secularism "because it is stated in the sacred texts of Christianity" (Farefuturo 2019, 8-9), a history of clashes with Islam. In this sense, it is hinted that "*European identity was also characterised by its difference from Islam*" (Farefuturo 2019, 70). However, the argument goes, Europe has lost its identity, and this makes it more vulnerable to Islamization.

In relation to this, criticism emerges against the European Union, which should learn to be "a union of peoples and not of bureaucracies, of finance, of submission" (Farefuturo 2019, 62). In this sense, Europe is 'complicit' in the incoming replacement that will destroy its identity. Blaming the élite for not being able – or refusing – to acknowledge the threat is indeed a recurrent theme of the contributions. The following quotation, for example, illustrates what is considered to be the ingenuity of the left: "*The phenomenon of leftist forces welcoming into their ranks and promoting the image and career of Muslim women on condition that they wear the veil is unfortunately common throughout the West*" (Farefuturo 2019, 161).

Broadly speaking, guilt is assigned to the supporters of the current Pope[12] (whom the Italian right considers too soft on migration – see for example Giorgi 2021), the 'left', European institutions, the European Court of Human Rights, European governments, NGOs, mainstream media, scholars and scientific institutions, former USA President Barak Obama, Soros' Open Society Foundation, and, more in general, 'do-gooders' and those who *exoticise* the others and praise 'political correctness'.

Emerging from the Dossier is also a general tone of daring to speak the truth against the attempts of downplaying the threat and the accusations of Islamophobia that 'mainstream power' moves to right-wing actors. This

[12] However, other Christian leaders are praised – such as the late Italian Cardinal Biffi, well known for his warnings against Islam.

'courage' to be different, who is also assigned to Houellebecq, is reclaimed as a general attitude of political coherence and faith. In assessing and detailing the threat, many authors also utter fierce statements, by saying, for example, that: "*We will not hand over our Italy either to the Nigerian mafia or to the muezzins, because we still prefer to hear the bells ring rather than hear the minarets sing*" (Farefuturo 2019, 60).

The contributions in the dossier also suggest 'solutions', among which: increasing border controls against 'illegal migration'; selective immigration policies, that would favour immigrants of Christian background; birth promotion policies; safeguard of Judeo-Christian roots of Europe; fund and protect Christian minorities in Muslim-majority countries. Particularly relevant is, of course, also acknowledging the threat.

## 6. Discussion and conclusions

The contribution has focused on the narrative of the demographic threat posed by Muslims, a 'politics of fear' adopted by right-wing and far-right actors all over Europe according to which Muslims will replace Europeans in the near future, because of a combination of birth rates and migration patterns. In Italy the narrative includes both the core elements and the others pointed out by the literature: the criticisms against the European élite, demography as an act of warfare, nationalism. The underlying understanding is that 'power' is in numbers and that there is a radical difference between Europeans and Muslims that will continue generation through generation.

Three elements are worth pointing out in these conclusions. The first element is connected to the fact that the discursive strategy adopts the politics of reference to legitimise and normalise the narrative. This politics of reference works in three directions. A first direction is related to the authors: the contributions are authored by individuals whose expertise is put forward in the line of bio below their names, particularly their connections with universities and higher education. A second direction concerns data. The production of data based on 'numbers', and statistics from well-reputed sources, such as the PEW research centre, are constantly referred to, so as to anchor the narrative to 'hard facts'. A third direction is related instead to the scientific discourse, which is often quoted and repurposed – this is the case for example of the long-term debate over Islamophobia, taken as a point of reference to undermine the heuristic value of the concept. The mobilisation of 'civil', scientific, arguments is an illustration of the mechanisms through which 'uncivil' narratives, such as the 'great replacement' conspiracy, are recontextualized and normalised in the public sphere (see Ekman and Krzyzanowski 2020).

Even though the reference to scientific discourse and experts for political reasons has a long history, it is particularly relevant in contemporary Europe for two main reasons. First, contemporary reference to scientific discourse and experts is particularly relevant in times of proliferation of regimes of 'post-truth' – that is, a situation in which: "*multiple regimes of truth co-exist in the same field of knowledge [...] and compete for hegemony in multiple arenas, in which active audiences undertake their own truth games in segmented epistemic communities*" (Giorgi 2022, 234). Second, right-wing and far-right parties have increased their attention towards the definition and the production of knowledge as a hegemonic practice to counter scientific theories and analysis, such as gender studies, scientific evidence, such as in the case of Covid-19, or to frame phenomena and trends, as in the case of immigration or 'Islamization' (see Saresma and Palonen 2022; Eslen-Ziya 2020; Pető 2022). Farefuturo think tank, in this sense, is part of an increasing number of right-wing oriented think tank and scientific institutions connected to right-wing and far-right parties. In this sense, the reference to demography and demographic statistics can be interpreted in the broader frame of epistemological controversies (see for example Eslen-Ziya and Giorgi 2022) and emergence of politicised epistemologies (Galanopoulos and Stavrakakis 2019).

Connected to this is also the characterization of the Dossier as an 'inconvenient truth' (Giorgi 2022), which is a second element worth pointing out, because it seems to be less relevant with respect to other iterations of the narrative of demographic threat. The concept of truth is particularly relevant in contemporary politics, in relation to politicised epistemologies and what scholars call 'judicialization' or 'tribunalization' of politics (for which judicial logic is increasingly relevant in contemporary politics – see Kelemen 2011; Rosanvallon 2008). In this sense, the authors of the Dossier depict themselves as a minority that has the courage to tell a political truth that nobody wants to hear. This 'truth' is characterised as objective, 'non political' – and, because of that, more credible and valuable.

The last element I wanted to highlight here concerns the role of the demographic narrative in Italian politics. Fratelli d'Italia (FDI) was, at the moment of the publication of the Dossier, a minority, whose electoral success was around 4%. It presented itself as a courageous minority, daring to stand by unpopular positions and suggesting unpopular measures such as selective immigration policies. Like other right-wing populist parties, it adopted the rhetoric of the underdog, opposing 'politics-as-usual' and challenging the power. In 2022, the party leads the Italian political sphere, and the government – even though it does not represent the majority of Italians, with its 26%. As other 'populists in power' (Albertazzi and McDonnell 2015), they would likely re-adjust their message to maintain the government. Yet, selective immigration informed one of the first act of FDI government, as only women, children, and 'vulnerable' individuals were allowed to disembark from an NGO boat with migrants on board.[13] Moreover, in April 2023, the Italian Minister of Agriculture, Food Sovereignty and Forestry, Francesco Lollobrigida, from the Fratelli d'Italia (FDI), brother-in-law of the prime minister Giorgia Meloni, warned that Italy's low birth rates had fallen even further, and, because of that, there was the need of strengthen border controls as there was the risk of ethnic replacement. While the statement has sparked outrage all over Europe, it can be seen as yet another illustration of how repetition of 'uncivil' narratives combined with reference to more acceptable arguments can pave the way to the normalisation of those narratives. It remains to be seen if this politics of fear and the narrative of demographic threat would become mainstream in Italian politics.

## References


Albertazzi, D. and McDonnell, D. (2015). *Populists in power.* Routledge, Abingdon.

Amar, P. (2011). "Middle East Masculinity Studies: Discourses of "Men in Crisis," Industries of Gender in Revolution". *Journal of Middle East Women's Studies*, 7(3), 36-70.

Anderson, B. (1984). *Imagined Communities: Reflections on the Origin and Spread of Nationalism.* Verso, London.

Angelucci, D., De Sio, L. and Paparo, A. (2021). "Beyond the migratiom crisis, deep values. Where does hostility to immigrants come from?". *Partecipazione e Conflitto*, 14(1), 373-395.

Bracke, S. (2012). "From "saving women" to "saving gays": Rescue narratives and their dis/continuities". *European Journal of Women's Studies*, 19(2), 237-252.

Bracke, S. and Hernández Aguilar, L.M. (2020). ""They love death as we love life": The "Muslim Question" and the biopolitics of replacement". *The British Journal of Sociology*, 71(4), 680-701.

Brubaker, R. (2017). "Between nationalism and civilizationism: the Euro-


[13] See for example https://apnews.com/article/france-italy-banksy-germany-government-and-politics-8d5cb0ba2cc9a382613803d535ac3b4c (accessed 2 April 2024).

pean populist moment in comparative perspective". *Ethnic and Racial Studies*, 40(8), 1191-1226.
Caiani, M. and Carvalho, T. (2021). "The use of religion by populist parties: the case of Italy and its broader implications". *Religion, State & Society*, 49(3): 211-230.
Chateauraynaud, C. and Torny, D. (2005). "Mobiliser autour d'un risque. Des lanceurs aux porteurs d'alerte", in C. Lahellec (ed.). *Risques et crises alimentaires*. Lavoisier/Tec & Doc, Cachan, 329-339
Cousin, B. and Vitale, T. (2014). "Le magistère intellectuel islamophobe d'Oriana Fallaci. Origines et modalités du succès italien de la «Trilogie sur l'Islam et sur l'Occident» (2001-2006)". *Sociologie*, 5, 61-79.
De Bruin, R. (2022). "European union as a road to serfdom: The Alt-Right's inversion of narratives on European integration". *Journal of Contemporary European Studies*, 30(1), 52-66.
Deterding, N.M. and Waters, M.C. (2021). "Flexible Coding of In-depth Interviews: A Twenty-first-century Approach". *Sociological Methods & Research*, 50(2), 708-739.
Ekman, M. (2022). "The great replacement: Strategic mainstreaming of far-right conspiracy claims". *Convergence*, 28(4), 1127-1143.
Ekman, M. and Krzyżanowski, M. (2021). "A populist turn?: News editorials and the recent discursive shift on immigration in Sweden". *Nordicom Review*, 42(s1), 67-87.
Eslen-Ziya, H. (2020). "Right-wing populism in New Turkey: Leading to all new grounds for troll science in gender theory". *HTS Teologiese Studies / Theological Studies*, 76(3), 9.
Eslen-Ziya, H. and Giorgi, A. (2022) (eds.). *Populism and Science in Europe.* Palgrave Macmillan, Cham.
Evolvi, G. (2019). "Emotional Politics, Islamophobic Tweet. The Hashtags #Brexit and #chiudiamoiporti". *Partecipazione e Conflitto*, 12(3), 871-897.
Farris, S.R. and Scrinzi, F. (2018). "'Subaltern victims' or 'useful resources'? Migrant women in the Lega Nord ideology and politics", in J. Mulholland, N. Montagna and E. Sanders-McDonagh (eds.). *Gendering Nationalism: Intersections of Nation, Gender and Sexuality.* Palgrave Macmillan, Cham, 241-257.
Fassin, E. (2010). "National Identities and Transnational Intimacies: Sexual Democracy and the Politics of Immigration in Europe". *Public Culture*, 22(3), 507-529.
Froio, C. (2018). "Race, Religion, or Culture? Framing Islam between Racism and Neo-Racism in the Online Network of the French Far Right". *Perspectives on Politics*, 16(3), 696-709.
Galanopoulos, A. and Stavrakakis, Y. (2019). "Populism, anti-populism

and posttruth in crisis-ridden Greece". *POPULISMUS* working paper 10, available at http://www.populismus.gr/wp-content/uploads/2019/10/WP-10upload-2019.pdf.

Giorgi, A. (2021). "Hijack or Release? On the heuristic limits of the frame of instrumentalization of religion for discussing the entanglements of populism, religion and gender". *Identities,* 29(4): 483-499.

Giorgi, A. (2022). "Inconvenient truths? Populist epistemology and the case of Portugal", in H. Eslen-Ziya and A. Giorgi (eds.). *Populism and Science in Europe.* Palgrave MacMillan, Cham, 231-254.

Giorgi, A. (2023). "Religious feminists facing populism in Italy", in A. Giorgi, J. Garraio and T. Toldy, (eds.). *Gender, Religion and Populism in the EU-related Mediterranean*, Routledge, Abingdon, 55-72.

Giorgi, A. and Vitale, T. (2017). "Migrants in the public discourse, between media, policies and public opinion", in S. Marino, R. Penninx and J. Roosblad (eds.). *Trade Unions, Immigration and Immigrants in Europe in the 21th Century: New Contexts and Challenges in Europe.* ILO-Edward Elgar, Cheltenam (UK), Northampton (USA), 66-89.

Giorgi, A., Garraio, J. and Toldy, T. (eds.) (2023). *Gender, Religion and Populism in the EU-related Mediterranean*, Routledge, Abingdon.

Giuliani, G. (2020). *Monsters, Catastrophes and the Anthropocene: A Postcolonial Critique.* Routledge, London.

Harsin, J. (2015). "Regimes of posttruth, postpolitics, and attention economies". *Communication, Culture & Critique*, 8(2), 327-333.

Hernandez Aguilar, L.M. (2023). "Memeing a conspiracy theory: On the biopolitical compression of the great replacement conspiracy theories". *Ethnography*, 14661381221146983.

Hodson, M. (2022). "Analyzing White Nationalist Fears of Changing Western Demographics". *Islamophobia Studies Journal*, 7(1), 108-120.

Hungtington, S.P. (1991). *The Clash of Civilizations and the Remaking of World Order.* Simon&Schuster, New York.

Kelemen D. (2011). *Eurolegalism. The Transformation of Law and Regulation in the European Union.* Harvard University Press, Harvard.

Korteveg A. (2019). "Gendered racializations: producing subordinate immigrant subjects, discrimination, and oppressive feminist and queer politics", in J. Solomos (ed.). *Routledge International Handbook of Contemporary Racisms.* Routledge, Abingdon, 344-355.

Kuhar, R. and Zobec, A. (2017). "The anti-gender movement in Europe and the educational process in public schools". *CEPS Journal*, 7(1), 29-46.

Lamont, M. and Molnár, V. (2002). "The Study of Boundaries in the Social Sciences". *Annual Review of Sociology,* 28, 167-95.

Maneri, M. (2001). "Il panico morale come dispositivo di trasformazione dell'insicurezza". *Rassegna Italiana di Sociologia*, 42(1), 5-40.

Marchetti, R., Righetti, N., Pagiotti, S. and Stanziano, A. (2022). "Right-Wing Populism and Political Instrumentalization of Religion: The Italian Debate on Matteo Salvini's Use of Religious Symbols on Facebook". *Journal of Religion in Europe*, 16(2), 144-171.

McDonnell, D. (2016). "The lega nord: The new saviour of Northern Italy", in N. Marzouki, D. McDonnell and O. Roy (eds.). *Saving the people. How populists hijack religion*. Hurst Publishers, London, 13-28.

Murru, M.F. (2022). "QAnon and Its Conspiracy Milieu: The Italian Case", in H. Eslen-Ziya and A. Giorgi (eds.). *Populism and Science in Europe*. Palgrave Macmillan, Cham, 163-184.

Norocel, O.C. and Giorgi, A. (2022). "Disentangling radical right populism, gender, and religion: an introduction". Identities, 29(4), 417-428.

Norocel, O.C. and Pettersson, K. (2022). "Imbrications of gender and religion in Nordic radical right populism". *Identities*, 29(4), 429-446.

Okin, S.M. (1999). "Is Multiculturalism Bad for Women?", in J. Cohen, M. Howard and M. Nussbaum (eds.). *Is Multiculturalism Bad for Women?*, Princeton University Press, Princeton, 7-23.

Osservatorio Carta di Roma (2021). *Notizie ai margini. Nono rapporto Carta di Roma, Associazione Carta di Roma,* available at https://www.cartadiroma.org/wp-content/uploads/2021/12/Notizie-ai-margini.pdf.

Ozzano, L. (2013). "The Many Faces of the Political God: A Typology of Religiously Oriented Parties". *Democratization*, 20(5), 807-830.

Ozzano, L. (2020). *The Masks of the Political God: Religion and Political Parties in Contemporary Democracies*. Rowan&Littlefield, Lanham.

Ozzano, L. and A. Giorgi. (2016). *European Culture Wars and the Italian Case: Which Side are You On?* Routledge, Abingdon.

Pető, A. (2022). "The Illiberal Polypore State and Its Science Policy", in N. Mörner (ed.). *The Many Faces of the Far Right in the Post-Communist Space: A Comparative Study of Far-Right Movements and Identity in the Region*. Södertörn University, Centre for Baltic and East European Studies (CBEES), Huddinge, 33-42.

Rao, M. (2011). "Love Jihad and Demographic Fears". *Indian Journal of Gender Studies*, 18(3), 425-430.

Rosanvallon, P. (2008). *Counter-Democracy: Politics in an Age of Distrust.* Cambridge University Press, Cambridge.

Ruzza, C. (2018). "The Radical Right in Southern Europe", in J. Rydgren, (ed.). *The Oxford Handbook of the Radical Right*. Oxford University Press, Oxford.

Saresma, T. and Palonen, E. (2022). "On the Emergence of Alt-Science Counterhegemony: The Case of the Finns Party", in H. Eslen-Ziya and

A. Giorgi, (eds.). *Populism and Science in Europe*. Palgrave Macmillan, Cham, 117-140.

Scott, J. (2018). *Sex and Secularism*. Princeton University Press, Princeton.

Selby, J.A. and Beaman, L. (2016). "Re-posing the "Muslim Question"". *Critical Research on Religion*, 4(1), 8-20.

Singh, S. and Féron, É. (2021). "Towards an intersectional approach to populism: comparative perspectives from Finland and India". *Contemporary Politics*, 27(5), 528-549.

Vitullo, A. (2021). "The Online Intersection among Islamophobia, Populism, and Hate Speech: an Italian Perspective". *Journal of Religion, Media and Digital Culture*, 10, 95-114.

Wodak, R. (2015). *The politics of fear: What right-wing populist discourses mean*. SAGE Publications, London, Thousand Oaks, New Delhi, Singapore.

Chapter 7

# BECOMING A REFUGEE. ETHNOGRAPHIC NOTES FROM A CHURCH ASYLUM CASE IN GERMANY


## Carmen Becker



ABSTRACT: *Based on ethnographic fieldwork among Syrians, who took sanctuary in a church in 2016 in the city of Hannover, and volunteers, this chapter argues that the subject position of the 'Muslim refugee' is entangled in a network of materialities, texts, other subject positions, regulations and practices. These different elements form nodes in a specific dispositive situating the Muslim Refugee, hailing them into a specific existence. Through the ethnographic material, the chapter investigates how specific practices and regimes of differentiation operated in the sanctuary in the interactions between refugees and volunteers and involved specific materialities. In this dispositive, Muslim refugees are the addressees of pedagogical projects trying to educate Muslim refugees into what is understood to be the socio-cultural norm in Germany and, by extension, of progressive societies in general. However, they are not able to fully achieve this norm since the pedagogical projects perpetuate the difference they claim to overcome.*




## 1. Introduction

The so-called refugee crisis in Germany in 2015 was, in some ways, a discursive event (Jäger and Maier 2016, 129). In the course of its unfolding, new elements were added to the syntax regulating integration and asylum in the German context, and it appeared extensively in politics and the (mass) media for a prolonged period of time. Since 2015, the 'refugee crisis' has been called upon in order to explain the rise of right-wing populism and the *Alternative für Deutschland* (AfD) in German voter preference. Beyond the actual events summarized under the term 'the refugee crisis', it has become objectified and still circulates in politics and media. Thus, it keeps influencing the trajectories of the German integration discourse.

The newness can be grasped with the term "welcome culture" (*Will-*

*kommenskultur*) which encompassed the volunteer work of numerous citizens in Germany with those who made it across the German border, mostly from Syria, Iraq, and Afghanistan. The then chancellor Angela Merkel epitomized the shift in the perception of refugees with her famous statement, "*Wir schaffen das*". (We will manage/ We can do it) in September 2015.

The German government temporarily suspended the enforcement of the Dublin Regulation, which determines that the EU member state where fingerprints are taken first or where an asylum claim is lodged is in charge of processing and adjudicating the claim for asylum. This decision came under the pressure of Hungary, the chaos in front of German immigration offices, and the collapse of due bureaucratic procedures from the summer of 2015 onward. This situation had been partly created by the reduction of adequately trained administrative staff, shelters, and facilities in Germany as well as by ignoring reports from countries that had taken the brunt of the refugees and the World Food Programme (WFP) run by the United Nations. The WFP had already warned at the beginning of 2015 that it was running out of funds to provide the minimum for Syrian refugees in the camps in neighboring countries. By 2016, the sympathy of the German public for refugees was waning for different reasons and the Dublin Agreement had been reinstated.

It is in this broader setting that I became involved in 2016 with a group of volunteers supporting Syrians who had asked for temporary sanctuary at a local Protestant church in the vicinity of my home. *Kirchenasyl* (church asylum) is the reinvigoration of the old practice of providing sanctuary to people on church compounds. Its modern form in Germany dates back to the beginning of the 1980s in Berlin, witnessing the suicide of Cemal Kemal Altun, who feared his deportation to Turkey, and the hunger strike of several of his friends in the Holy Cross church in the Kreuzberg district of Berlin. Since then, Catholic, Protestant, and independent churches have established communicative structures with the relevant government bodies, set up procedures, produced guidelines, and coordinated their activities in the German Ecumenical Committee on Church Asylum (Ökumenische Bundesarbeitsgemeinschaft Asyl in der Kirche). In recent years, the government has increasingly prosecuted volunteers and church staff providing church asylum and breached sanctuaries, sending in special task forces of the police in order to enforce deportation orders. The forty-year tradition of church asylum has come under increasing pressure. According to the documentation of the Ecumenical Committee, the number of church asylum cases jumped to 430 in 2014 as compared to mostly 30 to 50 cases annually in the previous years. The numbers reached a peak in 2019 with

1,325 cases and have largely remained between 500 and 1,200 ever since. Most of the cases relate to the Dublin Regulation: individuals asking for sanctuary want to evade deportation to fellow EU-member states.

I got involved in 2016 by coincidence: I had just moved with my family into an apartment that the parish of the local Protestant church had originally rented from a private owner for one of their employees who decided to move out after a few months. Having been unable to stick to the three-month termination period, the parish was obliged to present the owner with a new tenant. We were the lucky ones. Through this, I got to know church members from whom I learned in May 2016 that three Syrians trying to evade their deportation orders to Bulgaria were living on the compound of another Protestant church in the vicinity. Having studied Arabic and lived in Syria for lengthy periods before 2011, I hoped I could help out with translation. I ended up spending part of my free time simply hanging out with Haydar, Rana, and Adnan, who, being in their early twenties, were fighting the boredom and anxiety of waiting for the redeeming news that would end their church asylum and assure them residence in Germany. After months of waiting, each of them was finally able to leave the church sanctuary and stay in Germany.

A few weeks after I got to know them, Haydar felt exhausted. Asking him whether he felt sick, he hesitated to answer, but then it came spurting out: "*I am not a refugee. I do not need help. I have not come here for help. You know that we have microwaves and computers in Syria*". The ensuing conversation between us inspired me to turn my involvement into a small ethnographic case study analysing the production of the refugee as a specific subjectivity. Haydar, Adnan, and Rana were surely thankful to all the volunteers and to the parish for providing sanctuary, assisting them, and trying to make the dull waiting time as comfortable and short-lived as possible. However, they struggled with the subject position of the refugee that was assigned to them and which petrified them into a subjectivity that was not of their choosing.

In the ensuing weeks, I wrote field notes, documented numerous conversations, collected information in order to understand the institution of church asylum better, and collected all kinds of data that, in the situation of the church asylum, was somehow relevant to the production of the refugee. In short, I engaged in part-time, eclectic ethnographic participant observation. I coded, analyzed, and theorized the data with the help of Maxqda, a software for qualitative data analysis. In this contribution, I present the results of this endeavor. First of all, I will theorize the refugee figure in order to provide the conceptual framework for this small case study. I then discuss practices from the context of my fieldwork through which Haydar,

Adnan, and Rana became refugees. In doing so, I will connect the micro level of daily interaction and acts to the meso and macro levels of discourses, structures, and institutions. In the conclusion, I return to Haydar's despair when he told me that he was not a refugee. By necessity, he had to inhabit this subjectivity in order to legally be in Germany and in order to acquire a legal status that would enable him to build a life. Concomitantly, by doing so, he succumbed to an interpellation that narrowly circumscribed his ambitions and hopes as well as his pasts and futures.

## 2. Theorizing "the refugee"

People classified in Germany as refugees are entangled in an administrative governmental apparatus that includes not only laws and regulations but also architectural structures (e.g., so-called reception centres, asylum homes), discourses, specific practices, terms, norms, affects, and subject positions. In this sense, one can speak of a refugee apparatus or *dispositif*.

Michel Foucault (1980, 194-95) describes a *dispositif* as

> "*[...], firstly, a thoroughly heterogeneous ensemble consisting of discourses, institutions, architectural forms, regulatory decisions, laws, administrative measures, scientific statements, philosophical, moral and philanthropic propositions – in short, the said as much as the unsaid. Such are the elements of the apparatus [original French:* dispositif*]. The apparatus [original French:* dispositif*] itself is the system of relations that can be established between these elements. [...] In short, between these elements, whether discursive or non-discursive, there is a sort of interplay of shifts of position and modifications of function which can also vary very widely. Thirdly, I understand by the term* dispositif *a sort of – shall we say formation which has as its major function at a given historical moment that of responding to an urgent need. The apparatus thus has a dominant strategic function. [...]*".

At the core of the apparatus are the relationships between its different nodes. As an analytical category, it guides our attention toward the linkages between, for instance, administrative procedures, subject positions, laws, and practices. This "system of relations" is not static but rather prone to modifications and shifts depending on the urgent need that reigns a specific historical moment. This specific analytic perspective enables us to empirically identify the relevant nodes and the qualities of their relationships in order to analyze the entanglement of the specific subject position of the refugee in the network of nodes that make up a *dispositif* and the reproduction of this subject position in the apparatus.

It is helpful to return to the French language in order to exemplify what a *dispositif* is. *A dispositive d'alarme*, for instance, includes an alarm installation (material and technological infrastructure attached to a property), specific signs and signals (e.g., alarm sounds), specific protocols that set in after an alarm has been triggered (e.g., notification of police stations, private security companies, or the owner's mobile devices), the notions of ownership and theft, land registries, laws and regulations pertaining to ownership, practices of owning and stealing, discourses on property crimes, police and security companies, and the subject positions of owner and thief. All these different elements can be found on different social levels, from the micro-level of practices and interactions up to the meso- and macro-levels of structures, institutions, and discourses. One could argue that the analytical lens of such an apparatus does not square with the idea of different levels common in the social sciences. Rather, it subscribes to a "flat ontology" (Schatzki 2016), which conceptualizes social reality on one single plane.

The quote from Haydar hints towards the violence and power inherent in the subject position of the refugee. Apparatuses produce specific positions from which individuals make sense of the world and from which they speak. With reference to Foucault, Stuart Hall (1997, 59) emphasizes that "*[individuals] will not be able to take meaning until they have identified with those positions which the discourse constructs, subjected themselves to the rules, and hence become the subjects of its power/knowledge*". This concept of the subject is deeply critical of the conventional notion of the subject as an autonomous individual with a stable, unified core from which it perceives and acts upon the world. Judith Butler (1997, 153) takes a closer look at how individuals come to inhabit a specific subject position produced within a discourse or a dispositive by resorting to the concept of interpellation:

> "*Interpellations that "hail" a subject into being, that is, social performatives that are ritualized and sedimented through time, are central to the very process of subject-formation as well as the embodied, participatory habitus. To be hailed or addressed by a social interpellation is to be constituted discursively and socially at once. This interpellation need not take on an explicit or official form in order to be socially efficacious and formative in the formation of the subject*".

She carves out the role of performativity in the formation of subjectivity. Subject positions are linked to social performatives, specific habits, and practices through which a person comes to inhabit them. As I hope to show in the following, different material structures, interactions, communication forms, procedural requirements, and media hail a person from Syria forced to leave home and to flee and involve this person in the performance of a specific way of being, namely that of a refugee.

Taking these theoretical considerations as the basis of my case study, I will in the following outline how the refugee as a specific form of subjectivity is reproduced through the ubiquitous and repetitive interpellation of people as refugees in official communication, media production, jurisprudence, and popular culture as well as through everyday social interactions with non-refugees. I do not deny the agency of people when inhabiting a specific subject position and responding to an interpellation. The reproduction of subjectivity does not foreclose the possibility of change, mutations, breaks, and ambivalence with every act from the vantage point of a specific subjectivity. I argue that the extent to which a subject position is forced upon a person and the agency this person retains is an empirical question and will differ depending on the historical context of the specific situation under investigation. However, taking into consideration the highly formalized, monitored, and juridical character of the situation of those being called refugees in Germany and the link of their status to existential questions of life (e.g., Can I find some safety and rest here? Will I be able to sustain myself? Is there a future? Will I be deported?), we should understand the high degree of powerlessness people like Haydar encounter as refugees.

## 3. Becoming a Muslim refugee

I will discuss the entanglement of the different nodes of the 'refugee dispositive' for the reproduction of the subject position of the refugee through the analysis of two practices taken from the case study of the church asylum. The first one is centred on what I call 'letter practices,' while the second one takes on the regime of differentiation constructing Germanness and its other, the refugee. Both instances provide a point of entrance into the dispositive and show how discourses, structures, norms, and institutions on the meso- and macro-level are linked with practices, interactions, and actors on the micro-level of social life. Furthermore, they were part of the everyday social interactions between 'refugees' and 'non-refugees' during the months of the church asylum, i.e., state authorities, volunteers, and lawyers. These practices occurred repeatedly and developed some kind of routine. Furthermore, they were shaped by specific assumptions, dispositions and attributions which can be reconstructed through the analysis of these practices.

### 3.1. Letter practices

Human beings are assigned specific subject positions through a variety of practices and structures. They may relate to the ongoing assignment of subjectivity in varying ways, from taking on and honing a specific subjectivity, to subverting it or resisting it. The governmental structures of states are very efficient and powerful actors in assigning specific subject positions, specifically in the case of refugees filing asylum cases with a state. In the German context of asylum procedures, letters play a vital role. After a case has been filed with all the necessary documents and interviews, the involved governmental agencies communicate with those seeking asylum via letters. Scholars have highlighted that the writing technique embedded in the production of paperwork lies at the core of the performance of states (Darling 2014, 485). As Caroline Desbiens, Alison Mountz, and Margaret Walton-Roberts (2004, 242) argue, "*[…] the state is not a unitary object but is, rather, a set of practices enacted through relationships between people, places, and institutions*". In order to understand how human beings become refugees in the sense of being hailed as refugees, we have to look at how specific state practices position and address them in specific situations.

During the church asylum of Haydar, Adnan, and Rana, letters from the Federal Office for Migration and Refugees (BAMF, *Bundesamt für Migration und Flüchtlinge*), the governmental agency in charge of processing and examining asylum applications, stood at the centre of what I term "letter practices". These letters were not only opened, read, and translated. They were passed around, shown to visitors, orderly stored together with other important documents, continuously re-interpreted, and sometimes responded to. The arrival of these letters solicited emotions of hopes, expectations, and also fear: Is this the final order for deportation? Will this be my entry into some kind of normal life? Do I have to stay much longer in church asylum? Usually, it was up to the lawyers to respond to the letters. Much of it was technical, juridical language, including passages discouraging direct answers. However, on some occasions, Adnan, Haydar, and Rana wanted to respond. We would sit together for hours around the table trying to figure out the best formulation that would express what they wanted to say. In the beginning, these were often vague notions of wanting to overcome the bureaucratic language of the letters. While discussing, drafting, and translating expressions back and forth in German, Arabic, and English, we laughed, we imagined how their case managers at the BAMF would read and react to their letters, we reminisced about our encounters with Syrian bureaucracy, discussed similarities and differences, and we cheered each other up in a sense of activism against what we perceived as an overwhelming, abstract bureaucratic entity encroaching on lives. The drafts would pass through the lawyers' hands in order to make sure that the letters would not affect the cases negatively. The lawyers general gave a pass while also stating that the letters would not achieve anything. They were probably right. None of them was ever responded to.

When we conceptualize these letters and the practices as nodes in a *dispositif* that administers, produces, handles, and responds to refugees, we can analytically grasp how they are intertwined with laws, state agencies, case managers, asylum rights lawyers, refugees, supporters/activists and writing as a specific technology. For sure, these collectively drafted letters did not change a lot in the way Adnan, Rana, and Haydar were subjected to being refugees. On the contrary, one can argue that they had to play the refugee card in order to achieve asylum status and that they were subjected to the laws and the assignment of this specific refugee position. However, the afternoons and evenings when we drafted the letters were crucial for honing and instilling some kind of resisting spirit and carving out some kind of agency while fully knowing that this agency does not include decisive power over the asylum procedures. Jonathan Darling (2014, 487-89) highlights three roles letters play in asylum procedures: (1) They inscribe authority of the state onto lives and "*position those receiving such letters as subject to this decision-making body*" (2014, 487). (2) Their arrival involves events that punctuate the long duration of inactive waiting. They are thereby linked to the specific temporality of church asylum. (3) They govern the geographic mobility of asylum seekers by tying them to known locations where letters can be sent to and are read. People in asylum procedures fear missing the arrival of a letter or a deadline communicated in a letter, as this threatens the success of their asylum case. The letters structured the time in the sanctuary. Their arrival sparked a series of letter practices that were beyond the intention of the BAMF staff. These letter practices culminated in the exhilaration of drafting responses. Upon sending the letter, the exhilaration would simmer on for a few days but ultimately transition into a long phase of waiting, boredom, and mixed emotions of despair and hope. It was this specific temporal rhythm that shaped church asylum.

Of course, there are numerous other practices, objects, and structures that reproduce and circulate the subject position of the refugee by addressing or interpellating certain people as refugees. The popular solidarity t-shirt with the slogan "Refugees Welcome" depicting the contours of people running in one direction, which are interpreted as people fleeing and seeking refuge, is a good case in point. The depiction became ubiquitous during the so-called refugee crisis and is linked to the above-mentioned welcome culture. The slogan, the depictions, and their different materializations were and are in support of refugees. This again underlines that resistance operates within the dispositive to which it resists. It needs to engage the subject positions and assignments in order to have a voice and to amplify the message. Therefore, resistance and non-hegemonic voices are part of the dispositive they aim to disrupt. This is not the same as complicity but rather points in the direction of relationality between hegemonic and marginalized positions.

## 3.2. Germanness and the refugee

A part of the activities during the church asylum consisted of a yoga course, German lessons and a drumming course. These activities were organized and carried out by the volunteers from the church. The volunteers offered them in order to help Adnan, Haydar and Rana to overcome boredom and, in the case of German lessons, in order to prepare them for the life after church asylum. All three of them accepted these activities and also enjoyed them, sometimes more sometimes less so. Whenever I was able to observe the lessons or to take part in the activities, the actions were clearly structured by two subject positions: learner/being taught and teacher/teaching. The former was equivalent to 'the refugee' and the latter to the 'volunteer'. Noticeably, especially the German lessons were used to explain to Rana, Adnan, and Haydar how Germany 'functions', what Germans think and belief, what they need to know about Germany, and what is central to German culture. Observing and, at times, being part of these teaching moments was the most revealing and intriguing part of my investigation. They reveal how the notion of 'Germanness' and its opposite, or the Other to 'Germanness', was constructed in the context of the sanctuary.

In one of his German lessons, a retired high school teacher and member of the local congregation showed an episode from the programme "Marhaba – Ankommen in Deutschland" (Welcome – Arriving in Germany), which was aired from autumn 2015 until early 2016 on the news channel n-tv and is still available on YouTube. The 18 five-minute long episodes are presented by the German journalist Constantin Schreiber in Arabic addressing refugees and migrants from the MENA region, in particular from Syria. The episodes are divided into two parts: an introduction to the topic by Constantin Schreiber followed by a conversation with a guest, often a person originating from an Arab country who functions as an insider or local informant on the issue of arriving in and understanding Germany. In

2016, Constantin Schreiber received the *Grimme Preis* for the programme, one of the most prestigious German television awards. His career has developed swiftly ever since. He has published several books, among which *Marhaba, Flüchtling! Im Dialog mit arabischen Flüchtlingen* (Welcome, Refugee! In Dialogue with Arabic Refugees, 2016), *Inside Islam. Was in Deutschlands Moscheen gepredigt wird* (Inside Islam. What is Preached in Germany's Mosques, 2017), and *Kinder des Koran. Was muslimische Schüler lernen* (Children of the Quran. What Muslim Pupils Learn, 2019). He is now one of the anchors of *Tagesschau*, the main news show of the German public broadcasting network ARD. In both his writings and TV productions, Schreiber employs an ethnographic mode to produce a specific narrative, in which his excellent Arabic language skills serve as a marker, underlining his 'unique' access to the 'secret worlds' of Arab refugees and Muslims in Germany (Becker 2020). Just like ethnographers, journalists employing an ethnographic mode strive to produce convincing narrative accounts of specific cultural sites. They narrate in order to translate the knowledge they have gained due to their access to a specific field to a broader audience, which does not necessarily share the dispositions and socio-cultural habitus of those who are part of the research field. These narrations, coupled with an air of investigative journalism – investigating realms that are barred for 'normal Germans' (i.e., mosques and the culture of Arab refugees) – authorize Schreiber's representation and construction of the life worlds of Muslims and Arabs in Germany.

The description of the episodes on n-tv's YouTube channel states that "*presenter Constantin Schreiber explains our country and us Germans in Arabic and provides practical information about life in Germany*".[1] This sentence indicates the structure of the imagined dichotomy between a homogenized, naturalized German group assigned to a 'we/us' and the group of Arab refugees who, due to their origin, are constructed as being in need of knowledge about certain rules, norms, traits, and aspects of German culture, sociality, and politics. The interesting question is how we/us and the Other are imagined through assigning specific qualities to one part of the dichotomy and, since the other needs explanation, concomitantly denying the other part these qualities. Ernesto Laclau discusses the dichotomization of the discursive space through two basic relations that can be established between two elements:

---

[1] n-tv Nachrichten: Marhaba – Folge 1 – So ticken die Deutschen, published on YouTube on 17 December 2015, https://www.youtube.com/watch?v=QILiBp19Yps [last accessed 15 March 2024]. All translations from Arabic or German to English have been done by the author.

"*On the one hand, each element of the system has an identity only as far as it is different from others: difference = identity. On the other hand, however, all these differences are equivalent to each other inasmuch as all of them belong to this side of the frontier of exclusion*" (Laclau 1996, 38).

The identity of an element appears through its quality of being different from other elements. These differences may align to each other in chains of equivalence represented by an (empty) signifier and delineating the border between the excluded and included elements of the hegemonic discursive formation. Martin Nonhoff (2010) develops three types of relations between discursive elements that specify the relation 'x is different from y'. (1) Equivalence is expressed by x being different from y, but coinciding with y in relation to a. (2) In a relationship of contrariness, x is different from y, and contrary to y in relation to a. (3) When x is different from y and in no way connected to y, Nonhoff uses the terms superdifference. He adds a fourth relation, that of representation: x represents y. Using this matrix of possible relations between discursive elements for the analysis of the 18 episodes of the programme *Marhaba. Willkommen in Deutschland*, I investigate how Germanness and its Other, the Arab refugee are socially constructed.

The episodes cover two thematic clusters: German culture and politics and specific aspects of everyday life, like German cuisine and going to the hairdresser. My analysis focuses on the first cluster. More specifically, the programme discusses the German Basic Law and sharia, the role of religion, women in Germany, xenophobia, the German welfare state, respect for values and norms, and Islamist terrorism.[2] By default, the episodes usually delineate what Germanness is about and thereby insinuating what Otherness is in relation to Germanness. Only on some occasions is Otherness more directly address as in the episode entitled *Das Grundgesetz und Scharia* (The Basic Law and Sharia). The result of the analysis of the discursive space is represented in Figure 1.

---

[2] One episode addresses the mood in Germany after the attacks of Paris on 13 November 2015.

Figure 1. Dichotomization of the discursive space.

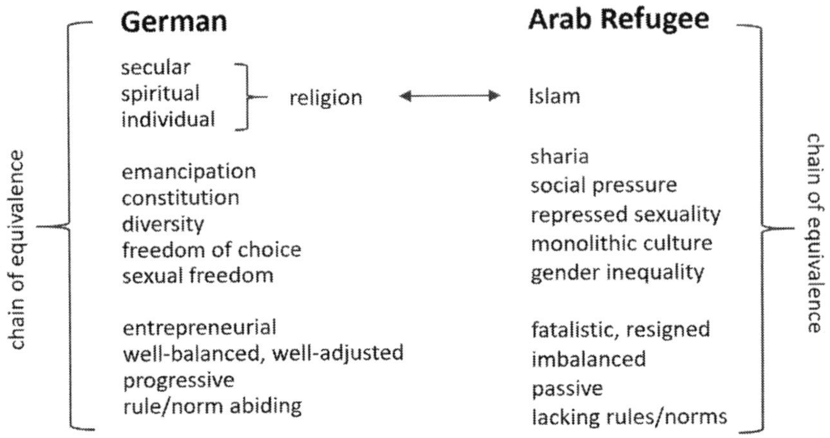


Source: Author's own elaboration.

On both sides of the discursive divide, we have a series of different discursive elements that come to form chains of equivalence in relation to the other side. For instance, the elements emancipation, constitution (Basic Law), diversity, freedom of choice, sexual freedom are different from each other. However, in relation to the Arab Refugees, they become equivalent in characterizing Germanness (us/we). German or Germanness comes to represent this chain of equivalence. Except for sharia, which is explicitly mentioned as contrary to the German Basic Law or constitution, the other side of the equation is not explicated. However, the implication of the discursive dichotomization and structuring is that the Arab refugee, who is explicitly addressed in the episodes with the second person personal pronoun (*antum*) in Arabic, comes to represent sharia, social pressure, repressed sexuality, monolithic culture, and gender inequality. Episode 12, entitled "Respekt für Werte und Normen" (Respect for Values and Norms), was produced after the large-scale occurrence of sexual assaults during New Year's Eve 2015/2016 in Cologne and other German cities involving men from Arab countries who came as refugees to Germany. Schreiber explains how German culture is different from Syrian culture in terms of how men and women behave in public spaces. He emphasizes that the clothing of women in Germany is usually an individual style and does not indicate an invitation to get closer. He states that "*women are by no means sluts because they dress as they please*".[3] Stand-

[3] n-tv Nachrichten: Marhaba – Folge 12 – Respekt für Werte und Normen, published on YouTube on 12 January 2016, available at https://youtu.be/7PDqv33_CHk?si=CvMRfsj3FtqbREtx (accessed 15 March 2024).

ing in front of a structure that seems to be a temporary housing for asylum seekers, Schreiber asks a man what he thinks about the assaults of New Year's Eve. The man is not introduced by name. However, his answer leads the viewer to conclude that he is a refugee from Syria. Schreiber puts forward the second issue that came up in the aftermath of New Year's Eve 2015/16: the lack of respect for law enforcement officers and laws. "*Respect for our law enforcement officers and laws is a basic precondition for everybody who wants to live with us. These incidents cannot be accepted*".[4] While rule- or norm-abiding behaviour, respect for freedom of choice, and emancipation are linked to Germanness, the insinuation is that Arab refugees at the very least have a problem with, if not a lack of, these qualities. It is not drunken (or intoxicated) masculinity, for instance, that is problematized but Arab refugee masculinity or, to be more precise, a specific imagination of Arab masculinity.

Episode six[5] on the role of religion underscores the secularity of Germany, which is understood as the separation of church and state. Religion, he argues, has been a matter of personal choice since the Enlightenment and all religions benefit from religious freedom in Germany. He talks in German to a man in a mosque – again, the person is not introduced; however, given the way he is addressed and responds in turn, he is identified as a Muslim with some kind of authority. Schreiber asks him what he thinks about the fact that throwing a copy of the Quran in the garbage bin is allowed in Germany. A bit further into the episode, he informs his Arab audience that Germans are unsure whether Muslims accept religious freedom in Germany. He states that "*on the other hand, many Muslim representatives and associations advocate an Islam that is compatible with our societal rules*". He closes the episode by saying that

> "*many people in Germany feel uncomfortable thinking about strict Islamic rules. This is the truth. At the same time, people who now come to us and engage with our clothing, traditions, and habits can gain a lot of sympathy. This is a chance for both sides*".

The dichotomization in these statements in this and other episodes touching on the issue of religion is again quite stark: Germanness and the way Germans engage with religion are linked to secularity, spirituality, and individuality. This is considered to be legitimate religion, while strict rules

---

[4] See footnote 3.

[5] n-tv Nachrichten: Marhaba – Folge 6 – Die Rolle der Religion, published on YouTube on 17 December 2015, available at https://youtu.be/v7Teru250V8?si=UR-XcUSM00O HY75j (accessed 15 March 2024).

and Islam are put into a relationship of contrariness to Germanness and 'legitimate religion'.

I cannot provide here a full analysis of the dichotomization of the discursive space. The examples illustrate how the discursive elements are part of a regime of differentiation. They form a dynamic network in which the different elements are put in relation to each other. Religion is part of the infinite play of difference and equivalence, which can only be temporarily arrested and fixed in social formations. Order and stability appear as relative fixations of the social (Laclau 2014). Regimes of differentiation have regulatory and classificatory power across multiple social fields in that they direct behavior, authorise subject positions, legitimate some traditions above others, and provide interpretive schemata of perception, conception, and actions. They thereby produce truth "*such that our epistemological certainties turn out to support a way of structuring the world that forecloses alternative possibilities of ordering*" (Butler 2001, 3). Therefore, regimes of differentiation include not only semiotic elements but also practices, subject positions, affects, discourses, material structures, and administrative procedures – in short, all elements that interconnect and produce differentiation on a societal scale.

Schreiber's 18 episodes of *Marhaba – Ankommen in Deutschland* were very popular and were used in interactions with refugees, as my case shows. Though they are part of a discourse circulating on the meso- level of society, they are also linked to practices on the micro-level: they were used in teaching German and in teaching about Germany/Germanness in the church asylum. The specific regime of differentiation at work around the continuous reproduction of German and the refugee as specific subject positions structures other practices and interactions I could observe and investigate during my time as a volunteer in the church asylum. Adnan, Haydar, and Rana were often presented with work and job training opportunities in order to "take life into their own hands", as one of the volunteers said. I observed on two occasions how a volunteer explained gender equality in Germany to Adnan and Haydar during a conversation by claiming that women and men are equal in Germany and that this has been a long struggle won by progressive movements. One evening, several volunteers came together with Rana, Haydar, and Adnan to the church compound in order to prepare and share a meal. We discussed what we would cook and checked on the ingredients. When the preparation of the meal started, Rana was jokingly barred from the kitchen by two volunteers, saying that in Germany, she does not have to work in the kitchen. Haydar and Adnan, who were already in the kitchen, received compliments for doing "traditional women's work" and were assisted by other volunteers. Adnan, Rana, and Haydar were confused and did not know what to make of the situation. When I asked Adnan later on how he understood the situation, he shrugged his shoulders and said that he was used to preparing meals and didn't mind. Asking the two volunteers who initiated the situation how they understood it, they said that they wanted to encourage the two men to adapt to how men and women interact in Germany and that they wanted to show appreciation for their willingness to do so. Most volunteers consulted me on and off as an 'Islam expert' during the duration of the church asylum. Often, they thought that they needed a better understanding of Islam in order to understand the situation and behaviour of Rana, Haydar, and Adnan. They thought that a thorough understanding of Islam in general would enable them to help in a better way.

These ethnographic snippets from the everyday interactions and practices in the sanctuary help to understand how specific subject positions such as 'the (German) volunteer' and 'the (Arab/Muslim) refugee' are enacted and reproduced on the micro-level. Discourses circulating across a range of social fields inform these interactions and practices as they communicate a specific regime of differentiation through which the refugee and the German (equated with us/we) appear as essentialized, homogenized, and naturalized subject positions.

## 4. Conclusion: Reproducing the refugee

I have argued that the refugee is a specific subject position within an apparatus. The ethnographic data from the case study suggest that the exchange of letters, a specific regime of differentiation through which Germanness and the refugee are signified, and the pedagogy of interactions are parts of the 'refugee *dispositif*'. They engender the reproduction of the refugee as a subject position and, interlocked, the subject position of the German. The relation between these two subject positions was marked by pedagogization: the education of the refugee within the hegemonic construction of a 'German norm'. Pedagogization entails the codification of a socio-economic, cultural, or political issue (e.g., health, racism, integration) whereby the pedagogical expands from the education sector into other social contexts. The pedagogical impetus works towards the re-shaping or reproduction of the subject (Höhne 2013). The volunteers maintained a very benevolent attitude towards Rana, Haydar, and Adnan. When I asked them why they were doing volunteer work, they underscored how much they wanted them to succeed in Germany and to build a new life. While doing this, they were engaged in practices that reproduced the regime of differentiation hinged upon the main dividing line: German/Refugee. The three 'refugees' also appreciated the sociality and company of the volunteers. Rana told me several times that she felt like being back in school. In this sense, the pedagogy of the interactions in the space of the church asylum might be understood as a specific effort to enculture the three adults: to make them "*acquire the mental representations (beliefs, knowledge, and so forth) and patterns of behaviour required to function as a member of a culture [...]*" (Rhum 1997). These mental representations and patterns of behavior, however, need to be socially produced, naturalized, homogenized and circulated in order to be available for practices of enculturation. It is through this effort that the Other of German subjectivity is produced while actually trying to transform 'the refugee' into being 'German'. However, there is a paradox in the effort to integrate refugees into German society while maintaining the regime of differentiation, positing the (Muslim) refugee in opposition to Germanness. Sara Farris describes this paradox at work in the discussions on Jewish integration in 19th-century Europe and the discussions on Muslim integration in contemporary Europe as

> "*a combination of (a) a "republican rigorist" position that inconsistently posits emancipation as a universal precept to be realized within the framework of political citizenship while requiring that subjective emancipation be achieved before or independently of such coordinates; and (b) "culturalist differentialism," which essentializes and establishes an insurmountable difference between cultures thereby effectively operating like biological racism*". (Farris 2014, 297)

While there is the universal notion of political citizenship at work, which is accessible to everybody, cultural differences – or regimes of differentiation – keep reproducing differences that the refugee can hardly overcome.

## References

Becker, C. (2020). "The Journalist-Ethnographer, Religious Diversity, and the Euphemization of Social Relations", in *Hijacked. A Critical Treatment of the Public Rhetoric of Good and Bad Religion*, ed. by L. Dorrough Smith, S. Führding and A. Hermann. Equinox, Sheffield-Bristol 87-97.

Butler, J. (1997). *Excitable Speech: A Politics of the Performative.* Routledge, New York.

Butler, J. (2001). "What Is Critique? An Essay on Foucault's Virtue".

*Transversal Texts*, May, available at https://transversal.at/transversal/0806/butler/en.

Darling, J. (2014). "Another Letter from the Home Office: Reading the Material Politics of Asylum". *Environment and Planning D: Society and Space,* 32, 484-500. https://doi.org/10.1068/d13067p.

Desbiens, C., Alison M. and Margaret W. (2004). "Introduction: Reconceptualising the State from the Margins of Political Geography". *Political Geography,* 23(3), 241-43. https://doi.org/10.1016/j.polgeo.2003.12.011.

Farris, S.R. (2014). "From the Jewish Question to the Muslim Question. Republican Rigorism, Culturalist Differentialism and Antinomies of Enforced Emancipation". *Constellations,* 21(2), 296-307. https://doi.org/10.1111/1467-8675.12087.

Foucault, M. (1980). *Power/Knowledge: Selected Interviews and Other Writings. 1972-1977,* ed. by C. Gordon. Pantheon Books, New York.

Hall, S. (1997). "The Work of Representation", in *Representation. Cultural Representations and Signifying Practices*, ed. by S. Hall. Thousand Oaks, Sage, New Delhi-London, 15-64.

Höhne, T. (2013). „Pädagogisierung als Entgrenzung und Machtstrategie. Einige kritische Überlegungen zum erziehungswissenschaftlichen Pädagogisierungsdiskurs“, in *Pädagogisierung*, ed. by A. Schäfer and C. Thompson. Wittenberger Gespräche. Halle: Martin-Luther-Universität Halle-Wittenberg, 7-35, urn:nbn:de:0111-opus-77227.

Jäger, S. and Florentine, M. (2016). "Analysing Discourses and Dispositives: A Foucauldian Approach to Theory and Methodology", in *Methods of Critical Discourse Studies*, ed. by R. Wodak and M. Meyer, 3rd ed. Thousand Oaks, Sage, New Delhi-London, 109-36.

Laclau, E. (1996). *Emancipation(s)*. Verso, London-New York.

Laclau, E. (2014). "The Impossibility of Society", in *The Discourse Studies Reader. Main Currents in Theories and Analysis*, ed. by J. Angermuller, D. Maingueneau and R. Wodak. John Benjamins, Amsterdam-Philadelphia, 122-26.

Nonhoff, M. (2010). „Hegemonieanalyse: Theorie, Methode und Forschungspraxis“, in *Handbuch sozialwissenschaftliche Diskursanalyse. Band 2: Forschungspraxis*, ed. by R. Keller, A. Hirseland, W. Schneider and W. Viehöver, 4th ed. VS Verlag für Sozialwissenschaften, Wiesbaden, 299-332.

Rhum, M. (1997). "Enculturation". *The Dictionary of Anthropology*, ed. by T. Jefferson Barfield. Blackwell, Oxford, 149.

Schatzki, T.R. (2016). „Praxistheorie als flache Ontologie“, in *Praxistheorie. Ein Soziologisches Forschungsprogramm*, ed. by H. Schäfer. Transcript, Bielefeld, 29-44. https://doi.org/10.14361/9783839424049-002.

Chapter 8

# DISPLACED POPULATIONS AS OTHER: A LEARNING APPROACH TO CONTRAST FEARS AND PROMOTE HUMAN RIGHTS

**Paola Perucchini, Sara Gabrielli and Bryan McCormack**

ABSTRACT: *This chapter will allow us to reflect on how the recent large migration flows produce contact and contrast between 'us' – European citizens – and 'others' – migrants. These contact and contrast can create fears, both in 'us' and 'others', that are investigated through Yesterday-Today-Tomorrow's (YTT's) learning program to promote human rights. The fears of displaced populations will be considered through the drawings they have produced in YTT workshops in refugee camps. As for the fears of Europeans, the YTT educational program will be presented. It focuses on displaced populations and ethnic prejudices in primary school children. The evidence-based primary school program is based on contact, empathy and perspective taking and aims to reduce children's prejudice toward migrants.*



## 1. Fear of the other

The recent large migration flows to Europe have produced day-to-day encounters, contact and contrast between 'us' – European citizens – and 'others' – displaced populations. These contact and contrast have generated fears in both communities. Displaced populations have multiple fears arising from difficulties that drove them to leave their countries of origin, as well as from the difficult conditions they find in refugee camps and centres and from their uncertain future. Europeans' fears are expressed in prejudice and discrimination. Stereotypes and prejudices are related to dichotomic social categories, which distinguish social groups between "us" and "others". This categorization can lead to intergroup discrimination (Tajfel and Turner 1979; Prati and Rubini 2015).

As other issues of relevance, migration flows in our society lends themselves to easy speculation that generates confusion and disinformation. When talking or thinking about migration, people often refer to their perceptions, more than to objective data. This mental categorization can easily lead to misconceptions, prejudices, and fears based on imagination, not on real data (Cerquozzi 2018). This process is confirmed also by surveys on Europeans' perception about migrants: for example, the Eurobarometer survey on migrants' integration in the European Union (n. 469) showed that most of the European citizens tend to overestimate the number of migrants residing in their country, estimating migrants to be 2,3 times more than the reality (EU 2018). Furthermore, a hostile reaction to migration flows is globally widespread (Paxton and Mughan 2006).

Immigrants are often blamed for threatening natives' economic and material interests (Blumer 1958; Hardin 1995), and the fear is heightened during economic down turns (Espenshade and Hempstead 1996; Olzak 1992) and emergencies, such as the ones characterizing our centuries: health emergency due to Covid-19, environmental crisis, etc. In this perspective, fear is associated to the "unknown" and to the absence of human control (Prosperi 2021). This increasing fear leads to conspiracy and loss of trust in science (Catarci *et al.* 2023), to which the only possible answer is knowledge (Prosperi 2021). In fact, as stated by the Annual Report on the ECRI's activity (ECRI – European Commission against Racism and Intolerance) in 2021, rising levels of hate speech and prejudice after the pandemic period can be regarded as obstacles for integration and inclusion efforts.

In this perspective, it is possible to share Furedi's idea that "*The only thing we have to fear is the 'culture of fear' itself*" (2007), recognizing fear to be influenced by the self and by the interaction of the self with others and shaped by culture. To answer this culture of fear it is necessary to rediscover the value of courage, risk tolerance, cooperation.

## 2. Hate feeling and hate speech

The feeling of fear and insecurity is strictly connected to the hate feeling and how it is reported in the media and in the public opinion. In this perspective fear and hate are connected to ethnicity and religion. In fact, hatred can be regarded as a defensive mechanism toward self-preservation and protection, especially in those periods in which social, economic, political and other conditions are perceived as threatening (Blee 2004; Zembylas 2007).

Fear also leads to a widespread propaganda, based on the migratory impact on society to justify the hate speech, which often characterized the public discourse. The expression "hate speech" refers to a category originated by case law in the USA to identify words and discourses aimed to express hate and intolerance against a person or a group, and that could possibly lead to violence (Cerquozzi 2018). Regarding the migratory phenomenon, migration flows are connected to an increase of racist expressions – both in everyday life and in politics – focused above all on extremism, terrorism, social coexistence (Ziccardi 2016).

Hate feeling can be regarded as a complex emotion, expressed in different ways. Recently, an article in the New York Times (Brooks 2015) defined hate in different forms: 1) Hot hate, based on anger; 2) cold hate, based on contempt, and express disgust for another person through sarcasm, dismissal or mockery; 3) anonymous hate, widespread thanks to Internet and social media.

The European Union addresses hate and hate speech in different recommendation and communication. In 1997 the Recommendation n. 20 of the Committee of Ministers on Hate Speech (COE 1997) recalls that

> "*the Vienna Declaration highlighted grave concern about the present resurgence of racism, xenophobia and anti-Semitism and the development of a climate of intolerance*" (*ivi*, 106).

It refers to hate speech

> "*as covering all forms of expression which spread, incite, promote or justify racial hatred, xenophobia, anti-Semitism or other forms of hatred based on intolerance, including: intolerance expressed by aggressive nationalism and ethnocentrism, discrimination and hostility against minorities, migrants and people of immigrant origin*" (COE 1997, 107).

The already mentioned European Commission against Racism and Intolerance (ECRI) in 2016 (ECRI General Policy Recommendation no. 15) extended the meaning of hate speech, including: "*the ground of 'race', colour, descent, national or ethnic origin, age, disability, language, religion or belief, sex, gender, gender identity, sexual orientation and other personal characteristics or status*" (3). In this way it refers to ethnicity and racism but also to any personal characteristics. Moreover, it recognizes the different forms in which hate can be expressed: harassment, insult, negative stereotyping, stigmatization or threat. The European concern for hate spreading is confirmed also by the statement of the ECRI in 2021, underlining the use of inflammatory rhetoric and the wide dissemination of hateful and dehumanising content, notably on the internet.

The idea of hate speech is extended also by the United Nations strategy and plan of action on hate speech (UN 2019), defined as:

> "*any kind of communication in speech, writing or behaviour, that attacks or uses pejorative or discriminatory language with reference to a person or a group on the basis of who they are, in other words, based on their religion, ethnicity, nationality, race, colour, descent, gender or other identity factor*" (*ivi*, 2).

United Nations considered hate to be a "weapon" against the so-called "Other" and a menace for democratic values and peace.

In fact, minorities are often victimized by violence, motivated by fear and stereotypes on differences of religion, ethnicity or other personal characteristics. Social stereotypes and biases, together with non-inclusive practices, create a hostile environment towards minorities (Perry and Scrivens 2018; Syed and Ali 2021). It is a social problem which deserves to be analysed not only regarding the horrifying incidents that reach the public consciousness but also investigating the social process (Jenness and Grattet 2001).

Regarding the Italian context, in 2014 the UN Special Rapporteur already pointed out the use of hate speech against migrants in Italy, a concern repeated also in 2017 and 2018. It led to the creation of the "Jo Cox" Commission in 2016, aimed to investigate intolerance, xenophobia, racism and hate phenomena.

The Commission adopted a widespread metaphor to explore hate and hate speech is the Pyramid one (ADL 2018), "*a theoretical and visual image of how the seeds of hate, once planted, can quickly grow from biased ideas to harmful behaviours and violence*" (Syed and Ali 2021, 44). It allows us to distinguish between different levels (stereotypes, threats, violence, etc.) and proposes an overview of the phenomenon (Faloppa 2020).

At the pyramid's basis (Biased Attitudes) there are stereotypes and shared and generalized categorization, offending or non-inclusive language, microaggressions or insensitive remarks. This level can easily lead to fear, hate and bad feelings about a person or a group, and can be easily shared by public discourse and media. The second level (Acts of Bias), in fact, consists of biased attitudes against groups and people, for example bullying, social avoidance, scapegoating, offensive and biased jokes, insults, and name-calling. It directly contributes to the third level of the pyramid (Discrimination), based on explicit discrimination and entitled sharing of the hate speech. Discrimination moves the biased attitude "*I don't like or trust those people*" to discrimination, "*I won't hire those people to work in my factory*". (Syed and Ali 2021). It can create social conditions for hate crimes and violence, at the fourth level (Bias-Motivated Violence), which culminate in Genocide at the top of the pyramid.

The pyramid contributes to clarify how the lower level can directly influence violence and hate crimes. In this perspective, working on stereotypes and prejudices means to start from the basis of the hate phenomenon, preventing its climax.

Prejudices, stereotypes and discrimination toward immigrants can be viewed as key determinants of receiving societies and of the migrants who seek to make these societies their new home (Goldin *et al.* 2011; Esses 2021). Attitudes toward migrants are particularly important as they influence migration policy, life outcomes of migrants and their treatment, intergroup relations and social cohesion (Esses 2021).

Based on the connection between fears of the Others and discrimination attitudes to stereotypes and prejudices, we adopted an interdisciplinary approach, focused on psychology and pedagogy, to address both migrants/refugees' fear – expressed through drawings – and the fear of the Europeans. On this purpose, the chapter will present an educational program aimed to reduce ethnic prejudice in Italian primary school children.

## 3. Displaced populations' expression of fear through drawing

UNHCR (2023) states that global forced displacement has reached 108.4 million at the end of 2022, children accounted for an estimated 41 per cent of all refugees, and women and girls accounted for 51 per cent of the total. More than 1 in 74 people worldwide remained forced to leave his/her house due to violence, war, persecution, etc. and it is estimated that, in the next 20 years, migrant population could reach around 150-300 million people (UNHCR 2016).

For their inclusion, for social wellbeing and as guaranty of Human Rights, it is essential to recognize their existence and cultural legacy.

In this perspective, the artist Bryan Mc Cormack founded the Yesterday-Today-Tomorrow association (YTT), which is an independent Paris-based Educational & Humanitarian Non-Profit which combines visual language with learning tools to facilitate migrants' and refugees' inclusive processes, promote human-rights, the prevention of violent extremism, freedom, diverse, multi-ethnic and multi religious societies. YTT is also aimed at positively affecting national and international migration policy-making. Since 2016, YTT has been collaborating with thousands of refugees/migrants (from more than 50 nationalities, aged from 3 to 70 years old) in over 40 camps and squats across Europe/North Africa. They receive 3 sheets of paper and coloured pens and are invited to draw 3 sketches: one of their life before: Yesterday; one of their current life: Today; and one of their life imagined in the future: Tomorrow. These drawings define the YTT visual language, a raw, emotional and explicative language that speaks logically and directly to the audience. Figures 1, 2 and 3 shows the YTT drawings by a 9 year old Iraqi girl, living in the Miksaliste Refugee Camp (Belgrade, Serbia). In her Yesterday she represented what she saw when on a Sunday morning, coming back from church, she found both her parents and brother killed. In her Today, she drew her hands and arms with the cuts she self-inflicts on her body. In her Tomorrow, she drew her dream to be a doctor, so that she can help others.

Figure 1. The Yesterday drawing by a 9 year old Iraqi girl currently living in Miksaliste Refugee Camp, Belgrade, Serbia.

Source: Yesterday-Today-Tomorrow Association.

**Figure 2.** The Today drawing by a 9 year old Iraqi girl currently living in Miksaliste Refugee Camp, Belgrade, Serbia.

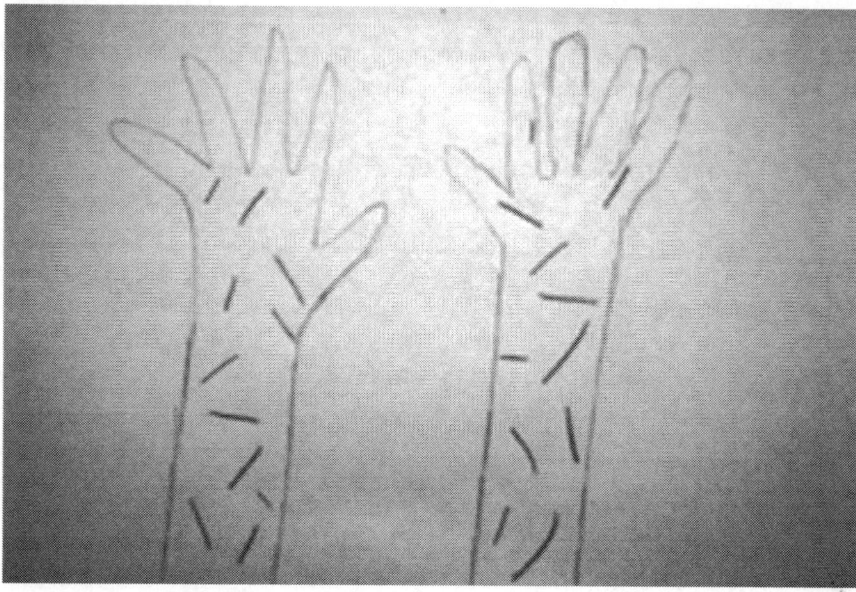

Source: Yesterday-Today-Tomorrow Association.

**Figure 3.** The Tomorrow drawing by a 9 year old Iraqi girl currently living in Miksaliste Refugee Camp, Belgrade, Serbia.

Source: Yesterday-Today-Tomorrow Association.

As it is well known, through drawing, people can clearly express their thoughts and feelings independently of dialect, nationality or education (Arizpe, Colomer, and Martínez-Roldán 2014). Thus, migrants can leave their own trace, creating their own contemporary culture and voice, whereas simultaneously losing all traceability of their inherited culture.

## 4. The YTT learning approach for primary schools

As underlined by the cited metaphor of the Pyramid, stereotypes and prejudices are at the basis of the hate speech phenomenon and its development. In this perspective, it is essential to start from this basis in order to stop the hate feeling at its beginning. Allport (1954) considered hate feelings toward other ethnic, racial and cultural groups as fundamental emotional features of the prejudiced personality (Zembylas 2007). Prejudice and discrimination lead people not to value those who are dissimilar to themselves (Aronson 1992), distinguishing between us and others and idealizing one's own group and demonizing the others (Zembylas 2007). Children develop prejudices from the early years of their life (Bigler 1999). Ethnic prejudices can impact on children's attitudes and behaviours, already in preschools and primary schools (Bigler and Liben 2007; Dovidio *et al.* 2010).

Starting from the cooperation between the Yesterday-Today-Tomorrow Association and Roma Tre University, coordinated by the last author, we designed an educational program to reduce ethnic prejudices towards migrants and refugees in Italian primary schools (Gabrielli *et al.* 2022). Our YTT educational program had the following multiple aims:

- to stimulate awareness of the living conditions of migrants and refugees;
- to promote deconstruction of prejudice, stereotypes and reduction of discrimination practices;
- to foster awareness among the school children of fundamental human rights, and of cultural differences, inclusion, and citizenship.

In order to answer to its aims, the educational program adopted an interdisciplinary approach and strategies considered to be effective in prejudices' reduction in social psychology literature, which recognize a central role to contact (direct and indirect), empathy and perspective taking (e.g., Allport 1954; Batson *et al.* 2002; Birtel and Crisp 2012). Meta-analyses provided converging evidence that interventions can contribute meaningfully to the reduction of outgroup bias between groups (Beelmann and Heinemann 2014; Ulger *et al.* 2018). Results from both studies showed that: i) intergroup contact, empathy, and perspective taking are the most promising components in educational programs; ii) programs that involve multiple strategies are highly effective; iii) interventions should involve multiple sessions rather than one-shot interventions; iv) interventions are particularly more effective for children over 8 years old; iv) interventions actively led by trained teachers, students or researchers yield significantly greater benefits with respect to those led by untrained teachers.

For the methodological approach, our YTT program uses student-centred strategies and an active learning approach, which are designed to activate emotive and cognitive empathy and perspective taking, and to promote anti-discrimination practices. By fostering the concepts of identity and ethnic differences, along with social comprehension, the program creates a contrast between the children's own experiences and those of migrants, to stimulate a more profound understanding of the minority experience (Gabrielli *et al.* 2019). On this basis, the educational program is composed of four phases:

- the first phase focuses on personal experiences of Italian children, investigating their previous knowledges about migration;
- the second phase is based on indirect contact, mediated by drawings collected by the YTT Association and realized by migrants' children. It allows a comparison between migrants and italians experience;
- the third phase is based on activities to promote empathy, perspective taking and emotional comprehension;
- the last phase focuses on the migrants' identity, thanks to direct contact with privileged witnesses.

Our YTT educational program developed in 8 lessons (Gabrielli *et al.* 2022):

1) During the first lesson, children were asked to draw their own Yesterday, Today, and Tomorrow. Drawing is followed by a collective discussion on the contents and a paperwork with open questions to verbalize it. This first lesson allows children to reflect on their personal experience and their dreams for the future.
2) In the second lesson, children were then asked to draw what might be their Yesterday, Today, and Tomorrow if they were a migrant child. As for the first lesson, drawing is followed by a collective discussion on the contents and a paperwork with open questions to verbalize it. In this activity, children start to wear the shoes of a migrant child, trying to imagine his/her life.
3) The third lesson opened with children divided into small groups. Groups have the aim to reflect on three drawings by a migrant child (furnished by

the YTT Association) and to reconstruct the history of the child and what he/she wanted to draw and communicate. After this activity, teachers explain the real history of the drawings and their meaning. Further drawings by migrant children of the same age as the Italian children are shown. Children compare their drawings with the YTT drawings through a collective discussion. Therefore, through their reflections on the differences between their own experiences, their idea of a migrant's experiences, and an actual migrant's experiences, the children were able to reach emotional comprehension of the migratory phenomena.

4) The lesson was focused on imagined indirect contact. After a short survey on children and their family origins, the children were asked to write an interview that might be administered to a familiar migrant about his/her migratory experience. Children first write the questions in small groups and then realize a complete interview for the whole class. Indirect contact appears to be important as a preparatory strategy that encourages people to seek real contact, to help them to overcome any initial inhibitions that might affect the intergroup interactions and future contact (Vezzali *et al.* 2012).
5) In this lesson children were asked to narrate their interviews in the class. Some of the children succeeded in conducting the interview with migrants living in Italy (e.g., shopkeepers, neighbours), thus turning the indirect contact into direct contact, while others conducted the interview with Italians (often family members) who had moved from the south to the north of Italy, or who had moved from the countryside into the city. This activity stimulated a discussion about the reasons for migration, the different experiences, and the acceptance and hospitality in the new place. It also allowed a focus on Italian migratory history and background, to analyse experiences near to the children's reality, compared to the refugee reality.
6) In the next lesson, the children were involved in three activities that were focused on their identities and on perspective taking. The first activity referred to the *Who are you?* approach by Kuhn and McPartland (1954), which allowed the children to identify their identity aspects, including their personal qualities and characteristics (i.e., their personal identity), and their membership of social groups (i.e., their social identity). In the second activity, the children were asked to imagine giving up some of their identity aspects that they previously indicated. Then they were encouraged to reflect on the feelings that this loss had created, and to compare their feelings with those that a migrant might experience, for example, in changing their name, abandoning their job, or leaving their family. In the third activity, the children were asked to imagine

which resources (as materials or personal traits) they would take with them that would help them on a long-trip and draw them as items of luggage. Then they discussed which resources a migrant might take on their migration that would help them in their new life.

7) The seventh lesson involved direct contact: young migrants (19-26 years old) were invited into the classrooms to share their histories and experiences with the children. During the meetings migrants showed their own YTT drawings and answered questions from the children's interviews. They then involved the whole class in some proposed activities from their own countries (e.g., stories, songs).
8) In the last lesson a paperwork with open questions was administered to verify changes in children's knowledge of the migratory phenomena and their satisfaction for the educational program.

To verify the effectiveness of the educational program on reducing pupils' implicit ethnic prejudice toward migrants, we conducted a study (Gabrielli *et al.* 2022). Participants were 77 fifth grade children from six primary school classrooms in Rome (34 females, 43 males). These children were assigned to two different conditions (groups): (i) the control group (n = 39; 15 females, 24 males); and (ii) the experimental group (n = 38; 19 females, 19 males). Only those who were assigned to the experimental group participated in the educational program, which lasted for a total of 20 h. Implicit prejudice was evaluated with the child version of the Implicit Association Test (Child-IAT) that was adapted to comply with the recommendations by Baron and Banaji (2006) and was designed by Pirchio *et al.* (2018).

Preliminary results show a statistically significant reduction in implicit prejudice in the experimental group [$F(1, 64) = 4.77$, $p = .03$, $\eta 2 = 0.07$] but not in the control group.

Pupils and teachers involved in the program showed great appreciation and interest, and schools' principals have asked to include other classes and continue next year (McCormack *et al.*, 2019). During the lessons, children expressed emotional engagement, non-verbally and verbally, and understood the migrants' condition.

## 5. Conclusion

As noted by Portera (Portera and Milani 2021), globalisation has caused "*the intensification of worldwide social relations which link distant localities in such a way that local happenings are shaped by events occurring many miles away and vice versa*" (Held 1991, 9). In this sense, societies are now multiethnic and multicultural (Bauman and Portera 2021), experiencing new relationships and interactions. There is an increasing debate to manage those changings (Grant 2017; Torres 2017; Habermas 1992; Held 1991) and the rising of ethnic, religious, linguistic and cultural diversity (United Nations 2015).

Schools can be ideal contexts to promote social inclusion and cohesion and to contrast the development of fear, stereotypes and prejudices. As seen referring to the hate speech development, stereotypes and prejudices are the basic level of the Hate Pyramid (ADL 2018). Interventions to reduce them can be considered as protective factors for the hate development.

Using drawings realized by migrants and refugees is regarded both as a medium to give them voice and recognize their experiences and as a medium to create a real contact between migrants and locals. In this perspective, migrants' drawings can promote knowledge of their real experiences, avoiding misconception and disinformation which can lead to fear.

## References

ADL (2018). *Pyramids of hate.* Available at https://www.adl.org/sites/default/files/documents/pyramid-of-hate.pdf (accessed 13 September 2024).

Allport, G.W. (1954). *The Nature of Prejudice.* Addison-Wesley, Cambridge, MA.

Arizpe, E., Colomer, T. and Martínez-Roldán, C. (2014). *Visual journeys through wordless narratives: An international inquiry with immigrant children and the arrival.* A&C Black, London.

Aronson, E. (1992). *The social animal.* W.H. Freeman, New York.

Baron, A.S. and Banaji, M.R. (2006). "The development of implicit attitudes: Evidence of race evaluations from ages 6 and 10 and adulthood". *Psychological Science*, 17, 53-58, https://doi.org/10.1111/j.14679280.2005.01664.x.

Batson, C.D., Chang, J., Orr, R. and Rowland, J. (2002). "Empathy, Attitudes, and Action: Can Feeling for a Member of a Stigmatized Group Motivate One to Help the Group?". *Personality and Social Psychology Bulletin*, 28(12), 1656-1666.

Bauman, Z., Mazzeo, R. and Portera, P. (2021). *Education and Intercultural Identity: A Dialogue between Zygmunt Bauman and Agostino Portera.* Routledge, Oxon-New York.

Beelmann, A. and Heinemann, K.S. (2014). "Preventing prejudice and improving intergroup attitudes: A meta-analysis of child and adolescent training programs". *Journal of Applied Developmental Psychology*, 31(1), 10-24. http://dx.doi.org/10.1016/j.appdev.2013.11.002.

Bigler, R.S. (1999). "The use of multicultural curricula and materials to counter racism in children". *Journal of Social Issues*, 55, 687-705. https://doi.org/10.1111/0022-4537.00142.

Bigler, R.S. and Liben, L.S. (2007). "Developmental intergroup theory: Explaining and reducing children's social stereotypes and prejudice". *Current Direction in Psychological Science*, 16(3), 162-166. https://doi.org/10.1111/j.1467-8721.2007.00496.x.

Birtel M.D., and Crisp R.J. (2012). ""Treating" prejudice: an exposure-therapy approach to reducing negative reactions toward stigmatized groups". *Psychological Science*, 23, 1379-1386.

Blee, K. (2004). "Positioning hate". *Journal of Hate Studies*, 3, 95-105.

Blumer, H. (1958). "Race prejudice as a sense of group position". *Pacific Sociological Review*, 1, 3-7.

Brooks, A.C. (2015). "The Thrill of Political Hating". *The New York Times*, 8 June 2015, available at http://www.nytimes.com/2015/06/08/opinion/the-thrill-of-political-hating.html?_r=0 (accessed 19 September 2024).

Catarci, M., Fiorucci, M., Giorda, M.C., Gervasio, G., Merluzzi, M. and Perucchini, P. (2023). "'Don't be afraid': preventing discrimination through intercultural education", in M.C. Fabbri (ed.). *Understanding Radicalization in Everyday Life*. McGraw-Hill Education, Milano, 59-77.

Cerquozzi, F. (2018). "Dall'odio all'hate speech. Conoscere l'odio e le sue trasformazioni per poi contrastarlo". *Tigor: rivista di scienze della comunicazione e di argomentazione giuridica*, X, 1, 42-53.

COE. (1997). *Recommendation n. 20 of the Committee of Ministers on Hate Speech*, available at https://rm.coe.int/1680505d5b (accessed19 September 2024).

Dovidio, J.F., Hewstone, M., Glick, P. and Esses, V.M. (eds.). (2010). *The SAGE handbook of prejudice, stereotyping and discrimination*. Sage,New Delhi.

ECRI – European Commission against Racism and Intolerance (2016). *General Policy Recommendation no. 15 on Combating Hate Speech*, available at https://rm.coe.int/ecri-general-policy-recommendation-no-15-on-combating-hate-speech/16808b5b01 (accessed 19 September 2024).

ECRI – European Commission against Racism and Intolerance (2021). *Statement of the European Commission against racism and intolerance on preventing and combating ultra-nationalistic and racist hate speech and violence in relation to confrontations and unresolved conflicts in Europe*, available at https://rm.coe.int/statement-of-ecri-on-preventing-and-combating-ultra-nationalistic-and-/1680a20d58 (accessed 19 September 2024).

ECRI – European Commission against Racism and Intolerance (2022). *An-*

*nual Report on the ECRI's activity. Covering the period from 1 January to 31 December 2021*, available at https://rm.coe.int/ecri-2021-annual-report-24052021-en/1680a6a6d3 (accessed 19 September 2024).

Espenshade, T. and Hempstead, K. (1996). "Contemporary American attitudes toward US immigration". *International Migration Review*, 30, 535-570.

Esses, V.M. (2021). "Prejudice and Discrimination Toward Immigrants". *Annual Review of Psychology*, 72, 503-31.

EU – European Union (2018). *Special Eurobarometer 469: Integration of immigrants in the European Union*, available at https://europa.eu/eurobarometer/surveys/de-tail/2169 (accessed 19 September 2024).

Faloppa, F. (2020). *#Odio: manuale di resistenza alla violenza delle parole.* Utet, Torino.

Furedi, F. (2007). *The only thing we have to fear is the 'culture of fear' itself*, available at http://www.spiked-online.com/index.php?/site/article/3053/ (accessed 19 September 2024).

Gabrielli, S., Catalano, M.G., Maricchiolo, F., Paolini, D. and Perucchini, P. (2022). "Reducing implicit prejudice towards migrants in fifth grade pupils: efficacy of a multi-faceted school-based program". *Social Psychology of Education*, 25, 425-440, 10.1007/s11218-022-09688-5.

Goldin, I., Cameron, G. and Balarajan, M. (2011). *Exceptional People: How Migration Shaped Our World and Will Define Our Future.* Princeton University Press, Princeton.

Grant, C.A. (2017). "Education in Urban Spaces: Neoliberal Rhetoric and Social Justices for the Global World", in A. Portera and C.A. Grant (eds.). *Intercultural Education and Competences. Challenges and Answers for the Global World* (pp. 85-114). Cambridge Scholars Publishing, Cambridge.

Habermas, J. (1992). "Cittadinanza politica e identità nazionale. Riflessioni sul futuro dell'Europa", in J. Habermas (ed.). *Morale, Diritto, Politica.* Einaudi, Torino, 113-146.

Hardin, R. (1995). *One for all: The logic of group conflict.* Princeton University Press, Princeton.

Held, D. (1991). "Democracy and Globalization". *Alternatives*, 16, 201-208. https://doi.org.10.1177/030437549101600205.

Jenness, V. and Grattet, R. (2001). *Making hate a crime: From social movement to law enforcement.* Russell Sage Foundation, New York.

Kuhn, M.H., and McPartland, T.S. (1954). "An empirical investigation of self-attitudes". *American Sociological Review*, 19, 68-76, https://doi.org/10.2307/2088175.

McCormack, B., Perucchini, P., Catalano, M.G. and Maricchiolo, F.

(2019). "Yesterday-Today-Tomorrow: An e-Learning Program on Migration. Connecting through Educational Technology". *Proceedings of the European Distance and E-Learning Network 2019 Annual Conference Bruges*, 16-19 June.

Olzak, S. (1992). *The dynamics of ethnic competition and conflict*. Stanford University Press, Stanford.

Paxton, P. and Mughan, A. (2006). "What's to Fear from Immigrants? Creating an Assimilationist Threat Scale". *Political Psychology*, 27, 4, 549-568.

Perry, B. and Scrivens, R. (2018). "A climate for hate? An exploration of the right-wing extremist landscape in Canada". *Critical Criminology*, 26, 169-187.

Pirchio, S., Passiatore, Y., Panno, A., Maricchiolo, F. and Carrus, G. (2018). "Chip off the old block: parents' subtle ethnic prejudice predicts children's implicit prejudice". *Frontiers of Psychology*, 9, 110, https://doi.org/10.3389/fpsyg.2018.00110.

Portera, A. and Milani, M. (2021). "Intercultural education and competences at school. Results of a exploratory study in Italy". *Profesorado. Revista de Currículum y Formación de Profesorado*, 25 (3), 49-67, DOI: 10.30827/profesorado.v25i3.21527.

Prati, F. and Rubini, M. (2015). Categorizzazioni, appartenenze sociali multiple e riduzione del pregiudizio intergruppi. *Psicologia sociale, Social Psychology Theory & Research*. 1/2015, pp. 13-34, doi: 10.1482/79435

Prosperi, A. (2021). *Tremare è umano. Una breve storia della paura*. Solferino, Milano.

Syed, J. and Ali, F. (2021). "A Pyramid of Hate Perspective on Religious Bias, Discrimination and Violence". *J Bus Ethics*, 172, 43-58, https://doi.org/10.1007/s10551-020-04505-5.

Tajfel, H. and Turner, J.C. (1979). "An integrative theory of intergroup conflict", in W.G. Austin and S. Worchel (eds.). *The social psychology of intergroup relations*. Brooks/Cole, Monterey, CA, 33-37.

Torres, C.A. (2017). *Theoretical and Empirical Foundations of Critical Global Citizenship*. Routledge, New York-Oxon. https://doi.org/10.4324/9781315452579.

Ulger, Z., Dette-Hagenmeyera, D.E., Reichle, B. and Gaertner, S.L. (2018). "Improving outgroup attitudes in schools: A meta-analytic review". *Journal of School Psychology*, 67, 88-103. https://doi.org/10.1016/j.jsp.2017.10.002.

UN – United Nations (2019). *United nations strategy and plan of action on Hate Speech*, available at https://www.un.org/en/genocideprevention/documents/UN%20Strategy%20and%20Plan%20of%20Action%20 on%20Hate%20Speech%2018%20June%20SYNOPSIS.pdf (accessed 19 September 2024).

UN – United Nations, Department of Economic and Social Affairs, Population Division (2015). *World Population Prospect: The 2015 revision. Key Findings and Advance Tables*, available at https://population.un.org/wpp/publications/files/key_findings_wpp_2015.pdf (accessed 19 September 2024).

UNHCR – United Nations High Commissioner for Refugees (2016). *With 1 human in every 113 affected, forced displacement hits record high*, available at https://www.unhcr.org/news/press/2016/6/5763ace54/1-human-113-affected-forced-displacement-hits-record-high.html (accessed 19 September 2024).

UNHCR – United Nations High Commissioner for Refugees (2023). *Global Trends Report 2022*, available at https://www.unhcr.org/global-trends-report-2022 (accessed 19 September 2024).

Vezzali, L., Stathi, S. and Giovannini, D. (2012). "Indirect contact through book reading: Improving adolescents' attitudes and behavioral intentions toward immigrants". *Psychology in the Schools*, 49, 148-162. https://doi.org/10.1002/pits.20621.

Zembylas, M. (2007). "The affective politics of hatred: implications for education". *Intercultural Education*, 18, 3, 177-192, 10.1080/14675980701463513.

Ziccardi, G. (2016). *L'odio online. Violenza verbale e ossessioni in rete*. Raffaello Cortina, Milano.

Chapter 9

# INTERCULTURAL EDUCATION: WHY IT IS NECESSARY, ITS CHARACTERISTICS AND ITS OBJECTIVES *

**Marco Catarci and Massimiliano Fiorucci**

ABSTRACT: *The chapter focuses on intercultural education as an approach aimed at promoting dialogue and cultural exchange between natives and foreigners. In particular, reasons, characteristics and aims of this approach are explored. In this perspective, diversity (cultural, gender, social class, etc.) becomes a relevant reference point in educational processes, providing an opportunity for everyone to develop from who they are.*



## 1. The reasons for an intercultural approach in education

"Why do we need an intercultural approach to education today?" In order to answer this first question we need to remember that issues concerning migration and the so-called multicultural society are now of central importance for the world of education and, as is increasingly evident, for society in general, for governments, for the media and for public opinion. These are complex topics which only too easily can be exploited in order to divide public opinion and to create easy consensus. Educationalists have the undeniable merit of having understood from the very start the central importance of these issues, taking on the role of interpreting these problems and formulating innovative and far-reaching visions and proposals to deal with them.

Pedagogy is once again faced with new challenges. Among these, one of the most pressing is building the conditions for dialogue between people coming from sometimes very different cultural and value systems, by formulating a proposal aimed in an opposite direction to that of the "clash of civilizations" (Huntington 1996). Constructing the conditions for positive

* Massimiliano Fiorucci is the author of paragraph 1. Marco Catarci is the author of paragraphs 2 and 3.

coexistence and dialogue is an educational issue that first of all has to come to terms with an extremely powerful toxic narrative which has been created and continued by the "entrepreneurs of fear" (Boeri 2019). By skilfully manipulating feelings of fear and insecurity, especially in a period of profound economic, social, cultural, and today also health, not to forget moral, crisis, the entrepreneurs of fear continue in that eternal process of "inventing the enemy" and the scapegoat (Eco 2012; Stella 2010), which is always useful for diverting public opinion from real problems and for steering election campaigns towards xenophobia and racism.

Among the many possible answers to the question "what is racism?", the reflections of Clelia Bartoli seem useful. As she sees it, racism is above all a social strategy that is often practised even by self-styled progressives and democrats in order to guarantee advantages for themselves in the competition for material and symbolic resources. Seeing yourself as a member of the "superior race" club would seem to grant the exercise of the right to pre-empt resources, privileges and prestige. In order to do this, while it may not always be necessary to use brute and blatant violence, it is never sufficient. What is needed is rather an order, a structure, a set of laws which both establish and legitimise the divide effectively, yet without drawing attention to themselves (Bartoli 2016, 125-126).

In other words, racism is a hierarchical system of power based on 'inferiorization', on a dehumanisation of the other, which is then legitimised by the institutionalisation of difference understood as inferiority. Language, urban structures which segregate, and indeed protection of citizenship based on the right of blood all contribute to this.

Étienne Balibar has dwelt particularly perceptively on the issue of citizenship: historically, the expression "democratic citizenship" can define only a recurring problem, a set of conflicts and contradictory definitions, an enigma without definitive solutions (Balibar 2015).

At the basis of the idea of exclusive citizenship, of the inferiorization of the other, there is clearly a vision and a model of representation of the other, a dominant paradigm that some scholars have identified very precisely. Palestinian intellectual Edward Said defines the Eurocentric approach as

> "*a collective notion identifying 'us', the Europeans as against all 'those' non-Europeans, and indeed it can be argued that the major component in European culture is precisely what made that culture hegemonic both in and outside Europe: the idea of European identity as a superior one in comparison with the non-European peoples and cultures. There is in addition the hegemony of European ideas about the Orient, themselves reiterating European superiority over Oriental backwardness, usually overrid-*

*ing the possibility that a more independent, or more sceptical, thinker might have had different views on the subject*" (Said 1979, 7).

The Algerian sociologist Abdelmalek Sayad has developed a radical critique of the ethnocentric perspective through which the issue of immigration is managed and studied: this perspective is usually from the point of view of the host society, without any investigation into the other fundamental component, namely that of emigration, i.e. the conditions of crisis that guide the departure of migrants.

> "*Power relations, precisely those which generated emigration-immigration, do not spare the science and, more particularly, the science of the migratory phenomenon*" (Sayad 2002, 163). "*Like two sides of the same coin, complementary aspects and supportive dimensions of the same phenomenon, emigration and immigration mutually imply one another*" and have implications of all kinds (Sayad 2002, 169).

His criticism focuses on the reductionist approach which is used to evaluate the "costs" and "benefits" of immigration, defined through the language of economics as "simple movement of labour force". Instead, there are ethical and political issues to be considered, including the fundamental responsibility of colonisation.

Reflection on immigration therefore refers to "state thought": thinking about immigration means thinking about the state. The state thinks about itself by thinking about immigration:

> "*because immigration represents the limit of the nation state, that limit which shows what the state intrinsically is, its fundamental truth. The state discriminates by its very nature, and thus equips itself in advance with all the appropriate criteria necessary to carry out discrimination, without which there is no national state*" (Sayad 2002, 368).

The way in which the State deals with immigration reveals its true colours and all those mechanisms/systems on which it is based. One of these is discrimination: the State recognises, and recognises itself in this, those who hold nationality. Viceversa, those who do not hold nationality represent the outer borders of the State, for which it has no responsibility. In this way, the State reaches a supposed homogeneity and preserves national order intact. It follows that immigration represents a threat which needs to be defended against.

In this respect the reflections of Tzvetan Todorov are particularly helpful, according to whom the "*fear of barbarians is what risks making us bar-*

*barian* (Todorov 2010, 6). The only way forward is that of seeking dialogue starting from what unites people and their needs regardless of their specific cultural backgrounds. The very definition of the barbarian presupposes a strong ethnocentrism that sees otherness as a threat and a form of inferiority. Barbarism consists in not recognizing the humanity of others, while civilization is precisely the ability to see others as others while at the same time admitting that they are human like us. Overcoming distrust linked to negative prejudice implies a cognitive effort, an intercultural mind and a hermeneutic attitude.

> "*In today's and tomorrow's world* – Todorov argues – *encounters between people and communities belonging to different cultures are destined to become more and more frequent; the participants alone can prevent them turning into conflicts*" (Todorov 2010, 11).

Since every human being belongs simultaneously to different cultures, the possibility of peaceful coexistence is beyond dispute. Nevertheless, this happens and continues to happen every time we move from the individual to the collective level, reifying cultures and interpreting cultural systems as monolithic, pure, static, impenetrable and unchangeable blocks. In reality, as Marco Aime clearly states, today more and more often when we say *culture*, we are thinking about *race* (Aime 2016, 43-67).

Todorov offers the tools necessary to deconstruct this erroneous interpretation and proposes a complex analysis of the current situation, by taking into consideration the notions of barbarism and civilization, reflecting on collective identities and European identity and making a well-reasoned critique of the simplifications proposed by Huntington and his followers. Huntington's theses have had a huge and far-reaching impact and have influenced certain political choices (think, for example, of the Bush doctrine in the field of international relations). The success of Huntington's views stems from the fact that his study offers a simple and simplistic explanation of the complexity of the international world. Basically, according to Huntington, the well-being of Westerners (North Americans and Western Europeans) is threatened, and he proposes a remedy for this threat.

> "*The survival of the West – says Huntington – depends on Americans re-affirming their Western identity and Westerners accepting their civilization as unique, not universal and uniting to renew and preserve it against challenges coming from non-Western societies*" (Huntington 1996, 20-21).

After the fall of the Berlin Wall, according to Huntington,

"*it is no longer ideological and political blocs that confront one another, but cultural areas, and groups of countries belonging to the same civilization. These groups, he says, are eight in number, and the civilizations are Chinese, Japanese, Hindu, Muslim, Orthodox, Western, Latin-American and, potentially, African. Their relations consist in rivalries that inevitably lead to a clash; the greatest danger for us Westerners, thus comes from other civilizations. Concretely, this threat is embodied above all by two particular civilizations – those of China and Islam*" (Todorov 2010, 88).

As may be seen even from a superficial and not very careful reading, the eight groups are identified according to inconsistent criteria: language, religion, geography. It is a simplistic and dangerous analysis, but functional to an aggressive and imperialist policy. All civilizations, all cultural systems, all people are in constant change and transformation, they never remain the same, and each individual is the bearer of multiple cultures. On the contrary Huntington

"*writes as if it were possible to identify, once and for all, the hard core, or essence, of every civilization – the thing which it must, as a matter of sacred duty, never betray; the same number of civilizations has been maintained right from the start. However, even a rapid glance at world history reveals that this is far from the case: Western culture – supposing that such a generalization has any meaning – was profoundly transformed between year zero, year 1000, and year 2000. As is also well known, the representation that it chooses to give of itself is the result of bitter conflicts between influential groups and of compromises that change from one generation to another*". (Todorov 2010, 88).

From the perspective of intercultural dialogue, Todorov's considerations on the theme of identity appear to be particularly useful. In fact, according to Todorov, each of us has not one but numerous cultural identities that overlap and intersect. Each individual is inherently pluricultural.

"*Individual identity stems from the encounter of multiple collective identities within one and the same person; each of our various affiliations contributes to the formation of the unique creature that we are*". (Todorov 2010, 54).

Each of us continually redefines the balance of their different affiliations. Individual identity is the result of the intersection of different collective identities in the same way that there are no pure cultures on the one hand and mixed cultures on the other: "*all cultures are mixed ('hybrid', 'crossbred'). Contacts between human groups go back to the origins of the species and they always leave traces.*". (Todorov, 2010 54-55). Defining, accepting and insisting on identity – as Francesco Remotti argues – is dangerous and leads to what he has defined as "identity obsession": therefore, *identity* is a *poisonous* word, because "*it promises what is not there*" (Remotti 2010, XI-XII).

Identity therefore is division and separates 'us' from 'others', nipping in the bud any possible relationships of similarity. Prior to any division, however, the so-called others are similar to us and, as Remotti states, after every division the similarities burst into new growth due to the strength of their unexepected resilience (Remotti 2019).

The danger consists in considering identity as substance, a sort of stable and permanent core that needs to be defended to prevent it from being modified and, consequently, infected. If identity is essence or substance, then it must be defended and affirmed in its integrity and purity and this will inevitably lead to clashes and wars in the name of something that does not actually exist but which is interpreted as real. Identities can therefore become dangerous, bloody and deadly, just as the reification of diversity can become dangerous: diversity is not an objective property that is inherent in itself to the structure of a certain culture, but it is a perceived quality of a relative and interactive nature. It is not an entity but a relationship (Anolli 2006, 20).

The reduction of multiple identities to a single identity is one of the conditions that determine the outbreak of violence (Sen 2008).

Before I kill my neighbor because he is a Tutsi, I need to forget all his other kinds of belonging: to a profession, an age, an environment, a country – or to humanity. Violence carried out in the name of identity is no less violent because the groups that practice it consider themselves, rightly or wrongly, to be the victims of other groups, threatened in their very existence, or in that of their nearest and dearest (Todorov 2010, 65).

What we need to do then within the educational system is to redefine the very paradigms of education, encouraging a critical reflection on the idea of cultural identity, on our multiple affiliations, on the problematic nature of national cultures and national histories, on the dangers inherent in the invention of traditions.

> "*'Traditions' which appear or claim to be old are often quite recent in origin and sometimes invented*". (Hobsbawm and Ranger 1983; 2012, 1).

Unlike "custom", that is old-established but still living, "invented traditions" are those sets of practices which are intended to instil, by repetition, certain values and norms of behaviour which consequently imply continuity with the past. Every society has accumulated a stock of seemingly ancient material: used to reinforce national ties, to more precisely recognise the identity of parties or classes, or to dilute that sense of insecurity which comes when faced with a future full of radical change and innovation. This kind of social and cultural engineering has in general characterised the formation of modern nations, which have sought to legitimise their most recent "history" by looking for roots in the past (Hobsbawm and Ranger 1983; 2012, 1-13).

Pure cultures and identities, therefore, do not exist and never remain the same, they are an invention. Another characteristic of cultures, in fact, is that they are in constant transformation, they change continuously, more or less rapidly, and for many reasons. Since each culture incorporates others or intersects with others, the different elements of a culture form what Todorov terms "an unstable equilibrium" (Todorov 2010, 55). Alongside the internal tension, there are contacts with the outside world (with close and distant cultures) which

> "*in turn lead to new changes in direction. Before it influenced other cultures in the world, European culture had already absorbed Egyptian, Mesopotamian, Persian, Indian, Islamic and Chinese influences*". (Todorov 2010, 56).

Cultures therefore have two characteristics that cannot be overlooked: *plurality* and *variability*. However, the unstable identity of cultures should not lead us to completely give up the notion of culture. We can recognize

> "*the necessity of talking about cultures without falling into the misperceptions of 'culturalism', or the deduction of all of an individual's characteristics, from his or her cultural belonging, in the way that racism proceeded in the past*". (Todorov 2010, 56).

However, it should not be forgotten that culture is a construct, since it is based on the collective memory of the group that bears it and memory is in itself a construct, i.e. the selection of past events and their hierarchization according to an order assigned by the group members themselves. Each human community – through the action of certain power groups – selects some events and leaves others out: both memory and oblivion are constitutive elements of identity.

Human beings are always born within a cultural system but this does not mean that they are destined to remain prisoners of it. Cultures exist but they are neither immutable nor impermeable and it is not legitimate to chain individuals to their group and culture of origin, denying them the capacity for autonomy, one of the principle characteristics of the human being. In fact each individual continuously redefines their relationship with their culture of origin in a new way by virtue of education (formal, non-formal and informal), the environment (natural, historical and social), and individual characteristics. Some external conditions can, however, positively or negatively modify the relationship of individuals with their cultural system of origin.

Therefore the issue of coexistence both at the local level (in multicultural societies) and at the global level requires a strong educational commitment that rests firmly on dialogue. However, in order to go beyond pure rhetoric, some clarifications are necessary. Intercultural relations have some basic requirements which can perhaps be better defined as conditions of possibility. To be defined as such, dialogue must take the form of a relationship between "equals", or rather it must be a relationship between subjects who are able to have their subjectivity, their needs, their interests and their rights recognised. However, as already mentioned, very often minorities (especially immigrants) live in a situation that has been defined as "*subordinate inclusion*" (Cotesta 1992) or "*subordinate integration*" (Ambrosini 2001) which results in an effective condition of "relative citizenship". Therefore, there is a radical asymmetry of power between natives and migrants that precludes the very possibility of an authentic dialogue. To be truly effective, dialogue

> "*must satisfy a twofold requirement. On the one hand, it must recognize the difference of voices engaged in the exchange, and must not presuppose that one of them constitutes the norm [...] If you are not ready to question your own certainties [...] dialogue cannot take place*" (Todorov 2010, 196).

Dialogue is destined to fail unless those who participate in it accept a shared common framework for their discussion, and agree on permitted topics and on the possibility of seeking justice and truth together.

Relationships between individuals, like relationships between groups, can develop on an equal footing through an attitude of "dialogic understanding", without one of the two sides having necessarily to prevail. What is needed is a dialogue in which neither of the two sides has the last word, in which neither side reduces the other to the role of an object. Dialogue makes it possible to reread one's own culture by deconstructing it in the light of what is gathered from the voice of the other (Todorov 1984).

Therefore coexistence is neither easy nor assured and requires a strong pedagogical and political commitment, as Alexander Langer had already understood in the 1990s (Riccardi, 2016). Coexistence is a difficult art that must be practised daily and constantly in order to become the norm and no longer the exception. Langer dedicated his famous 'Attempt at the Decalogue for inter-ethnic coexistence' to these issues (Langer 2011, 365-375).

In order to make possible the move from a condition of conflict to one of inter-ethnic coexistence, courageous people are needed, who are capable of voluntarily placing themselves on the border between affiliations and ready to promote mutual knowledge, dialogue and cooperation, committed to fostering awareness and mediation between different groups. These are the kind of people who Langer defined as "traitors to ethnic solidity", that is, people who engage in the exploration and transcending of borders and who are able to be critical even towards their own reference group. However they must never become displaced people, that is, they must maintain credibility with their own community. Langer sees in these "traitors of ethnic solidity" the first tool of coexistence. To some extent

> "*we are all traitors to our original identities. And the gesture of breaking away from a belonging that becomes a cage often turns out to be a necessity, it is sometimes a risky but noble choice*" (Lerner 2007, 184, my translation).

## 2. The characteristics of intercultural education

"What then exactly is intercultural education?" We can offer a first, although by no means complete, definition by saying that it consists of an *intentional political project* to be carried out by means of educating towards dialogue and cultural exchange, directed towards everyone, the native subjects of the hosting society just as much as the foreign subjects. In this way, forms of diversity (cultural, gender, social, biographical, etc.) can become the privileged point of view for educational processes, giving everyone the opportunity to develop according to what they actually are (Barn 2012; Fiorucci 2008; Gundara 2000; Pinto Minerva 2007; Portera 2006; Santerini 2010; Zoletto 2007).

Intercultural education requires an intentional political project:

a) *An educational project*, in that it requires that a society make an active investment towards encouraging relations between subjects coming from different cultures based on the "interactionist" model. This means that there is a commitment which involves many different areas of the subjects' lives: social, economic, political, as well as cultural. This project would make it possible and practical for everyone to define and realise their own individual projects, with the same possibilities in education, work and citizenship. In this sense, intercultural education requires a basic connection with the striving towards a perspective of social justice, that is, an outlook aimed at significantly affecting conditions of disadvantage in order to guarantee not only equal educational opportunities, but also equity and educational success for foreign students, as an essential criterion for evaluating the effectiveness of the educational system at all levels.

b) *A political project*, in that it looks to the future, linked to an idea of a society yet to be constructed. Discussing education always means working out a project to follow at the level of the community and of the men and women who will inhabit it. It is not possible to talk about intercultural education without first asking the fundamental question regarding what type of society we want to create by means of this kind of education. In this respect, as has been stated, the intercultural dimension is linked to a co-existence based firmly on indispensable principles such as democracy, pluralism and social justice. This represents the fundamental starting point, since in a sort of 'mirroring', the migrant reflects a representation of the society into which they have been integrated and thereby draws attention to its structural weaknesses, incoherence and dangers, as well as the failure to translate formal recognition of rights into a practical exercise of rights. The vast breadth of the problems posed by intercultural education may be seen, for example, when discussion on issues linked to immigration inevitably leads to dealing with the question of exactly what kind of Europe we want to construct. This may be seen by recent events in the 'Refugee Crisis' which developed in Europe, beginning in 2015. This crisis was certainly not caused by the number of refugees arriving in Europe, which is far less than the number of refugees moving from place to place in the South of the world. It should be remembered that the most industrialised countries receive only a fifth of the world total of people forced to flee from their home countries, while the greatest movement of forced migrants is from one country of the South of the world to another country of the South of the world, usually adjacent to the migrants' country of origin (UNHCR 2022). If it is indeed legitimate to talk about a 'crisis', then it should be done so in the context of the disappearance/clouding/loss of the project of Europe as the 'cradle' of human rights, a proposal which ran to ground in the light of episodes of resistance and refusal to accept immigrants, blocks and even violence towards people arriving in Europe, fleeing from war and persecution (precisely those people who according to international treaties should be protected). Today, the presence in Europe of people who did not actually choose to come here – as, for example, in the case of people who are simply fleeing – has the effect of "upending" the question of social integration, which is usually considered as uniquely one-way in the view of assimilation, as the simple integration of migrants. It may be seen as a touchstone to understand fully the quality of our democracy, and in particular, the response we are able to offer when confronted with those global processes which, by causing social dissolution, disruption and the impoverishment of huge areas of the world, give rise to the flight of millions of people. The presence of forced migrants in our societies is thus an "ethical" presence which points the finger above all at societies in the industrialised world and their responsibilities for the origin of many of the processes which cause the flight of refugees.

c) *Intentional*, because it will be brought about by precise choices and the outcome of a specific process of project and vision, of a critical reflection, of study, not certainly by mere chance. This approach therefore brings with it a commitment to bring about to take on consciously and continuously, in both formal educational contexts (school, university, etc.) and non-formal educational contexts (associations, social organisations, etc.), with a long-lasting perspective which involves not just people of immigrant origin (young migrants) and their families), but the whole population (all young people, schools and the whole of society), tailored to the various age groups, in a vision of permanent education. The question of intercultural education must be faced in terms of an educational commitment directed towards all levels of school and all pupils and students, towards all aspects of society and towards all members of society.

From this point of view, it can be stated that education is in itself intercultural. In fact, the adjective 'intercultural' used in the above consideration could be omitted without affecting the argument and the simple term 'education' could be used. In other words, education is intercultural, or else it is not true education.

## 3. The objectives of intercultural education

"What are the objectives of intercultural education?" To answer this question, it must be remembered that discussions on intercultural education very often have to take into consideration difficult areas of life as well as life and work situations which present people with problems and contradictions. The root for a potential intercultural framework for education fundamentally rests on the problem of protecting the dignity and the self-respect of human beings.

For this reason, putting aside any rhetoric, we need to recognise that an immigrant is regarded as such by society essentially because they are 'poor', that is, because they are disadvantaged in terms of opportunities, be they social, economic, cultural or political. A 'rich' foreigner is never considered to be an 'immigrant', and often arouses merely cultural curiosity. An immigrant however is 'poor' and arouses no curiosity whatsoever.

It is indeed the condition of socio-economic difficulty, stemming from migration, which produces disadvantages. It is certainly not a cultural difference which produces disadvantages. This point is important because an immigrant is a vulnerable subject not because of their displacement, but rather he or she becomes vulnerable as a result of contact with the context in which he or she attempts to integrate. In other words, it is precisely the environment of integration which makes an immigrant socially weak.

In this respect, Hans Magnus Enzenberger has illustrated the need for a critique of the processes of integration which do nothing more than reproduce the dynamics of social subordination. As he says: "*Foreigners are the more foreign, the poorer they are*" (Enzenberger 1992, 26, my translation).

Racism plays an important part in the apparatus which generates subordination. In its most extreme mode, that is, "systemic-institutional" racism, racism acts fundamentally as a form of discrimination, which is not rooted so much in individuals or in groups, but rather in processes at the very roots of the way society functions, which lead to situations of inequality and disadvantage (Basso 2010; Ben Jelloun 1998; Wieviorka 2000).

Then, the objectives of intercultural education are precisely to have a far-reaching and incisive effect on the educational, cultural, social, economic and political spheres which, through their processes of social differentiation, transform the migrant into a vulnerable subject. Among the various forms of differentiation, the formal and non-formal processes of education play a crucial and determining role.

## References

Aime, M. (2016). *Una bella differenza. Alla scoperta della diversità del mondo*. Einaudi, Torino.

Ambrosini, M. (2001). *La fatica d'integrarsi. Immigrati e lavoro in Italia*. Il Mulino, Bologna.

Anolli, L. (2006). *La mente multiculturale*. Laterza, Roma-Bari.

Balibar, E. (2015). *Citizenship*, translated by T. Scott-Railton. Polity, Cambridge. Originally published in Italian (2012) as *Cittadinanza*. Bollati Boringhieri, Torino.

Barn, R. (2012). "Interculturalism in Europe: Fact, Fad or Fiction – the deconstruction of a theoretical idea", in M. Farrar *et al.*, *Debating Multiculturalism 1*. Dialogue Society, London.

Bartoli, C. (2016). "Concentrare, segregare e assistere. Così il razzismo diventa Sistema", in M. Aime (eds.). *Contro il razzismo. Quattro ragionamenti.* Einaudi, Torino.

Basso, P. (ed.) (2010). *Razzismo di stato. Stati Uniti, Europa, Italia*. Franco Angeli, Milano.

Basso, P. and Perrocco, F. (eds.) (2003). *Gli immigrati in Europa. Diseguaglianze, razzismo, lotte*. Franco Angeli, Milano.

Ben Jelloun, T. (1999). *French Hospitality: Racism and North African Immigrants*. Columbia University Press, New York.

Bevilacqua, P. *et.al.* (eds.) (2001). *Storia dell'emigrazione italiana.* Vol. I, *Partenze*. Donzelli, Roma.

Bevilacqua P *et al.* (eds.) (2002). *Storia dell'emigrazione italiana.* Vol. II, *Arrivi*. Donzelli, Roma.

Boeri, T. (2019). "Gli imprenditori della paura". *lavoce.info*, 4 June, available at https://www.lavoce.info/archives/59482/gli-imprenditori-della-paura/.

Campani, G. (2008). *Dalle minoranze agli immigrati. La questione del pluralismo culturale e religioso in Italia*. Unicopli, Milano.

Cotesta, V. (1992). *La cittadella assediata. Immigrazione e conflitti etnici in Italia*. Editori Riuniti, Roma.

Covato, C. (2014). "Milani Lorenzo", in G. Chiosso and R. Sani (eds.). *Dizionario bibliografico dei pedagogisti e degli educatori 1800-2000*. Editrice Bibliografica, Milano.

Eco, U. (2012). *Inventing the Enemy*, translated by R. Dixon. Houghton Mifflin Harcourt, Boston.

Enzensberger, H.M. (1992). *Die grosse Wanderung*. Suhrkamp, Frankfurt.

Fiorucci, M. (eds.) (2008). *Una scuola per tutti. Idee e proposte per una didattica interculturale delle discipline*. Franco Angeli, Milano.

Freire, P. (1971). *La pedagogia degli oppressi*. Mondadori, Milano.

Freire, P. (2008). *Pedagogia della speranza. Un nuovo approccio alla Pedagogia degli oppressi*. EGA, Torino.

Ginsborg, P. (2003). *A History of Contemporary Italy: Society and Politics, 1943-1988*. Palgrave Macmillan, Basingstoke.

Goody, J. (2007). *The Theft of History*. CUP, Cambridge.

Gundara, J. (2000). *Interculturalism, Education and Inclusion*. Paul Chapman, London.

Hobsbawm, E. and Ranger, T. (eds.) (1983; 2012). *The Invention of Tradition*. CUP, Cambridge.

Huntington, S.P. (1996). *The Clash of Civilizations and the Remaking of the World Order*. Simon & Schuster, New York.

Langer, A. (1994), *Tentativo di decalogo per la convivenza inter-etnica*, available at http://www.alexanderlanger.org/it/32/104 (accessed 17 April 2024).

Lerner, G. (2007). *Tu sei un Bastardo*. Feltrinelli, Milano.

Levi, F. (2007). *In viaggio con Alex*. Feltrinelli, Milano.

Lorenzoni, F. (2015). *I sogni senza limiti di Alexander Langer*, available at https://www.internazionale.it/opinione/franco-lorenzoni-2/2015/07/02/alexander-langer (accessed 17 April 2024).

McIntosh, P. (1998). "White privilege and male privilege: A personal account of coming to see correspondences through work in women's studies", in M. Andersen and P.H. Collins (eds.). *Race, class, and gender. An anthology*. Wadsworth Publishing, Belmont.

MIUR Ministero dell'Istruzione, dell'Università e della Ricerca (2014). *Linee guida per l'accoglienza e l'integrazione degli alunni stranieri*, Roma.

MIUR Ministero dell'Istruzione, dell'Università e della Ricerca (2015). *Diversi da chi? Raccomandazioni per l'integrazione degli alunni stranieri e per l'intercultura*. Roma.

MPI Ministero della Pubblica Istruzione, Osservatorio nazionale per l'integrazione degli alunni stranieri e per l'educazione interculturale (2007). *La via italiana per la scuola interculturale e l'integrazione degli alunni stranieri*. Roma.

Pinto, Minerva F. (2007). *L'intercultura*. Laterza, Roma-Bari.

Portera, A. (2006), *Globalizzazione e pedagogia interculturale. Interventi nella scuola*. Centro Studi Erickson, Trento.

Remotti, F. (2010). *L'ossessione identitaria*. Laterza, Roma-Bari.

Remotti, F. (2019). *Somiglianze. Una via per la convivenza*. Laterza, Roma-Bari.

Riccardi, V. (2016). *Costruire la cultura della convivenza. Alexander Langer educatore*. Franco Angeli, Milano.

Said, E. (1979). *Orientalism*. Vintage, New York.

Santerini, M. (2010). *La qualità della scuola interculturale. Nuovi modelli per l'integrazione*. Centro Studi Erickson, Trento.

Sayad, A. (2002). *La doppia assenza*. Raffaello Cortina, Milano.

Scuola di Barbiana (1967). *Lettera a una professoressa*. Libreria Editrice Fiorentina, Firenze

Sen, A. (2007). *Identity and Violence: The Illusion of Destiny*. Penguin, London.

Sofocle. (2006). *Edipo re – Edipo a Colono – Antigone*. Oscar Mondadori, Milano.

Stella, G.A. (2010). *Negri, froci, giudei & co. L'eterna guerra contro l'altro.* Rizzoli, Milano.
Susi, F. (1998). *L'educazione interculturale fra teoria e prassi.* Università degli Studi Roma Tre, Roma.
Todorov, T. (1984). *The Conquest of America: The Question of the Other.* Harper & Row, New York.
Todorov, T. (2010). *The Fear of Barbarians: Beyond the Clash of Civilizations.* Polity, Cambridge.
Toso, F. (2011). "Minoranze linguistiche". *Enciclopedia dell'Italiano Treccani*, available at http://www.treccani.it/enciclopedia/minoranze-linguistiche_(Enciclopedia_dell'Italiano)/ (accessed 17 April 2024).
UNHCR (2022). *Global Trends: Forced Displacement in 2021.* Geneva.
Wieviorka, M. (1998). *Le Racisme – une introduction.* La Découverte, Paris.
Zoletto, D. (2007). *Straniero in classe. Una pedagogia dell'ospitalità.* Raffaello Cortina Editore, Milano.

# Chapter 10
## *SHOUT OUT/SHUT UP!*

**Isabella De Paolis, Gennaro Gervasio and Maria Chiara Giorda** *

ABSTRACT: *The academic and public debate on stereotypical representations of Islam, on Islamophobia or 'fear of Islam' has been growing internationally in the last couple of decades.*
*Much less attention has been devoted, so far, to ways Muslims act and re-act to these representations, do create their own representations.*
*The case of Italy is rather peculiar both in terms of lateness in the debate on representations of Islam and Muslims as well as in the still scarce interest in listening to and engaging with Muslims' multiple voices and representations, despite a few recent contributions. They are often called and socially recognized as a minority, while they are not even juridically recognised by the State. In this chapter, we will be focusing on the self-representations and the fears emerging from within the Muslim communities in Italy today. We will rely on a corpus of primary sources made of interviews realised within the activities of PriMED project (www.primed_miur.it) – of which we were part – together with structured interviews with a sample of Italian Muslim leaders and young Muslim people.*

SUMMARY: 1. Studying, researching and framing Islamophobia. – 2. Italian Muslims speak out. – 3. The World Café gives the floor to Muslims. – 4. Conclusions. – References.

The academic and public debate on stereotypical representations of Islam and on Islamophobia has been growing internationally in the last couple of decades. Much less attention has been devoted, so far, to ways Muslims act and *re-act* to these representations, do create their own representations and self-representations.

The case of Italy is rather peculiar both in terms of delay in the debate on representations as well as in the still scarce interest in listening to and

* Our gratitude and a special thank is extended to the professors Antonio Angelucci and Alessandro Ferrari (University of Insubria), Laura Sabrina Martucci (University of Bari), Roberta Ricucci (University of Turin), Annita Larissa Sciacovelli (University of Bari) who took part in the scientific committee of the PriMED project and read this contribution. This chapter is the the result of the collaboration between the three authors, however the first paragraph is attributed to Gennaro Gervasio the second to Isabella De Paolis and the third to Maria Chiara Giorda.

engaging with Muslims' multiple voices and representations, despite a few recent contributions.

In this chapter, we will be focusing on the Italian debate on representations of Islam and fears, unpacking the cultural and political positions through the results of some recent European and Italian researches (first section) in order to understand if there is a solution of continuity or not between the orientalisms put into light from the first historical observations and today's forms of mystification and representation on Islam.

Even if few researches have been dedicated to the self-representations and the fears arising from within the Muslim communities in Italy today, some bottom-up ideas and representations have emerged from our interviews to Italian teachers and policemen and women realized within the activities of PriMED project (Prevention and interaction in the Mediterranean Sea, www.primed_miur.it) that Gennaro Gervasio and Maria Chiara Giorda coordinated at Roma Tre with Paola Perucchini (second section).

The third section is based on an original collection of bottom-up and insider perspectives, thanks to the participation in the experience of *s* in 2022 of more than a hundred Muslim young persons in Turin and Bari, discussing issues that affect the cultural, social and political life of a group of stakeholders.

## 1. Studying, researching and framing Islamophobia

Research into Islamophobia and the public debate on historical and current stereotypical representations of Islam have recently become an interesting topic within academic studies.

A successful academic project on religious stereotypes and consequent prejudices cofounded by the Erasmus+ Programme of the European Union called SORAPS [1] reflected the increasing religious-historical significance of Islamophobia.

The SORAPS report pointed out the spread both in the public sphere, and also in some cultural, pedagogical and intellectual circles of the negative and reductionist interpretations of Islam, making it a violent religion tout court, practised by radical and fanatical people. On the other hand, the view that violent Islamists are the true and genuine expression of Islam

[1] https://soraps.unive.it/files/2019/04/PROFREAD-IO1-Stereotypes-and-prejudices Guidelines_V4-05_01_19-2.pdf (accessed 20 September 2024). The SORAPS project was the continuation of an earlier project called "Intercultural Education through Religious Studies" (IERS 539803-LLP-1-2013-1-EN-COMENIUS-CMP) and implemented by the same European Consortium.

is likewise the result of a monolithic reading of the practices and beliefs of a religion that must, like all, be contextualised and interpreted in light of its many expressions (SORAPS 2018, 9).Therefore, the SORAPS project can be seen as a pedagogical model, which includes an analytical part related to the negative aspects anchored in the vulgate about Islam, but also provides a lexical and conceptual framework based on notions and terms that overturn this view, with the aim of promoting mutual understanding, improving integration and addressing radicalization.

The outputs of this project were Digital modules and ICT applications to be used in the classroom by teachers to foster intercultural understanding of different religions. Hereinafter, we report some examples of impressive statements taken from interviews, bibliography, textbooks and school tools collected during the project (SORAPS 2018, 62).:

- "Muslims do not act upon their own free will, but solely on their fear for the consequences in this life and on Judgement Day. They submit themselves like slaves".
- "The terms 'Islam' and 'Muslim' are translated into 'submission' and 'one who is submitting him/herself (to Allah)".
- "Allah is like an Oriental despot, who threatens and punishes the submitted worshippers".
- "Jihad is 'holy war' directed and fought against infidels, non-Muslims, Westerners and Muslims who have been deemed inadequate".
- "Sharia is 'the divine law of Allah' – a well-defined body of articles, stating the precise rules and regulations regarding punishment for violations of the law".
- "Islam is 'a religion of law' (over against Christianity – the religion of love, free will and faith)".
- "Islam is a political ideology".
- "Muslims strive for an Islamic system covering the whole world. This system is totalitarian by nature and in direct opposition to democracy".
- "Islam is a religion of extremism, radicalism, fundamentalism and terrorism".
- "Islam is an old-fashioned religion".
- "Real Muslims are narrow-minded fanatics, jihadists and terrorists".
- "Islam is a male-dominated religion, and the veil expresses the oppression of women".
- Muslim women are all 'under the thumb' of the Muslim macho man
- "Muslims are Arabs".
- "Islam and Muslims are intolerant".
- "Islam is a monolith – static, with no internal differences, and discussions. They have no tolerance in regard to a plurality of truths".

- "Islam constitutes a culture on its own, isolated from other cultures, and with no interest in any intercultural communication".
- "Islam and the West are by nature direct opposites".
- "Islam and Muslims constitute the significant 'other' over against 'us'".
- "Islam and Muslims are barbaric, irrational, sexist and primitive (Westerners are civilised, progressive, etc.)".
- "Islam is by nature violent and belligerent. It has been so ever since its beginning and spread, and it is so in today's world too, where it is 'at war' with everything Western.

What emerges is clearly the spread of a reassuringly monolithic and essentialist vision of Islam which is strictly related to a popular stratified misconception about a fragmented ideological, religious and political view of the overall Muslim culture. As a consequence of that, a wrong dual polarisation is often associated with Islam, thus evoking a widespread negative representation of gender relations (man/woman), conflict management (war/peace), openness to modernity (tradition/innovation).

The case of Italy is rather peculiar in terms of delay in the debate on representations of Islam and Muslims in general (Giorda and Giorgi 2018; Bombardieri, Giorda and Hejazi 2019) as well as in the analysis of the issue of Islamophobia (Proglio 2020) and its prevention. It is certainly due to the latest historical background and the lack of terrorist attacks in Italy, unlike what happened in the USA or in other European countries. However, recently the written debate has become intriguing and stimulating, in particular on the web. In his edited book, Proglio has collected some noteworthy contributions which offer an authentic depiction of the Italian scenario through a multiple analysis, from the anthropological side to the sociological one, from the economic point of view to the media one focusing, in particular, on the migration issue within the securitisation narrative.

In a recent contribution, Alessandra Vitullo (2023, 203) has described Islamophobia "*as the unfounded hostility toward Islam and the resulting discriminatory practices that disadvantage Muslim individuals and communities*". Vitullo's references are some classic studies on the topic (Allen 2010; Poole and Richardson 2006; Bakali 2016, Beydoun 2018): these studies depict the role of the media, the position of Muslims in the public space, and investigate whether and how Islamophobia can be read as a continuation of historical anti-Muslimism or anti-Islamism, a completely contemporary concept. With a focus on the United States, the topic of Islamophobia is considered mainly from a local or global perspective (Taguieff 1994; 1999; Halliday 1999; Trust 1997; Gallup 2016; Waldron 2012; Bleich 2012; Tibi 2010).

Yet, as a number of scholars, including Richardson (2009) and Bunzl (2005), have shown recently, the concept of "phobia" is inappropriate because it refers to a phenomenon that is not an irrational, spontaneous, individual fear, but is a collective, iterated and perpetrated emotion with the often conscious purpose of pursuing discriminatory behaviours.

Actually, fear of Islam is widely diffused in the western societies and Islamophobia is recognizable at an institutional level, in the media and in everyday life.

As it was reported recently in a collective article about the fear of diversity, in the SETA Foundation's report *Islamophobia in Italia. Rapporto nazionale 2018*,[2] we read:

> "*the xenophobic and anti-Islam climate fuelled by the political actors of the traditional right, Lega Nord and Fratelli d'Italia, by far-right movements (Casa Pound and Forza Nuova) and by the more conservative sectors of the mass media, such as Il Giornale, has had very negative effects at a social level, legitimising racist behaviour. Physical and verbal aggression against migrants, asylum seekers, refugees, and Muslim citizens has increased both in the North and in the South, culminating in dramatic events*" (Catarci *et al.* 2023, 67).

In the same article it is remembered how these words have been confirmed by the fact that Italy ranks last in the survey of European countries on the familiarity of accepting a Muslim in the family or as a neighbour (Catarci *et al.* 2023, 67).

In her chapter in this volume, Alberta Giorgi (87-106) focuses on the narrative of the "demographic threat" as it relates to different groups, so-called minority groups, which are treated as "other" in a dynamic of simplification and stereotyping: dimensions of gender, religion, linguistic and ethnic affiliation that assembled in a fixed way produce discriminated enclaves. Through the data of Amnesty's Hate Barometer 2021, Vox's Maps of Hate – Italian Observatory on Rights, Against Hate – BIT 2021, Giorgi recalls how hate speech, Islamophobia and suspicion and hatred against immigrants and LGBT+ people are constantly increasing: according to certain political narratives, Italy as well as Europe are white and Christian and the risk of 'replacement' based on the demographic threat is the most widespread reason for the fear and resulting hatred (*ivi*). The population is at risk of demographic upheaval.

---

[2] Aletti, A. and Padovan, D. (2020). *Islamophobia in Italia. Rapporto nazionale 2018.* Seta, Istanbul: https://setav.org/en/assets/uploads/2020/04/R156It.pdf (accessed 20 September 2024).

## 2. Italian Muslims speak out

One of the most intriguing yet most contested issues in the debate on Islamophobia in Italy has to do with the 'authentic' voice of the Muslims: whereas some of them avoid a direct involvement in interviews or informal conversations, others show the need to share their experiences. As much of the discussion of the current literature is focused on the theme of immigration or on the generation gap between first and second generation Muslims, Our interest is to bring to light the inner thoughts and emotions aroused by Islamophobic attitudes, from first hand testimony of Islamic people living in Italy.

In 2021 we had the opportunity to gather testimonies among Muslims and collect authentic, informal narratives concerning Muslims during the two Academic Advanced Training Courses *The trans-mediterranean space and Islam: integration in the public sphere* dedicated to public sector employees (municipality offices, policemen and policewomen, nursing field) and *The trans-mediterranean space and Islam: integration in the scholastic public sphere* for teachers and school headmasters[3] organised within the PriMED project (Prevention and interaction in the Mediterranean Sea).

Before making our point and discussing our project's outcomes, there are some initial considerations central to our path that represent a *fil rouge* of our narrative.

Unlike other European countries, Italy has experienced a surge in Muslim immigration over the past several years as a result of the migration from the Mediterranean Sea (Africa and the Middle-East/West Asia), even though there was already a significant presence – but highly fragmented – of Muslims in the country beforehand.

First, recently the number of projects dealing with Islamophobia has increased a lot in Italy and, at the same time, they have spread around the web through dissemination actions, thus showing a great concern for the issue. Islamophobia has promoted a multidimensional analysis within the public sphere which enhanced the promotion of educational action plans in order to foster social integration and to prevent radicalisation. The redefinition and reshaping of the urban space due to the interactions of global discourses as migration, secular experiences, new spiritual movements and super-diversity have fostered social sciences scholars (Bombardieri,

[3] Due to the Covid-19 pandemic, the courses have been held online. The Moodle platform enabled teachers and tutors to customise the audience learning experience thus creating a stimulating educational environment. The participants had the opportunity to acquire knowledge about the Muslim community in Italy from an historical, legal, sociological and anthropological perspective and, at the same time, have engaged in a respectful intercultural exchange of views.

Giorda and Hejazi 2019; Cuciniello and Pasta 2020; Proglio 2020) and teachers – from the primary school to the upper secondary school – to take part in EU-funded projects[4] which promote inclusion and tackle discrimination. And as a result, many educational seminars and training workshops have been organised, effective toolkits and shared platforms have been implemented with the result to bring together people, share experiences and reveal emotions.[5] Thus being definitely a good mean to explore effective methods to fight anti-Muslim hatred and discrimination.

Second, Muslim women – in particular veiled ones – seem to be particularly vulnerable to hate speech and hate crime. Amidst many cases of hate speech against veiled Muslim women, it is worth recalling what happened to Silvia Romano[6] and the hate campaign she has been subjected to. The reference to what Federico Faloppa wrote about her "*Donna, giovane, cooperante, e… musulmana*" (Faloppa 2020, 5) ("*Woman, young, aid worker, and… muslim*") lead to a harsh awareness of the coexistence of multifaceted and uncontrolled racism.

Much has been written about veiled Muslim women and religious identity and many pages have been dedicated to the cultural and symbolic capital of Islamic veils (Giacalone 2021; 2020; Abdel Qader 2019; 2008; Muzzarelli 2016; Acocella and Pepicelli 2015; Farris 2015; Zatti 2013; Greco 2014; Pepicelli 2010; 2012; Vanzan 2006; Riviera 2005; Trevisani 2003) within the academia; under-reporting and under-recording[7] have been discussed and analysed within the army and social organisations. However,

---

[4]https://home-affairs.ec.europa.eu/policies/migration-and-asylum/legal-migration-and-integration/integration/action-plan-integration-and-inclusion_en; https://ec.europa.eu/migrant-integration/library-document/european-islamophobia-report_en; (both accessed 20 September 2024).

[5]*Discorsi d'odio e Social Media, criticità, strategie e pratiche di intervento* https://www.arci.it/app/uploads/2018/05/progetto_PRISM_-_bassa.pdf; https://www.osservatorio.it/lislam-nei-social-media/; *DICO DI NO, Discorsi d'odio e cultura giovanili*, conducted by the Center for Religious Studies Bruno Kessler, during the academic year 2018/2019 (https://isr.fbk.eu/it/; www.amnesty.it/entra-in-azione/discorsi-dodio-online-combattiamoli-insieme/); https://associazione.acmos.net/scuter/; https://associazione.acmos.net/hate-campagna-per-la-cittadinanza-20172018/; http://www.voxdiritti.it/la-nuova-mappa-dellintolleranza-7/ (all accessed accessed 20 September 2024).

[6]Silvia Romano is a 25-year-old Italian aid worker who converted to Islam during an 18-month detention by Somali Islamist militants. Immediately following her release (10 May 2020), she was labelled as a terrorist https://www.ansa.it/english/news/2020/05/13/house-row-after-leaguer-calls-silvia-romano-neo-terrorist_abea263c-84e7-4d5f-b5b5-2d46e623dbac.html (accessed 20 September 2024).

[7] *TRUST Tackling Under-Reporting and Under-Recording of Hate Speech and Hate Crimes Against Muslim Women*, 101049611, available at https://www.trust-project-eu.info/en/home/ (accessed 20 September 2024).

what remains under-researched is an inquiry on the emotional involvement of veiled Muslim women and their self-representation.

Third, Muslims – or Arabs, according to an unfair biased belief but popular misconception[8] – are considered a threat to Italian national security (Vitullo 2023; Proglio 2020; Vidino and Marone 2019; Graziano 2018; Vidino 2014; 2008; Perocco 2010). A complex political system which is coping with the rising numbers of migrant arrivals, on one hand, and the proliferation of hatred against Islam *tout court,* on the other, are triggering a sort of "*normalisation of Islamophobia*" (Calculli 2020, 55) within the Italian public opinion. According to this interpretation, the anti-Muslim hatred is recognised as leading cause of our country's instability and insecurity.

In this context, PriMED has fostered the debate for an academic reflection on social integration and interreligious dialogue, thanks to two Academic Advanced Training Courses organised in 2021 by the Humanities Department and the Educational Science Department of Roma Tre University.

"The trans-mediterranean space and Islam: integration in the public sphere" was dedicated to public sector employees (municipality offices, policemen and policewomen, nursing field) and "*The trans-mediterranean space and Islam: integration in the scholastic public sphere*" was framed for teachers and school headmasters. Due to the Covid-19 pandemic, the courses have been held online. The Moodle platform enabled teachers and tutors to customise the audience learning experience thus creating a stimulating educational environment. The participants had the opportunity to acquire knowledge about the Muslim community in Italy from an historical, legal, sociological and anthropological perspective and, at the same time, have engaged in a respectful intercultural exchange of views.

Apart from the course relevance within the Italian social context – in particular by partnering with the Minister for Internal Affairs and the Minister of Education – the most important outcome for the academia is undoubtedly represented by the courses' participants' interviews.

Therefore, we present in this section the results of more than 800 structured interviews[9] conducted by the PriMED courses participants as their

---

[8] Many Arabs are not Muslim: Muslims are followers of Islam, Arabs are an ethnolinguistic group of people, most of whom are Muslim in religion but many of whom are not. There are several different Arab Christian groups in the Middle East, for example the Coptic Christians of Egypt.

[9] We refer to the interviews collected from 746 participants of the Academic Advanced Training Course *The trans-mediterranean space and Islam: integration in the public sphere and* 94 participants of the Academic Advanced Training Course *The trans-mediterranean space and Islam: integration in the scholastic public sphere.* About 90% of

final tasks. What emerges from these interviews is their heuristic power: the following questions suggested by the scholars ("*1. Do you know how many Muslims there are in Italy? And how many mosques are there in Italy? – 2. Is Islam formally recognised in Italy? – 3. Have you ever experienced prejudice or witnessed an incident of discrimination or hate against Islam or Muslims? How did this make you feel? – 4. What are the opportunities and tools within the Italian educational system to acquire knowledge about Islam? – 5. What kind of effective changes could enhance a better knowledge of Islam? – 6. What are you afraid of?". The questions 4 and 5 have been thought for the advanced academic course for teachers and school headmasters)* are intended to represent a way to collect a large amount of data which is quite difficult to achieve. Each participant has conducted an on-line or live interview with a Muslim man or woman (aged from 18 to 70), thus providing us a huge amount of information for academic purposes.

Namely, these interviews represent an interesting primary source for this chapter, focusing on the ways Muslims respond to Islamophobic behaviours. Among the questions suggested for the interviews we focused our attention on the following one: "What are you afraid of?" Amidst many given answers, we cannot fail to consider the remarkable recurrence of the terms *ignorance, threat, security*. Even though we will not deal with the thousands of definitions of the term *fear* and its diverse interpretations, our thoughts go to Baumann: "*fear is at its most fearsome when it is diffuse, scattered, unclear, unattached, unanchored, free floating [...] fear is the name we give to our uncertainty: to our ignorance of the threat*" (Baumann 2006, 2). It seems clear that what emerged from the Muslim answers lead us to the "*derivative fear*" (Baumann 2006), or a common shared emotion which can be related to particular historical times or peculiar social frames. *Security, ignorance* and *threat* reveal emotional connotations linked to a kind of fear and vulnerability experienced within the social sphere, thus evoking the presence of a binary opposition between *us* and *the others*.

Referring to the overall outcome of the interviews, it is noteworthy that many Muslims (especially young ones) tend to minimise (Vicini 2022), as a straight first response to the question "What are you afraid of?", the Islamophobic episodes they have experienced. Then, little by little, the memories of violence and hatred come back to mind and the interviewed Muslim refer to experiences of harassment and bullying. It clearly concerns Vicini's contribution about memories of "*micro-racism*" (Vicini 2022, 68), as a con-

---

the participants conducted an interview with a Muslim, as a final task that has been evaluated by the teachers involved in the formation path. The interviews were conducted in different parts of Italy, from Piedmont to Sicily.

firmation "*that Islamophobia is not a marginal phenomenon, it appears embedded in other forms of racial prejudice and discrimination*".[10] Considering the large dataset analysis (more than 800 structured interviews) it is clear that many Muslim do not still have the means to cope with the enormous flow of hatred and prejudices within Italian society. In this context, even an effective support from the institutional authorities has been shown in different occasions and through official declarations and pleas,[11] the interviewed people agree that there is a lot more to do. The collected interviews have given voice to a large spectrum of Muslims: from the Maghreb countries to Sub-Saharan ones, from the Middle East to Pakistan and Bangladesh. They are aged from 18 to 70, several of them are migrants, others are born in Italy; and there are even Italians converted to Islam.

The analysis of the responses to the interviews brought out three relevant clusters.

First, there are shared common narratives linked to the words Islamophobia and racism. Many Muslims agree with the statement that the Islamophobic era has begun since the Twin Towers attack. From that day, an intense attack against the Islamic community has spread worldwide and most of the Muslims have been considered as terrorists, violent jihadists and major threats to security and stability. This misconstrued rhetoric of hate is expressed in the interviews by the following recurrent words: extremists, terrorists, fundamentalists, fanatics thus contributing to reveal the menacing external portrait of Islam.

It is worth noting that next to the word Islamophobia, much attention has been given to the term racism that is articulated, according to the interviewees, in different ways. It is racism against the skin colour and against ethnicity and race especially among Muslim coming from Senegal or Nigeria; it is also gender racism against veiled women, which could be read in the frame of a complex intersectionality.

Referring to the above, we have collected a few sentences that clearly show the link between negative experiences (being compared to terrorists or the difficulty to rent a house due to prejudices against Muslims) and their related emotions (fear, anger, disillusion...).

---

[10] *Islamophobia and its consequences on Young People,* European Youth Centre Budapest 1-June 2004, Published by the Directorate of Youth and Sport of the Council of Europe, Council of Europe, 2004, 6.

[11] Reading and analyzing the rhetoric found on the websites of the major Islamic associations in Italy a fairly homogeneous picture emerges, albeit in the differentiation of styles, topics covered and modes of communication. https://www.coreis.it/, https://ucoii.org/, https://www.facebook.com/centroislamicoculturale, https://www.facebook.com/confederazioneislamicaitaliana/?locale=it_IT (accessed 20 September 2024).

*"I'm afraid people will hate us because they associate Islam with terrorism"*. (I.B)

*"In my opinion, episodes of discrimination rarely concern religion itself, but rather skin colour or ethnicity. For example, if a black Muslim is discriminated against, it is due to the colour of his skin, not his religion"*. (S.M.F)

*"Yes, Muslim women suffer many examples of discrimination. My wife wears a veil and tells me that when she has to enter the city hall or public offices she has problems because of her veiled head"*. (E.F.)

*"I was looking for a rental apartment. On the phone the owner was nice and helpful. As soon as he saw me wearing the veil, excuses and problems began"*. (F.M.)

*"There are many negative attitudes towards immigrants and Muslims. There is Islamophobia and it is perceived in a very violent way. Unfortunately, many episodes are not reported, they are concealed but there are. There is racism as well as Islamophobia"*. (T.P.)

In terms of both racisms it is clear that the occurrence of being a Muslim veiled woman from a Nigerian tribe can provoke a multidimensional hatred. Within this context, the feedback to racisms provokes two different attitudes: in everyday life most of the Muslim tend to consider hate speech as a routine habit, looking the other way. In cases of more evident violent episodes of intolerance or discrimination, the Muslims – especially women – usually discuss them with other Muslims, even though under-reporting [12] them to the police.

Second, the acknowledged triggering causes that have been pointed out as sources of discriminatory events and prejudicial attitudes are related to press and mass media. Too often a twisted version of a warlike culture of Islam is brought to screen arenas, too many pages are full of distorted depictions of violent Muslims and their submissive veiled women. Research has been demonstrated with fieldworks and scientific studies that prejudices and discrimination are relevant issues of the day. As a result of this negative discourse produced by the media there is a social urge to cope with this question, or to fight disinformation and foster a correct perception of Islam.

Among the interviewed Muslims it is clear the reference to a widespread

---

[12] "Under-reporting is the phenomenon whereby victims of and witnesses to hate crimes tend, for different and complex reasons, not to report. Under-recording is the phenomenon whereby the police sometimes do not recognise the discriminatory matrix of hate crimes and the reported crime and, consequently, do not record or investigate it as such. The planned activities also aim to raise awareness among Muslim women who have suffered hate crimes to perceive themselves as victims of illegal actions and train representatives of the above categories so that they acquire the necessary skills.": https://www.agenformedia.com/projects/trust/ (accessed 20 September 2024).

unawareness and ignorance towards Islam, from ordinary life experiences to the media system.

> "*Yes, I have experienced discrimination as an Arab, as a Muslim because many people are ignorant, because of television. They should not speak because they do not know about other religions. They do not read, do not inform themselves and remain closed in their misconceptions*". (L.M.)
>
> "*When people talk about Islam, they think of jihadists, of wars, of ISIS, of terrorists. So I often had to explain that these organisations use religion for their aims.... because Islam is a peaceful religion*". (I.D.A.)
>
> "*What we watch on TV or read in magazines is the mirror of a popular ignorance about Islam*". (G.D.)

Third, what emerges from the interviewees' conduct is, on the one hand, the emotions revealed and, on the other hand, the concrete demands. The Muslims expressed mainly sadness, anger and fear (or blendings of these) often related to feelings of anxiety, frustration, and disappointment. The interviewees' replies are concerned especially with feelings of contempt, guilt and shame. However, it is evident that a sincere bond of empathy has united interviewers and interviewees, as in the following claims:

> "*I felt empathy, especially when she told me about the causes of her fear. The fact of not being understood for her inner thoughts, for her religious faith*". (M.H.)
>
> "*I felt sad and discouraged...the fact that an Italian citizen (but Muslim) working regularly in Italy lives in a condition of fear and worry because of her skin colour and her faith, made me conscious that Italians are not good people*". (A.G.)
>
> "*While I was conducting the interview I realised the importance of dialogue among people of the same community but of different religious faith*". (G.R.)
>
> "*Dialogue means the conviction that prejudices are born from ignorance and the only way to a path towards change*". (E.D.P.)

In the end, what emerges from the interviews is a demand for a better integration which is to attribute to the importance of engaging in a real knowledge of Islam.

Besides various good practices and relevant projects towards a correct understanding of Islam, Muslims are yet often portrayed as a homogenous group prone to violence. One of the reasons can be traced back in a weak follow-up after the projects' dissemination actions which call into question stakeholders but also institutional agencies. In the next session we will recount one of the relevant experiences on the national territory, allowing for the emergence of a good practice that took place in 2022 and reflecting on its consequences and repercussions.

## 3. The World Café gives the floor to Muslims

It is therefore not (only) a matter of collecting good practices, of observing and raising or denouncing open questions, but of accompanying processes of self-reflection and position-taking.

As Clelia Bartoli wrote [13] in her review of the volume *Subaltern Studies. Modernity and (post)colonialism* edited by Guha and Spivak,

> "*The operation of giving back the word to the subalterns is not assumed to be easy and straightforward: the question is not only whether from the available historical sources, i.e. almost exclusively those produced by the dominant groups, one can derive clues to the worldview of the subaltern subjects, as from a cast one reconstructs the form of the absent; but ours comes to the question of whether there is a subaltern consciousness to be exhumed, to what extent a will can be assigned to a collective subject, and whether the work of constructing a subaltern identity, artificially carried out by the historian, is not yet another fanciful and constricting objectification for those who fall under this appellation*". [14]

These reflections stemmed from the reading and reworking of the work produced by Subaltern Studies, the manifesto of which is probably the valuable and disruptive contribution of G. Spivak, *Can the Subaltern Speak?* (1988).

Twenty years later, in Italy, subalterns are still oppressed by narratives that are not only religious (eg. "Muslims are fanatics") but also social and political ("Muslims are terrorists"). The ways to break these drifts are based on the construction of new and entirely innovative (counter) narratives (Premazzi 2023).

One of the ways, however, if not uncommonly ingrained and widespread, to stimulate awareness, to speak out and to foster active participation is that of the s, whose specific format is based on a method aimed at initiating concrete and constructive informal conversations on issues that

---

[13] Bartoli wrote *Subalternità, rappresentazioni sociali e rappresentanza politica* (2004) on the possibility of the oppressed-subalterns to represent themselves and redeem themselves from foundation myths, paternalist and colonialist narratives by getting out of the logic of puppets in the hands of ventriloquists.

[14] https://www.juragentium.org/books/it/spivak.htm (accessed 20 September 2024).

affect the cultural, social and political life of a group of stakeholders.

The collection of reflections, ideas and different points of view is the basis of the lively and interactive discussion that has been made in the working tables: the session saw the active involvement of all the participants, whose fundamental cornerstones were discussions, mutual understanding and dialogue.

Within this framework, in a system that is organised but at the same time based on the spontaneity of discussion and debate, the Integra project, the result of a project of the Ministry of the Interior and promoted by the University of Insubria [15] in collaboration with the University of Bari Aldo Moro, the University of Turin and the LUM University of Casamassima, arranged two events. [16]

On 19th May in Bari, at the Conference Hall of the Port System Authority of the Southern Adriatic Sea, and on 26th May in Turin, at the Luigi Einaudi Campus, the two s were divided into two key moments: during the morning there was a discussion on six thematic tables, dealing with peculiar issues of the day. The topics were identified by a number of scholars and researchers belonging to the academic network and familiar with the sociology of contemporary Islam in Italy. Each table was managed by a facilitator, with the support of a trainer who had prepared fact sheets, case studies, and crucial issues to foster active involvement and encourage discussion. The outcome of these tables was discussed with national and local institutions in the second part of the day, with the participation of the table leaders, who presented their shared documents and interacted with the authorities that have intervened.

In this framework, the was a very important moment not only for the cohesion of the Islamic Community living in our country, since the young people were selected from among the members, affiliated or linked to the organisations that signed the *Pact for Italian Islam,* but it was an almost unique moment of gathering and building a positive narrative with respect to other instances rather aimed at denouncing and recognising discrimina-

---

[15] The was one of the actions of the Ministry of the Interior project, entrusted to the Inter-University Research Centre International Forum Democracy and Religions (FIDR), supported by the FAMI 2014-2020 Asylum, Migration and Integration Fund, coordinated by A. Ferrari, P. Naso, M. Giorda and A. Angelucci.

[16] Report edited by Report: Coord. Maria Chiara Giorda (University of Roma Tre) Antonio Angelucci (University of Insubria) – Natascia Marchei (University of Milan Bicocca) – Laura Sabrina Martucci (University of Bari) – Roberta Ricucci (University of Turin) – Milena Santerini (University Cattolica del Sacro Cuore, Milan) – Annita L. Sciacovelli (University of Bari) – Wisam Zreg (University of Turin). Special thanks to Dr Sciacovelli and Dr Zreg.

tion and problems. Far be it from the writer to think that practical and rapid solutions could have been found, it is beyond symbolic the importance of having been able to give them voice, to listen, to set down in writing drafts of cultural, social, educational and political proposals that are an answer to the legislative and political holes that our country presents in the face of the question of minorities and in particular the fragmented and pulpy Islamic universe.

The thematic tables have been planned following the most relevant issues of the Italian political agenda on which the participants were invited to share their ideas and experiences, on:

- Public schools and religious freedom;
- Stereotypes, fears and new challenges in the fight against discrimination;
- Volunteering and local and global solidarity practices and associationism in the two socio-religious dimensions;
- Youth civic activism starting from cities;
- Social media and networking.

With regard to the chosen topics, the participation of young Muslims was fostered by the relational activity carried out by trainers and especially by facilitators with members of the various institutions representing the Muslim world, as well as the more transversal group of the GMI, the Italian Muslim Youth association.

The lively participation of young Muslims and students or ex-students from local universities, involved as facilitators of the tables, gave rise to informal, pragmatic but at the same time very dense and constructive conversations on the suggested issues focused on the daily lives of the young people involved.

In particular, interesting indications emerged from the working table on "Stereotypes, fears and new challenges in the fight against discrimination" regarding the following questions:

> *What are the most widespread stereotypes about Islam? Which ones do you consider the most serious? What is their history? What are their causes? What are your fears?*
>
> *What are the consequences of the entrenchment of such stereotypes?*
>
> *How do we combat these forms of ignorance?*
>
> *What could the institutions and in particular the Ministry of the Interior do about it?*

As Laura Sabrina Martucci wrote in her opening dossier: [17]

> *"The fight against and prevention of discrimination and the hypotheses of breaking action of stereotypes and pre-constituted opinions on Islam require the choice of precise guidelines, coordinated within a framework of multi-level action, which must be constantly contextualised, due to social priorities and to what is foreseen and recommended by international bodies and institutions to national policies for the maintenance of the rule of law and the protection of fundamental rights. One of the goals of the UN 2030 Agenda is to make cities and communities safe and peaceful through the 'implementation of effective, accountable and inclusive institutions at all levels'. One of the ways to work towards this is to holistically promote interreligious and intercultural integration, particularly of communities of the Islamic faith, which are overwhelmed by the persistence of stereotypes.*
>
> *(...)*
>
> *The condition of second and third generations of young people of the Islamic faith deserves not only monitoring of the drifts, but mainly the development and/or implementation of intervention, action and prevention plans functional to their effective social integration and valorisation. Plans that from the macro-levels of inter-institutional relations can gradually take shape in the micro-levels of cities and their suburbs, passing through all the frameworks at risk (schools, communities, prevention and punishment institutes, reception camps, the Web, etc.) and the unavoidable cooperation – at various levels – of all the other social actors involved"*.

In this sense, to avoid simplification through a scheme of stereotypes based on keywords such as violence, radicalisation, recruitment, failure, and ignorance linked to Islam, the tables overturned such narrative systems into positive narratives (and actions) and revitalisation not only religious but also cultural, social and political.

In Bari [18], the working table came up with five proposals, starting from the key word 'Awareness', related to the creation of a Ministerial Body:

- A technical working table with the task of clearly and unambiguously defining the concept of 'Islamophobia' and discriminatory acts revolving around the concept of 'Islamophobia';
- Consequent sanctioning apparatus for non-compliance arising from the identification of discriminatory acts as referred to in the previous point;

---

[17] Laura Sabrina Martucci, Aggregate Professor of Comparative Ecclesiastical Law at the University of Bari.

[18] Work Table in Bari, report by A. Sciacovelli.

- Observatory with the following tasks: collection of data on incidents of discrimination (linked to the definitions and cases of discriminatory acts identified by the technical roundtable mentioned in the previous point); reporting; drafting of an annual report;
- Training work for Public Officials and Teachers (training motivated by the lack of knowledge of certain issues and the high frequency of relations with the public). This training should in fact focus on the right intercultural approach that each of these actors must take towards citizens;
- Organisation of events and awareness-raising campaigns against Islamophobia. As well as the establishment of a national day against Islamophobia (already present at an international level).

The proposals that emerged from the Turin [19] table focused on the urgent need for institutional recognition of official interlocutors, a need linked to the more than topical issue of an understanding with Islam. Mention was made of the need to train primary, lower and upper secondary school teachers, who often display cultural illiteracy concerning the history and religious history of Islam, both globally and in Italy.

The three proposals formulated are:

a) Reaching an understanding between Islam and the Italian state that would facilitate institutional dialogue;
b) Creation of an observatory whose main task would be to monitor episodes of discrimination linked to Islamophobia;
c) Training primary, middle and high school teachers in order to make them knowledgeable about Islam and enable them to deconstruct the stereotypes that still often permeate textbooks and school narratives.

## 4. Conclusions

In a general obscuration of fear of Islam, experienced but often not communicated as a problem of prejudice and stereotypes and therefore normalised, few voices are emerging to denounce the side effects of such emotion.

In fact, the problem lies both in understanding the reasons for the fear, in order to address them, to counter them and resolve them, but also in understanding what are the side effects of such widespread fear, and what is the attitude of citizens who inhabit public spaces.

There is a widespread illiteracy that does not allow this cultural but also

[19] Work Table in Turin, report by W. Zreg.

solid mechanism in terms of collective psychology to be addressed with effective tools.

Within this context, the interviews with the Muslims have shown the coexistence of two narratives. On the one hand the presence of a widespread exposure to fear against Islam, on the other hand the lack of a formal and institutional response to this issue. Without doubt the activities promoted by PriMED – from the advanced courses to the World Café – are to be considered good practices to be enhanced and replicated in wider official settings. Then, on this basis, hopefully new trajectories will be defined.[20]

As far as the World Café's tables are concerned, a complex Muslim pride emerged from them based on the awareness of a double, yet hybrid, identity. Most of the participants are, in fact, both Muslims and Italians. In looking at young Muslims across Italian society, it is clear a sort of perception of the otherness that is coping with religious pluralism and multilayered identities.

The topic and the word Islamophobia are central and really seems to be crucial to the reflections of young people who have often been in contact with forms of suspicion, fear or discrimination at different levels. At opposite poles there is the demand for correct information, education, transmission of data and news, the fight against fake news or fallacious narratives and, on the other hand, the call for the possibility of sanctioning and inventing just punishment for hate crimes and discriminatory forms.

## References

Abdel Qader, S. (2008). *Porto il velo, adoro i Queen*. Sonzogno, Milano.

Abdel Qader, S. (2019). *Quello che abbiamo in testa*. Mondadori, Milano.

Acocella, I. and Pepicelli, R. (2015). *Giovani musulmane in Italia. Percorsi biografici e pratiche quotidiane*. Il Mulino, Bologna.

Basso P. (2010) (eds.). *Razzismo di stato*. Franco Angeli, Milano.

Baumann, N. Z. (2006). *Liquid fear*. Polity, Cambridge.

Bleich, E. (2012). "Defining and Researching Islamophobia". *Review of Middle East Studies,* 46, 2 (Winter), 180-189.

Bombardieri, M. *et al.* (eds.) (2019). *Capire l'Islam. Mito o realtà?*. Scholé, Brescia.

[20] We refer to the issues *communities, pluralism and welfare* analysed in the text Ambrosini A., Molli S.D. and Naso P. (eds.), *Quando gli immigrati vogliono pregare*. Il Mulino, Bologna, 2022.

Bunzl, M. (2005). "Between anti-Semitism and islamophobia: Some thoughts on the new Europe". *American Ethnologist*, 32(4), 499-508.

Calculli, M. (2020). "Sicurezza nazionale, ma di chi è esattamente? L'estrema destra, l'islamofobia e la politica mediterranea dell'Italia", in G. Proglio (ed.). *Islamofobia e razzismo. Media, discorsi pubblici e immaginario nella decostruzine dell'altro*. Ed. Seb 27, Torino.

Catarci, M. *et al.* (2023). "'Don't be afraid': preventing discrimination through intercultural education" in L. Fabbri and C. Melacarne (eds.). *Understanding Radicalization in Everyday Life*. McGraw-Hill, Milano, 59-77.

Cuciniello, A. and Pasta, S. (2020). *Studenti musulmani a scuola*. Carocci, Roma.

Evolvi, G. (2018). *Blogging my religion: Secular, Muslim, and Catholic media spaces in Europe*. Routledge, London.

Faloppa, F. (2020). *Le parole e le cose in G. Proglio (ed.). Islamofobia e razzismo. Media, discorsi pubblici e immaginario nella decostruzione dell'altro.* Ed. Seb 27, Torino.

Faloppa, F. (2020). *Odio: manuale di resistenza alla violenza delle parole*. Utet, Torino.

Farris, S. (2015). *Il femonazionalismo in Italia*. Gaia, G. (2015) (ed.). *Il colore della nazione*. Le Monnier, Firenze, pp. 172-195.

Gallup (2016). *Islamophobia. Understanding Anti-Muslim Sentiment in the West*, available at: https://news.gallup.com/poll/157082/islamophobia-understanding-anti-muslim-sentiment-west.aspx (accessed 20 September 2024).

Giacalone, F. (2020). "Islamofobia e sessismo nella rappresentazione delle donne musulmane in Italia". *Voci*, XVII, 198-221.

Graziano, P. (2018). *Neopopulismi. Perché sono destinati a durare*. Il Mulino, Bologna.

Greco, M.C. (2014). "Le donne dell'Islam, una vita s-velata". *Mobilità umane e nuove geografie migranti*, 193-208.

Guha, R. and Spivak, G.C. (2002) (eds.). *Selected Subaltern Studies*. Oxford University Press, Delhi.

Halliday, F. (1999). "'Islamophobia' reconsidered. *Ethnic and Racial Studies*, 22, 5, 892-902.

Muzzarelli, M.G. (2016). *A capo coperto: storie di donne e di veli*. Il Mulino, Bologna.

Pepicelli, R. (2010). *Femminismo islamico. Corano, diritti, riforme*. Carocci, Roma.

Pepicelli, R. (2012). *Il velo nell'Islam. Storia, politica, estetica*. Carocci, Roma.

Perocco, F. (2010). *L'Italia, avanguardia del razzismo europeo*. Franco Angeli, Milano.

Peterson, K.M. (2022). *Unruly Souls: The Digital Activism of Muslim and Christian Feminists*. Rutgers University Press, Rutgers.

Premazzi, V. (2020). "Secolarizzazione e nuove forme di protagonismo nella seconda generazione musulmana in Italia", in G. Salmeri, *Troppa religione o troppo poca. Cristiani e musulmani alla prova della secolarizzazione*. Marsilio, Venezia, 106-116.

Premazzi, V. (2021). "Young Muslims and islamophobia in Italy: What is at Stake?". *Culture e Studi del Sociale*, 6(1), 51-64.

Premazzi, V. and Ricucci, R. (2014). "La religione conta ancora? Fra secolarizzazione e riscoperta", in P. Cingolani and R. Ricucci, *Transmediterranei. Generazioni a confronto tra Italia e Nord Africa*. Accademia University Press, Torino, 56-71.

Proglio, G. (2020) (eds.). *Media, discorsi pubblici e immaginario nella decostruzione dell'altro*. Edizioni SEB27, Torino.

Richardson, R. (2009). *Islamophobia or anti-Muslim racism – or what? – concepts and terms revisited*, available at http://www.insted.co.uk/anti-muslim-racism.pdf (accessed 30 August 2024).

Ricucci, R.C (2015). *Cittadini senza cittadinanza. Immigrati, seconde e altre generazioni: pratiche quotidiane tra inclusione ed estraneità*. Edizioni SEB27, Torino.

Rivera, A. (2005). *La guerra dei simboli. Veli postcoloniali e retoriche sull'alterità*. Dedalo, Bari.

Taguieff, P.A. (1994). *La forza del pregiudizio*. Il Mulino, Bologna.

Taguieff, P.A. (1999). *Il razzismo*. Cortina, Milano.

Tibi, B. (2010). "Ethnicity of fear? Islamic migration and the ethnicization of Islam in Europe". *Studies in Ethnicity and Nationalism*, 10(1), 126-157.

Trevisani, I. (2003). *Il velo e lo specchio. Pratiche di bellezza come forma di resistenza agli integralismi*. Baldini Castoldi, Milano.

Trust, R. (1997). *Islamophobia: A Challenge for Us*, available at https://www.runnymedetrust.org/publications/islamophobia-a-challenge-for-us-all (accessed 20 September 2024).

Vanzan, A. (2006). *La storia velata: le donne dell'Islam nell'immaginario Italiano*. Edizioni Lavoro, Roma.

Vicini, F. (2022). "Il lato quotidiano dell'islamofobia. Micro-razzismo a scuola tra differenzialismo culturale e razzismo spirituale". *EtnoAntropologia*, 10(2), 60-78.

Vidino, L. (2008). "Islam, Islamism, and Jihadism in Italy". *Current Trends in Islamist Ideology,* August 4, svailable at: https://www.hudson.org/

research/9813-islam-islamism-and-jihadism-in-italy (accessed 20 September 2024).

Vidino, L. (2014). *Home-Grown Jihadism in Italy: Birth, Development and Radicalization Dynamics*. Report. Milan: Italian Institute for International Political Studies (ISPI) and European Foundation for Democracy, available at https://www.ispionline.it/it/EBook/vidino-eng.pdf (accessed 20 September 2024).

Vidino, L. and Marone, F. (2017). *The Jihadist Threat in Italy: A Primer. Analysis, No. 318. Italian Institute for International Political Studies (ISPI)*, available at: https://www.ispionline.it/sites/default/files/pubblicazioni/analisi318_vidino-marone.pdf (accessed 20 September 2024).

Vitullo, A. (2021). "The Online Intersection among Islamophobia, Populism, and Hate Speech: An Italian Perspective". *Journal of Religion. Media and Digital Culture*, 10(1), 95-114.

Vitullo, A. (2023). "Hate Speech or Hate Shot?". *Advances in Media, Entertainment and the Arts (AMEA)*, 203-219.

Waldron, J. (2012). *The Harm in Hate Speech.* Harvard University Press, Harvard.

Zatti, N. (2013). *Ho un cervello sotto il velo!*. Cavinato, Brescia.

# INDEX

## G



## H



## J



## K



## L



## M



## P



## P



## Q



## R

Papier | Fördert gute Waldnutzung
FSC® C083411

Kolibri 360 GmbH
Ferdinand-Jühlke-Straße 7
99095 Erfurt, Deutschland
produktsicherheit@kolibri360.de